ONE OF US

GEOFFREY GALT HARPHAM

ONE OF US

The Mastery of Joseph Conrad

THE UNIVERSITY OF CHICAGO PRESS

Chicago & London

GEOFFREY GALT HARPHAM is professor of English at
Tulane University. He is the author of *On the
Grotesque: Strategies of Contradiction in Art and
Literature* (1982); *The Ascetic Imperative in Culture
and Criticism* (1987); and *Getting it Right: Language,
Literature, and Ethics* (1992)—the latter two
published by the University of Chicago Press.

The University of Chicago Press, Chicago 60637
The University of Chicago Press, Ltd., London

©1996 by The University of Chicago
All rights reserved. Published 1996
Printed in the United States of America

06 05 04 03 02 01 00 99 98 97 96   1 2 3 4 5
ISBN: 0-226-31695-5 (cloth)
ISBN: 0-226-31696-3 (paper)

Library of Congress Cataloging-in-Publication Data

Harpham, Geoffrey Galt, 1946–
One of us : the mastery of Joseph Conrad / Geoffrey Galt Harpham.
p.   cm.
Includes bibliographical references and index.
ISBN 0-226-31695-5 (cloth : alk. paper).—ISBN 0-226-31696-3
(paper : alk. paper)
1. Conrad, Joseph, 1857–1924—Criticism and interpretation.
I. Title.
PR6005.04Z74188   1996
823.912—dc20   96-24571
CIP

⊗ The paper used in this publication meets the
minimum requirements of the American National
Standard for Information Sciences—Permanence of
Paper for Printed Library Materials,
ANSI Z39.48-1984.

For Clare

With Thoughts of Larks Past, Larks Present, and Larks Yet to Come

CONTENTS

PREFACE

The concept of mastery occupies a largely unexamined seam in contemporary thought, standing astride a thin line dividing an admirable self-control from a reprehensible will to power. Mastery gathers into itself psychological, political, technological, and formal energies in such an indiscriminately inclusive way that it can be considered a general term, a master term, for our relations with others and with ourselves. Once introduced or recognized, mastery is difficult to avoid: the only remedy for some kinds of mastery is, it sometimes seems, other kinds.

Conrad provides a perfect pretext for interrogating this issue and this seam because his work and reputation are so indelibly marked by mastery. Indeed, the concept has acquired the status of a critical category in the discussion of Conrad's work. F. R. Leavis begins *The Great Tradition,* the single most influential text in the history of Conrad criticism, by noting that Conrad was "a master of the English language" who "chose to write his novels in English for the reasons that led him to become a British Master Mariner" (17, 18). For many years, appreciation of Conrad confined itself to tracing his various masteries, as he was accounted a master of style, of literary form, of scenic and atmospheric description, of the secrets of the human heart, of the intricacies of political intrigue—a master of mastery itself. Two of Conrad's most powerful critics in recent years testify to the durability and flexibility of this trope. Edward Said, who, in his 1983 book *The World, the Text, and the Critic,* had written approvingly of Conrad's "evolving mastery" as a technical and more than technical triumph over the radical self-doubt that nearly crippled him early in his career, raised the issue once again a decade later in *Culture and Imperialism,* this time, however, linking stylistic and technical mastery directly to practices of imperial domination. In a famous chapter in *The Political Unconscious* (1981), Fredric Jameson noted in Conrad an exercise of mastery deployed as a "strategy of aestheticization" or "ideological containment" that concealed political and economic realities behind a mask of "ethics" or individual concerns. A careful study of Conrad discloses, it seems, a seam running through the very notion of mastery: an internal difference that demarcates, and fails to demarcate, the laudable from the culpable.

However, if Conrad continues to command the attention of intelligent and responsible people, it is because he bestrides another seam, or seme, as well, one that divides and joins together the experience of mastering and of being mastered. The man himself—dispossessed orphan, exile, largely unemployed sailor, mostly unsuccessful writer, perpetual debtor, alien and uncomfortable man—seems so little a master of anything that the ritual attribution of a superbly self-assured command seems almost a kind of historical mockery. His work, so far from reflecting the steady imposition of a self-aware control, often stimulates, in this reader at least, an uneasy indecision about whether, in a given passage, Conrad is succeeding in doing something extraordinary or failing to do something strictly routine. When we see Conrad as much mastered as master, we can begin to measure the comprehensiveness of his accomplishment, and the ways in which we mortals can still consider him to be, as Marlow says of Lord Jim, "one of us." When we understand the form and force of our cultural identification with him, we can begin to grasp what might be at stake in the otherwise unimportant issue of his reputation, or what I call, in the last chapter, his "greatness."

The structure of this book tracks that of Frederick Karl's biography, *Joseph Conrad: The Three Lives* (as well as that of a lesser known work, Olivia Coolidge's *The Three Lives of Joseph Conrad*). But while Karl, for obvious reasons, treats each phase—as Pole, seaman, and writer—as discrete stages in a remarkable human career, I regard each of these "lives" as an index to a particular obsession or imperative that structures Conrad's work in ways he himself could not recognize. I have, in other words, converted the biographical sequence into a conceptual simultaneity, locating not moments but strata. In this book, Pole, seaman, and writer, become, in their broadest formulations, Nation, Nature, and Language. Such a translation changes everything. Where biography posits sites of accomplishment and grounds for identity, I have placed concepts so large as to threaten to overwhelm individuality as such. To the extent that Karl's temporal epochs remain, unsublated, within my more general terms, however, this book will take the form of a dialectic or, to anticipate the first chapter, an oxymoron in which the truth of Conrad is cast in terms that enable it to communicate with other kinds of truth, other discourses than his own.

My divisions can, perhaps, be considered as the "unconscious" of Karl's, just as my approach to Conrad's work focuses on the "unconscious" aspects of those public and heroic themes for which it is so noteworthy. Said distinguishes between Conrad's personal psychology and "the psychology of Conrad's writing" in order to divert attention away from the tormented man and towards the enduring work (*WTC* 107). This book represents an attempt at a theory of production, a psychology of composition that does not simply shoulder the ill, distracted, desperate man off to the side. I use the term "unconscious" here as the proper name not simply of the individual's buried inner being—to which, out of respect for the actual conditions of human accomplishment, we must be attentive—but also of the various discursive, ideological, and material systems that circulate within and around people without their full knowledge. To explore Conrad's "unconscious" is, in this sense, to attend not only to the facts of the private individual Joseph Conrad but also to a range of other systems in which that individual was enmeshed and by which he was determined. Moreover, to employ the same term to denote the inner fastness of the individual and the extrapersonal systems and forces in which the individual participates is implicitly to suggest that, in their depths, people are engaged in collective systems and projects that no single person, or any limited group of people, can control or even fully comprehend; and to imply, too, that people truly become or realize themselves insofar as they connect with those systems and projects. The unconscious, in this account, is where the subject hemorrhages into the social, the economic, the legal, the national, the linguistic, the historic—and also where these macrophenomena become one's "own," components (however unmastered) of oneself. Conrad's "unconscious," I begin by presuming, provides a fascinating cynosure for many of the distinctive forces that defined the first generation of literary modernism.

Stephen Greenblatt has described literature in terms of a "circulation of social energy," a formulation that has been deployed as a rallying cry by those who seek to orient literary study in the direction of "history" or "culture" and against "theory." However emancipating the phrase—or historical criticism generally—may have been, the consequences of this struggle have been, to my mind, debilitating. Many now seem to believe that a serious interest in theoretical issues cannot coincide with an interest in material facts. But "theory" could be accounted a social energy. If it were, the literary text could be opened up even farther, and criticism could retain its theoretical sophistication even as it treated literature as a social phenomenon.

Another misunderstanding of Greenblatt's phrase holds that literature has no special distinction, that it can serve as a source of representations or articulations of social energy but has no special force or interest of its own. Theoretically inclined criticism has collaborated in this second misunderstanding, treating literature as a repository of narrative examples of concepts whose proper home is pure, nonnarrative thought. A more productive approach, and one I have tried to follow here, would set literature and theory on an equal footing, so that either could serve as the "example" of the other. A theoretical formulation could, in other words, be regarded as a clarifying instance of a concept whose native or natural discursive home was literature. Conrad's work, I have tried to show, is especially rich in such concepts.

Beyond the formidable task of representing Conrad accurately, I hope to have indicated here some ways of getting around a couple of the impasses that currently inhibit literary criticism. If this book still appears strange in its approach, that, too, may be read as a tribute to Conrad's peculiar genius.

ACKNOWLEDGMENTS

Just before I began writing this book, I attended my thirtieth high school reunion, and was amazed by—well, by everything, but in particular by the perfect recall several of my classmates had for the details of Mr. Roy Howarth's approach to *Heart of Darkness*. As everyone seemed to remember, this approach featured four levels of meaning, which all could recite in unison. Although I have sustained my fascination with Conrad for nearly all of those thirty years, and although I have always counted that class as a crucial and formative experience, I hadn't recalled anything about levels, and felt, when my friends chanted them, as if I were hearing about them for the first time; and yet, to my nearly certain knowledge, this is the first book on Conrad to be produced by a member of that class. My first expression of gratitude is, then, to Mr. Howarth, whose teaching became a creative force only after it had been forgotten.

My second is to the invaluable National Endowment for the Humanities, whose support was crucial to the timely completion of the project.

I wish, too, to thank Jacqueline Foertsch for her intelligence and care; Annie Wedekind, for the freshness of her response, which recalled to me my own long ago; Robert Storey, yet again, for his generosity and (increasingly aggressive, it seems) skepticism; Richard Rambuss and Molly Rothenberg for their invaluable early encouragement; Paul Kintzele for his spirited receptivity; and Joseph Valente, for the extraordinary stimulation of his ongoing interest.

Near the end of my labors, I was browsing through Frederick Karl's massive biography of Conrad, which I had kept at my elbow for many months, and came across a fact I had known long before but had misplaced somewhere—that during Conrad's period of greatest energy and productivity, his children were seriously ill. Whether his productive intensity during this time simply overwhelmed his distress, or his children's illness had somehow focused him in a way he was never able to reproduce when they were healthy, I cannot say. But, with reason to identify with my subject in this respect, I did draw a retroactive sustenance from his example—and cheer from his children's recovery.

To Be a Pole

Baby son, may this christening
Give you strength to live,
To look bravely into shadows
[. . .] when God allows
Poland to rise from the grave,
Of captivity—*our only Mother*
    Hushaby, my baby son! [. . .]
Bless you, my little son:
Be a *Pole!*
        —Apollo Korzeniowski, "To my son born in the 85th year of
Muscovite oppression, a song for the day of his christening" (1857),
                    in Najder, *Conrad under Familial Eyes*

THE NATION IN COFFINS

"What I saw with my own eyes"—Joseph Conrad recalled in 1919, a half-century after the event—"was the public funeral" (*PR* viii). After five years of exile in Russia, his father, the Polish patriot Apollo Korzeniowski, had died of tuberculosis, ending a disastrous period for the Korzeniowski family. Convicted of political agitation against Russian authorities in Warsaw, Apollo and his wife Ewa had been sent (on foot, as was the custom) to a penal colony in Vologda, 250 miles northeast of Moscow on the Moscow-Siberia road, and had brought their small child Konrad with them. Ewa had become ill on the journey and had died of tuberculosis in 1865, leaving Konrad alone with his increasingly melancholic and mystical father, a man who "used to cast gloom all round, posturing as a broken-hearted bard" (Perłowski 155). Ill himself, Apollo had been permitted to return to Poland, where his death in Cracow in May 1869 occasioned a procession at which, by Conrad's later estimate, half the city's population turned out. Alone at the head of the procession, conscious of a mighty following behind him, strode the eleven-year-old orphan, becoming a Pole as he observed "the cleared streets, the hushed crowds," the throngs of people, heads bared and eyes lowered, who had gathered

1

to mark the passing of "a man who believing in the spirituality of a national existence could not bear to see that spirit enslaved" (*PR* viii; see also *NLL* 169–70). Of the larger, as of the particular significance of the event, he comprehended little;

> but I understood perfectly well that this was a manifestation of the national spirit seizing a worthy occasion. That bareheaded mass of work people, youths of the University, women at the windows, school-boys on the pavement, could have known nothing positive about him except the fame of his fidelity to the one guiding emotion in their hearts. I had nothing but that knowledge myself; and this great silent demonstration seemed to me the most natural tribute in the world—not to the man but to the Idea. (*PR* viii)

What sort of national spirit manifests itself here? To which "guiding emotion" had Apollo Korzeniowski been famously faithful? To what Idea in particular were the silent crowds paying tribute? Conrad's silence on these questions fosters speculation, and recalls other, more famous Conradian moments, such as the conclusion of *The Nigger of the "Narcissus,"* where the narrator bids his crew of "Shades" farewell and asks them, "Haven't we, together and upon the immortal sea, wrung out a meaning from our sinful lives?"—without specifying which meaning it was (107); or the interview between Marlow and the Intended that finishes *Heart of Darkness* in which she asks, in a tone appropriate to the memory of a great public man, "Who was not his friend who heard him speak once? . . . But you have heard him! You know!"—and Marlow replies, "Yes, I know," bowing his head "before the faith that was in her" (74). Conrad understood how contradictory and uninspiring particulars could generate a vague idea that commanded fidelity.

Thus, when, in the course of writing this retrospective "Author's Note" to *A Personal Record,* one of a series of prefaces written near the end of his life for a collected edition of his works, Conrad abruptly introduces this recollection of "these Shades," and the Ideas that attach to them, he is following in his own tradition; or perhaps more exactly, he is summoning up the Shade of his Shades, not just the memory of his father but the father of his memories, the original instance of a remembered being whose mortal existence, while perhaps unimpressive—even perhaps "sordid" or "squalid," two favored Conradian words—in its details, meant something. In the case of his father, that meaning is defined by the Polish national Idea, which Conrad here seems to endorse. The unmentioned immediate provocation for the entire passage, however, was an essay by H. L. Mencken that attributed Conrad's distinctiveness to his "Sclavonism." Such criticism, Conrad says in his "Author's Note," "ascribed to racial and historical influences much, of what, I believe, appertains simply to the individual" (*PR* vi). Conrad insists, in other words, that he is not simply a Slav, much less a pseudo-Russian; he is himself alone. To be Polish, he claims, is to be an individual in the fully modern sense. As he says in the "Author's Note," "nothing is more foreign than what in the literary world is called Slavonism, to the Polish temperament with its tradition of self-government, its chivalrous view of moral restraints and an exaggerated respect for individual rights: not to mention the important fact that the whole Polish mentality, Western in complexion, had received its training from Italy and France and, historically, had always remained . . . in sympathy with the most liberal currents of European thought" (vi–vii).

However, Conrad, who on one occasion declared all "national egoism" to be "repulsive," was not simply a Pole either (Fleishman 19). Indeed, being a Pole in the nineteenth century was not a simple thing. After 1795, when Poland suffered the third and last of its partitions, being wholly divided among Prussia on the west, Russia on the east, and Austria on the south, Poland did not exist as a sovereign state, and was, rather, a theoretical entity, the absent cause of a defiant but literally groundless patriotism. As Apollo Korzeniowski put it in a poem written to his wife,

> In our Motherland life is hard and sad,
> For her breast is crushed by tombstones . . .
> Into an abyss our eyes gaze,
> For nowhere, nowhere can Poland be seen!
>
> (Najder, *JC* 12)

With the enemies of Poland in power, the project of "being a Pole" was in many ways impossible "in" Poland, where one could only be a captive subject, or, like Apollo Korzeniowski, a failed revolutionary. Partition occasioned not only heroic martyrdoms and doomed insurrections, but an enduring debate about the true nature, and even the location, of Poland. Those who, like the Korzeniowskis, found themselves in the Russian sector, often insisted, as Conrad does in the passage just quoted, that Poland was essentially a Western-style modern nation. But Poland had other, undeniable affiliations, and elsewhere Conrad himself would derive Poland's identity from its geographical situation "between Slavo-Tartar Byzantine barbarism on one side and the German tribes on the other" (qtd. in Karl, *JC* 78n). In this construction, Poland does not occupy a precarious space between the modernizing West and the archaic East, but is rather positioned geotemporally between two kinds of primitivism in a moment *before* either East or West discovered modernity, with Poland's politically advanced but ancient liberalism providing an anachronistic contrast to both. On another occasion, Conrad employed the figure of a purely spatial betweenness while retaining the Polish difference, describing Poland as being "compressed between Prussian Germanism on one side and Russian Slavonism on the other. For Germanism it feels nothing but hatred. But between Polonism and Slavonism there is not so much hatred as a complete and ineradicable incompatibility" (*NLL* 135–36).

Since so much of Poland was, in Conrad's time, part of Russia, and since Poland had traditionally been considered part of the transnational Slavic world, one might question how "ineradicable" this incompatibility really was (see Dvornik xxii). Conrad is also concerned in this passage to establish the radical difference between Prussia and Russia, and to situate the predicament of Poland in that inconceivable space. But his major political essay, "Autocracy and War" (1905), describes not only these radical differences between East and West, but also an unsettling "common guilt," which is "defined precisely" by the gigantic seam of "their frontier line running through the Polish provinces," a common guilt marked by a common frontier that indicates, one would think, a certain commonality (*NLL* 95). The essay is memorable most of all for its extended and extraordinarily lurid personifications of Russia as a gigantic and inhuman monstrosity, a thing apart, a "dreaded and strange apparition, bristling with bayonets, armed with chains, hung over with holy images; that something not of this world, partaking of a ravenous ghoul, of a blind Djinn grown up from a cloud, and of the Old Man of the Sea . . . with its old stupidity, with its strange mystical arrogance, stamping its shadowy feet upon the gravestone of autocracy." Russia, Conrad writes, is a vast "*Néant* . . . the negation of everything worth living for," and of "everything else that has its root in reason or conscience" (*NLL* 89, 100, 101). Still, the essay concludes with an abrupt switch, warning that, the crimes of Russia notwithstanding, "*Le Prussianisme—voilà l'ennemi*" (114). What Poland *means* in the geopolitical sense is the underlying identity of East and West, barbarism and tribalism, primitivism and modernity, even human and inhuman.

One begins to suspect that there is in fact no authentic *between* at all, no space—no matter how slender—that could be called simply Polish. (Indeed, one of the most disconcerting moments in "Autocracy and War" occurs when Conrad characterizes Russia as "a yawning chasm open between East and West," suggesting that Poland's distinctive betweenness may have been modeled on that of the hated enemy [*NLL* 100].) Genuine Polonism could not be located anywhere except on foreign soil, that is, on Polish soil effectively claimed by a military, political, and symbolic order hostile to Poland. The recognition of an "ineradicable incompatibility" between the resistant material base and the various symbolic, and not only symbolic, orders that might appropriate it has inflected Polish identity down to the present, leading to a characteristic uneasiness with the notion of identity itself. In a 1994 interview, the writer Adam Michnik reasserted that the key to the Polish national character is its militant refusal of identity: "I believe," he said, "that the greatest misfortune for my country and my nation is the tendency to impose a single identity on the whole of Poland. . . . In reality there is a common Polish identity which is pluralistic and heterogeneous; that is our strength, we have it in our genes" (28). As a nation, Poland is unique; and yet its uniqueness is determined by the fact that its nature is, to an uncertain extent, confused with precisely those oppressive and anti-Polish forces: nothing could be more foreign to it than the forces that, since the Partition, had dominated it. Thus, it is strictly in the Polish tradition, strictly in keeping with the Idea, when Conrad establishes his individuality, his difference from the West, by affirming his "ultra-Slav nature" and by naming his second son Borys, the patron saint of Russia, because he "wanted to have a purely Slavonic name" (qtd. in Fleishman 20; Najder, *CUFE* 221). It is strictly in the Polish tradition, too, when Conrad suggests, in 1914, that Polish hopes might best be realized by Poland's coming under the protection of an expanded Austria; or when, two years later, he proposes a Triple Protectorate involving England, France, and, amazingly, Russia, whom he generously includes in order to "allay to the fullest extent her possible apprehensions and satisfy her national sentiment" (Najder, *CPB* 303–04; *NLL* 139). Both proposals suggest an inability to think of Poland without thinking of, and through, others—even, in the second case, the absolute Other of Russia.

At the end of the nineteenth century, in the most unrestrained era of Western imperial violence, a more or less Russian-based Slavic nature could be a useful thing, a subnationalist and yet still "Polish" resistance to the forms of illiberalism that had arisen in the West in violation of its own ideals. Polishness, as we are just beginning to see, could be deployed as a means of justification, of disidentification with the crimes of the East and the West, a project close to the heart of Poles such as Conrad, who insists that "there was never a history more free from political bloodshed than the history of the Polish State" (*NLL* 132). Even today, Michnik can mime and mock and repeat the Polish tendency to self-justification: "None of us has ever done anything wicked" (26). The negative form of such statements is altogether characteristic of the terms of Polish self-assertion. The "national spirit" that articulated and celebrated itself at the funeral of Conrad's father possessed neither land nor state apparatus; but it could count among its resources a remarkable variousness that could always find a way to dissociate itself from its Others. It could, for example, describe itself—as Conrad does describe it in the "Author's Note" to *A Personal Record*—as defined by "the most liberal currents of Western thought. An impartial view of humanity . . . together with a special regard for the rights of the unprivileged of this earth, not on any mystic ground but on the ground of simple fellowship and honourable reciprocity of services. . . . [The Polish mentality is] removed as far as possible from that humanitarianism that seems to be merely a matter of crazy nerves or a morbid conscience" (vii). Neither mystic nor humanitarian, the Polish national spirit, based on a "view" and a "regard," seems to be "removed as far as possible" from any positive self-determination whatsoever.

The national idea seems most mobile and most negatively determined in the person of its most uncompromisingly faithful representative, Apollo Korzeniowski. John Galsworthy suggested that some features of Conrad's work could be traced to the fact that he was "the son of a Revolutionist," a suggestion to which Conrad took vehement exception: "No epithet could be more inapplicable to a man with such a strong sense of responsibility in the region of ideas and action and so indifferent to the promptings of personal ambition as my father" (*PR* vii). "No more revolutionary than the others," Conrad replied, Apollo Korzeniowski had been engaged not in "revolution" against a properly constituted state, but in one of a series of "revolts against foreign domination," actions that, however they might appear to the Russian occupiers, had a conservative purpose, seeking a mere reversion to an authentically Polish existence rather than "the subversion of any social or political scheme of existence" (vii-viii). His father had sought, in other words, no positive program, only the negation of the regime, the departure of the oppressors, the undoing of the wrong of Partition, a general liberation of Poles, Lithuanians, Belorussians, Ukrainians, and the freeing of the serfs. On 22 January 1863, the Central Committee he had been instrumental in forming issued an emancipation proclamation declaring the complete enfranchisement of every person in the Polish realm; but beyond a general wish to see the spread of freedom, Apollo Korzeniowski's goals were vague. "I could never make out his political and social beliefs," Tadeusz Bobrowski wrote of his brother-in-law, "except his vague leanings towards a republican form of government and towards something equally vague: *per modum* of [similar to] the rights guaranteed by the 3 May Constitution [1791]—which in our own day is already inadequate. . . . poets and people of imagination and ideals are generally unable to state their life postulates clearly" (Najder, *CUFE* 17–18). As Conrad wrote in "Poland Revisited" (1915), his father had been unswervingly faithful to "a creed which the simplest heart in that crowd could feel and understand" (*NLL* 169).

Indeed, perhaps *only* the simplest could understand it, for it lacked detail, as Korzeniowski himself had lacked positive accomplishment or contribution. The simplest hearts could rightly honor the memory of an impoverished, radical, tormented, highly educated but crucially uncertain member of the gentry not despite the fact that, but because, they "could have known nothing positive about him." "I had nothing but that knowledge myself," Conrad adds ambiguously (*PR* viii). Other than his funeral, Conrad records about his father only the fact that before he died he burned his manuscripts. Still, the mark of the father can be seen in the son's dedication to undifferentiated ideas—simplicity, solidarity, fidelity—and to negative formulations: *removed as far as possible from, nothing is more foreign than, no epithet could be more inapplicable to, no more revolutionary than the others.*

What the simplest hearts understood perhaps better than anything else was that the man, like the nation to which he was faithful, was dead. Under Partition, with, as one writer put it, "the nation in three coffins," living Poles felt a special kinship with the dead (qtd. in Lednicki 14). As Conrad comments about the bond between his father and his mourners, "The dead and they were victims alike of an unrelenting destiny which cut them off from every path of merit and glory" (*NLL* 169). Apollo Korzeniowski was never so much a man of the people as at his funeral.

The Cracow procession may in fact have been the defining moment of Apollo Korzeniowski's life. Permitted by the more liberal Austrian authorities in the semiautonomous Cracow because they feared a popular uprising if they did not permit it—or because they feared none if they did—the funeral defined "the national spirit" with eloquent precision. It took, in Conrad's account, the form of an assertion that was not quite a protest or even a true statement. How could the massive silence Conrad noted fail to express submission as well as solidarity? Decisively Polish, the event was still not exactly antiauthoritarian, and was perhaps most emphatically Polish in that it was not. Moreover, the procession commemorated not only a death but a failed and, for the most part, an extraordinarily unproductive and gloomy life, a life devoted to an "idea" that was never realized partly because, in exercising what agency he did have, Apollo Korzeniowski contributed to the establishment of an even more oppressive despotism than the one against which he protested. In the Russian sector, the Polish language, the teaching of Polish history, and any mention of "Poland" had been outlawed since the 1831 uprising; but after 1863, Russia eliminated the very last remnants of political autonomy. One highly effective means of doing so was to empower the peasants, any gains made by whom had to come at the expense of Korzeniowski's class, the *szlachta*, the largely dispossessed, subaristocratic hereditary intelligentsia who had traditionally ruled the country and owned the land. What seemed to constitute a liberalizing reform under Russian rule was actually intended "to destroy the *szlachta* as a class" and thus to eliminate the base of future political activism (Breuilly 119).

Conrad seems quietly to have absorbed the lesson of his father's career. Composing an "Author's Note" to his 1911 novel about Russia, *Under Western Eyes* in 1920, he gave, perhaps unwittingly, a comprehensively damning analysis of antiautocratic activism: "The ferocity and imbecility of an autocratic rule rejecting all legality and in fact basing itself upon complete moral anarchism provokes the no less imbecile and atrocious answer of a purely Utopian revolutionism. . . . These people are unable to see that all they can effect is merely a change of names. The oppressors and the oppressed are all Russians together" (*UWE* 51). Walking at the head of the procession as the representative of his dead father, Conrad occupied both the place of honor and the position of maximum impotence. He saw in the hushed crowds the visible form of an unrealized idea, fidelity to negation, and identification enabled by a lack of precise knowledge; they saw in the eleven-year-old boy the shadow of a Shade.

My argument in this chapter will be that the spirit of Poland was manifest in all its simplicity not only in this funeral and in Conrad's faithful account of it, but in Conrad's work generally; and this despite the fact that Poland is almost entirely absent from it. *Like* the Poles, and *as* a Pole, the adult Conrad did not (often) speak or write Polish, and (almost) never mentioned the name of Poland. His practice in this respect is critically different from, for example, James Joyce, an émigré who wrote exclusively and literally about his native land. Conrad wrote about Poland only in a manner so indirect and encrypted as to elude even his detection: he wrote about an erased Poland in a manner that reflected and repeated that erasure. His critics, to be sure, have not felt bound to silence with respect to Poland, but those who have written on Conrad's "Polish background" have tended to leave it in the background as a source of various characters, incidents, or attitudes, the foreground being claimed by Conrad's more conscious exercise of artistry, his "philosophy," his "politics," his technical innovations, his modernism or postmodernism, his prescient insight into the unconscious, his endorsement or critique of colonialism—by everything but Poland. In general, they have assimilated Conrad to the West as "one of us," to recall for the first time the phrase Marlow applies to Lord Jim, even if only to hold him responsible for the West's various crimes. Timothy Brennan, to take one example, situates *Heart of Darkness* among other "classic modernist" "novels of empire" that refuse to take in the "human realities" of domination, or to embrace a "comprehensive approach" based on "the work of those who have not merely visited but lived it" (48). Brennan and others who count Conrad among the ranks of Western imperialists interpret as a *lack* what is in fact an *excess*. Conrad's experience of domination was not merely touristic: he had actually been dominated, but he had also lived as a citizen and agent of the imperial nations. His experience, in other words, was *truly* comprehensive, a fact that confuses the moralizing mind and is, indeed, genuinely confusing.

A long tradition in Conrad criticism discovers Poland as secret or symbol. *Lord* Jim in particular has been read as an allegory of Conrad's feelings about Poland, especially about his own culpable "leap" from the beleaguered national ship (see Morf; Najder, *CUFE* passim). But the possibility of a deep determination of Conrad's sensibility by "the Polish spirit," an effect that is not empirically detectable as an "influence" and does not operate at the level of character, plot, or symbol, has gone unrecognized despite a remarkable quantity of archival information made available by Zdzisław Najder and others over the past thirty years. Meanwhile, Conrad has been canonized as a Western writer; as the heir of Rousseau, Burke, Carlyle, Matthew Arnold, Maupassant, and Flaubert; as part of the Great Tradition of the English novel or of the French tradition of literary "impressionism"; as the voice of cosmopolitan modernity itself—and attacked as a typical Western imperialist, racist, and phallocrat. As Conrad and countless other emigrés throughout the nineteenth century demonstrated, Poland was easy to leave, all the more so because it could not be located on the map of sovereign states to begin with; and like Conrad, his readers have also "emigrated," without realizing that emigration is a "Polish" phenomenon, a "Polish" tradition, a gesture distinctively expressive of the national character.

"Poland" must, in other words, be conceived differently, in a way responsive to the actual concrete particulars of its historical situation, particulars that rendered it very far from being concrete and even from being historical. In the concrete historical sense, Poland did not exist during Conrad's era except as an ideal object of bitter dispute. Even within the intensely patriotic world inhabited by Conrad's parents' generation, Polish specificity resisted what Michnik calls "single identity." Friedrich Nietzsche tried, in fact, to account for his "*Doppelgänger*" character by pointing to his ancestors: "Polish noblemen: I have many racial instincts in my body from that source—who knows?" and adding that he had been "merely externally *sprinkled* with what is German" (1:iii, 225). While Nietzsche's ancestors included German clergymen and butchers but no Polish noblemen, he struck upon Polishness as a sign of an oppositional temperament, a refusal to be "merely German," an insistently multiple identity. Conrad's own family efficiently summarizes the deep (*Doppelgänger*) division within the *szlachta* class between what Avrom Fleishman called "the romantic ne'er-do-well Korzeniowski side of his nature" and "the mature and enlightened Bobrowski heritage" represented by Tadeusz Bobrowski, the maternal uncle who oversaw the boy's upbringing after the death of his parents and provided funds, advice, and reproaches well into Conrad's adulthood (8). Fleishman speaks for those who see Conrad not as a Slavo-Dostoevskyan alien let loose in foreign lands to whose history and institutions he was only superficially attached, but rather as a true citizen of the liberal West who shared its concerns for individual freedoms, rights, and liberties, as well as its anxieties about the ethical status of such issues as race and empire. He speaks just as forcefully for any who regards the issue as determinable in one way or another by reference to either of Conrad's "fathers." A glance at these two men suggests the true complexity of the situation. It was the enlightened uncle who was, during the turbulence of the 1860s, one of the Appeasers, the party that sought accommodation with a Russia whose political dominance it did not seriously question; and the romantic father with his pointedly Western name who insisted on an absolute Polish difference from Russia, embraced liberty, and translated Hugo, de Vigny, and Shakespeare. If the uncle was Western (-Eastern), the father was Eastern (-Western).

If to be Polish at that time was to be defined by such oppositions as East and West, it was not necessarily to choose or to be able to choose one or the other, or even to understand precisely what those terms might mean in a Polish context. This passionate overdetermination, this intense investment in oppositions that refuse to remain opposed, stands as the primary mark of Poland in Conrad. The evident facts that Conrad is uneasy in any company, that his relation to contexts in general is unclarified and insecure, and that while he can always be made out to be one of us there is something that marks him as one of them as well suggest a dimension of Conrad not fully cognizable by the kind of mentality whose conceptual resources are exhausted by the binary opposition and its synthetic resolution, by what may be called the theoretical mind. This factor of excess may, I will argue, be conveniently and accurately called "Poland."

This not a question, then, of determining the proper historico-ideological referent of Conrad's fictions, but rather of giving a name to the difficulty of doing so. The force with which Poland determines Conrad's work is directly proportional to its literal nonappearance within it. Poland functions not as biographical background but as what Jacques Lacan (undoubtedly thinking of Poland) calls "the real," that which guarantees the consistency of the symbolic order, but which cannot appear within that order except as disfigurement or "stain." Thus, we can mark the appearance of Poland in such unlikely sites as the crushed face discovered in the mud by the river in Conrad's first book, *Almayer's Folly;* and in the misspelled forms of *Patna* (the ship from which Jim jumps: read "Patria" or "Polska," the Polish name for Poland) or of *Pelham,* a highly filagreed novel by Bulwer-Lytton about English *szlachta,* a gentry class devoted to cultivating its own trivial liberties, a book incongruously treasured by the nearly illiterate Singleton in *The Nigger;* and in the almost ludicrously extended conceit about the winds in *The Mirror of the Sea,* where the "Rulers of East and West" are said to divide the oceans between them, each with an autocratic "genius of supreme rule" (92).

Poland also has a more general applicability. If, "in" Poland, Poland was elsewhere, then Conrad's work is Polish inasmuch as the real pith or subject of his work, its *thing* or *matter,* is other than it seems to be. The real significance of Poland in Conrad's work is that the real significance is elsewhere; or, to put the matter otherwise, where the real significance is elsewhere in Conrad, there Poland is. Poland stands as the type and first formulation of an elsewhereness, a foreignness, that informs and infects such disparate Conradian phenomena as his heroes, his political ideas, his plots, his "universality," his settings, even some of his stylistic exotica. Poland provides, moreover, a concrete historical source of Conrad's mannered atmospherics, dominated by darkness, shadows, shades, obscurity, invisibility. Lastly, Poland is the proper name, the specific cultural origin for Conrad of that quality of canonical literature that encourages interpretive contestation, multiple signification, undecidability, dissemination. The "richness" or "excessiveness" of "great" literature, its irreducibility to its contexts, ideas, or ideologies—its capacity to mean more and other than any single, coherent account of it would suggest—has a root, in Conrad's case, in Poland.

POLAND AND THE THEORY OF NATIONS

A nation is a historically evolved, stable community of language, territory, economic life, and psychological make-up manifested in a community of culture.
—Joseph Stalin, "Marxism and the National Question"

What, then, is Poland? The question is easily answered: Poland is a nation, one of the oldest, largest, and most distinguished in the world. Among European nations, only France has a comparable antiquity, and during the sixteenth and seventeenth centuries, Poland could claim pre-eminence in Eastern Europe for its scientific and cultural achievements. Poland's most distinctive contribution to European civilization was, however, its unique form of government, a "Royal

Republic" where, in the most ambitious experiment with republican government since Rome, the monarch was elected by the gentry. Living in the freest and most tolerant multi-ethnic and multireligious state in Europe, the nobles possessed a unique responsibility for their kingdom; indeed, in the most extraordinary feature of their constitution, a single noble could invoke the *liberum veto,* instantly dissolving the Diet and nullifying all its proceedings. (Nietzsche counted the *liberum veto* among the "racial instincts in my body from that source" [225].) While the rest of Europe was engaging in religious wars and perfecting the despotism of kings and czars, Poland was experimenting with radical democracy, and was doing so to the cheers of Enlightenment philosophers, especially Rousseau, who wrote a pamphlet on behalf of the "gentry republic" (a weirdly Tory document that counsels against liberation of the serfs; blandly assumes that Poles will eventually become Russian subjects whose republic will exist only in their hearts; and advises Poles to change nothing, to "think well before laying hands upon your laws, especially those that have made you what you are" [26]). If representation was limited to a single class, that class included about ten percent of the entire population, with more formally "active citizens" than nineteenth-century France or than England before the introduction of universal suffrage (Walicki, "PN"; see also Walicki, *BMN.*) Moreover, Poland was neither dynastic nor susceptible to foreign domination. Nor did Poland seek an empire; the Polish Confederation included an ancient and voluntary union with Lithuania, and embraced Ruthenian (Ukrainian and Belorussian) peasants, who had not sought national autonomy.

Nor was Poland a mere state, a region united under a government whose inhabitants shared no other affiliation than that they lived in lands ruled by a single monarch. As an ethnically and religiously diverse polity whose inhabitants were yet "centered" in an idea of Polishness, Poland was a radiant anticipation and prototype of the modern nation; it was, as Conrad says, a "State which had adopted and brought them [modern nations] up in the development of its own humane culture" (*NLL* 133). The Ukrainian-American historian Roman Szporluk contends, in fact, that "the Polish case deserves to be placed alongside the French Revolution as a major historical event that had a direct ideological significance in the history of national-ism" because it demonstrated to intellectuals of "new" nations in Central and Eastern Europe that claims to nationhood could be based on "language, culture, and 'soul.'" Thus, Szporluk concludes, "while the Poles were unique, they became a role model" (84–85). In this way, Poland directly inspired the emergence of new nations—includ-ing, after a pause of about a century and a quarter, Poland itself, which reunited nation with state after the defeat of Germany in the Great War.

History was not, however, kind to Poland. Precursor to all nations, Poland was distributed among its enemies as those enemies began the process of becoming nations. The extinction of Poland as a con-sequence of three partitions—1772, 1793, and 1795, when Poland was finally consumed entire—constituted an historical crime on the grand scale, the victory of despotism and empire over republican government, a huge step backwards for modernity; and yet it was solemnly reaffirmed by representatives of the nations gathered at the Congress of Vienna in 1815, who recognized its rationale. Modernity did not protest. Indeed, as Mikhail Bakunin (whom Conrad would use as a model for Peter Ivanovich in *Under Western Eyes*) notes, in a tone of bitter irony (a tone that was Conrad's only access to humor), Frederick and Catherine were, at the time of Partition, "conducting a witty and philanthropic correspondence with the French philo-sophes" (65). Conrad argues in his 1919 essay "The Crime of Parti-tion" a suggestive and provocative case that, in being destroyed, Po-land "secured the safety of the French Revolution" by offering itself to Prussia and Russia as a more vulnerable sponsor of democratic ideals, "an immediate satisfaction to their cupidity" (*NLL* 117). "Thus," he notes, giving the matter a distinctively "Conradian" twist, "even a crime may become a moral agent by the lapse of time and the course of history" (118). Most intriguing, however, is the unusual conviction and emphasis with which Conrad states, "I am speaking of what I know when I say that the original and only formative idea in Europe was the idea of delivering the fate of Poland into the hands of Russian Tsarism" (126). Europe, Conrad nearly suggests, could form itself as a system of modern political entities *only* by first parti-tioning Poland, whose example suggested, perhaps, that nationalism did not have to await a revolution, that dynastic regimes could have been abolished long ago, that nationality was not the creation of the Western Enlightenment. Before European nations and nationalism itself could be born, Poland had to die.

Or—in a marginally less morbid formulation—modern nations and nationalism awoke from a dream of Poland that quickly receded into unconsciousness. Lord Acton commented that the Partition "awakened the theory of nationality in Europe, converting a dormant right into an aspiration, and a sentiment into a political claim . . . Thenceforward there was a nation demanding to be united in a State—a soul, as it were, wandering in search of a body . . . and, for the first time, a cry was heard that the arrangement of States was unjust—that their limits were unnatural, and that a whole people was deprived of its right to constitute an independent community." From this unprecedented severance of nation from state there arose "the theory of nationality," which carried fatal consequences for "the ancient European system" (413–14). That system included, however, the nation of Poland itself, which was among the first victims of this awakening, after which Polish patriots had to struggle to remember, in a radically changed world, what and where Poland was. The task fell largely to the literary rather than the political class. Post-Partition Poland existed solely as a phantasm, a collective dream, a fiction. Czeslaw Milosz remarks in a recent essay "On Nationalism" that "Poland, after it disappeared from the map of Europe at the end of the eighteenth century, was invented anew by a few poets" (16). Understanding the force of dreams, Czar Alexander II concluded a speech to a Polish audience in 1865 by warning, "Point des rêveries, messieurs!" (by which he really meant, Dream on!) (Najder, *CUFE* 35n). And Conrad, recalling his visit to Poland in 1914, records his relief at discovering that Poland, "if erased from the map, yet existed in reality; it was not a mere *pays du rêve*, where you can travel only in imagination" (*NLL* 148).

In a classic 1882 essay that stands at the origin of the theorization of the nation, Ernest Renan drew attention to the decisive role played in the formation of a national community by "forgetting" and "historical error." "Unity is always effected by means of brutality," he wrote, and a violence that must be repressed lies at the origin of every nation: "The essence of a nation is that all individuals have many things in common, and also that they have forgotten many things" ("WN" 11). From this bold statement the singular position of partitioned Poland in the theory of European nationality can be immediately inferred. Poland was a nation, but it had not achieved its unity through brutality; consequently, Poland had not had to suppress the memory of the means by which its original heterogeneity had been subdued. In short, Poland disproved the theory that other nations exemplified and made those nations' brutality appear inessential to their nationhood, a gratuitous rather than a lamentably necessary immersion in blood. As the relatively recent victim rather than the ancient perpetrator of violence, Poland had no founding crime to forget: thus, what Homi Bhabha calls the "minus in the origin" of the nation's narrative was not, in Poland's case, *in* the origin, which had been a glorious plus; the minus was in the present ("DN" 310). This was undoubtedly, in some abstract sense, Poland's ongoing offense. If nations, or at least most nations, begin by forgetting, then Poland stood as the most immediate and all-but-visible token of *that which did not forget and which must therefore be forgotten.* As Conrad almost puts it, forgetting Poland was "the original and only formative idea in Europe."

Emergent European nations found the spectacle, and the idea, of a nation of dreamers enlightening and instructive because of the formative role played by dreams and imagination in the construction of nations generally. This role is the burden of Benedict Anderson's classic 1983 study of nations as *Imagined Communities,* as it is for a number of others who have extended Anderson's claim with arguments that nations are "inventions" that occur independent of "material or [objective] structural factors"; or that "for the purpose of analysis nationalism comes before nations" (Greenfield 402; Hobsbawm 10). Poland seems to be the very type of an imagined community—and yet, astonishingly, it is altogether absent from Anderson's study. To understand why, we need to probe the theory of nationalism more deeply; to do this we can begin with Anderson's list of three "paradoxes" common to nationalism: "(1) The objective modernity of nations to the historian's eye vs. their subjective antiquity in the eyes of nationalists. (2) The formal universality of nationality as a socio-

cultural concept [the fact that everyone has a national identity] ...
vs. the irremediable particularity of its concrete manifestations [in
that these identities are all distinct from the others].... (3) The
'political' power of nationalisms vs. their philosophical poverty and
even incoherence" (*IC* 5). All three "paradoxes" ultimately reflect and
affirm a single fact, that nations are not natural or historically inevitable entities, but "cultural artefacts of a particular kind" that are
brought into being and sustained by collective imagination as limited,
sovereign communities based on "deep, horizontal comradeship" (4,
7). Each "vs." signals an effort to represent what has been created by
human agency as a deep-laid fact of that nation's being. Nations are
represented as ancient when they are in fact recent inventions; national identity is represented as particularizing when it is from another, more spacious, point of view a universal trait; and nations are
represented as clear and distinct ideas when, to the philosopher, they
are mere units of force.

The question is, however, whether "paradox" is the right term for
what might be considered differences in point of view between the
nationalist's "inside" and the historian's or philosopher's "outside."
Hasn't Anderson simply misnamed perspectival difference? Unlike
true paradoxes, the struggles he outlines are incapable of being resolved or absorbed into larger synthetic unities; the two simply co-
exist as different registers or kinds of facts, accessible from different
points of view. The larger category suggested by these conflicts is,
then, not real but apparent paradox, or simple complexity. If Anderson had wanted nationalist paradoxes, he could have found them
more readily in the "Royal Republic" of Poland than in his favored
example of Indochina—of which, like Conrad, he is a scrupulous observer. The properly paradoxical character of Polish nationalism, and
its real unassimilability to Anderson's theory of nationalism, emerges
into full view when we consider the relation of Poland in Conrad's
time to Anderson's three pseudoparadoxes.

In the first case, Poland, like other nations, was imagined in terms
of a temporal split, but one that reversed the usual sequence. Poland
was not "objectively" recent and "subjectively" ancient; following the
last partition, its objective existence was ancient, while its recent existence was entirely subjective. In the second, Polish nationalists of the

time typically did not regard nationality as "formally universal," but as distinctive of Poles; we have already seen how Conrad situated Poland not between two nationalities but between tribalism and barbarism, between the hated and the utterly alien. Nor did Poles regard the "natives" living within the boundaries of Poland as having any significant national identity that might interfere with Polish dominance. Not even the radical Apollo Korzeniowski, who urged the liberation of Ruthenians, Lithuanians, and ethnic Germans living within the pre-Partition boundaries of Poland, contemplated immediate nationhood for them. When, in 1863, Lithuanians fought with Poles against Russian domination, they did so in the trust that if the struggle had been successful, they would have been given their sovereignty by the Poles, most of whom in fact harbored no such ambition for them, Lithuania traditionally having been an acquiescent junior partner in the Confederation. Marx and Engels reaffirmed the Polish position by distinguishing between nations and nationalities. Unlike the reactionary and divisive "principle of nationalities" based on the claims of separatist ethnic groups (a "*Russian invention concocted to destroy Poland*"), the right of historical nations to self-government did not, they argued, conflict with the centralizing tendency of universal progress ("WC" 100). Therefore, they concluded, Poland should be free, but the "at least four different nationalities" within Poland should not (101). This conclusion precisely accorded with the traditional Polish sense of the matter, if not with Anderson's claim that national identity is "formally universal." The case of Lithuania demonstrates another Polish counterinstance to Anderson's hypothesis, for Lithuania was not simply a subnational ethnicity but something closer to a national identity. However, one could, without contradiction, be both a Pole and a Lithuanian: the great poet of *Polish* romantic nationalism, Adam Mickiewicz, begins his masterpiece *Master Thaddeus* with the salute, "Lithuania, my fatherland." Thus, within traditional, pre-Partition Poland, if only there, national identities were not altogether exclusive.

Anderson's third pseudoparadox is particularly painful to contemplate from a Polish point of view. As uprising after doomed uprising demonstrated beyond appeal, Polish nationalism had no political power whatsoever. It did, however, possess a philosophical richness and coherence that flourished in a climate of political impotence, where theory encountered no check in the material world. The most palpable Polish contribution to Enlightenment political theory, the Constitution of the Third of May 1791, reflected the influence of Locke, the French Encyclopaedists, Voltaire, and Rousseau. Burke thought it one of the noblest benefits received by any nation at any time, and Marx judged it "the only work of liberty which Eastern Europe has ever created independently" (qtd. in Walicki, *BMN* 152–53). The Constitution did take several steps forward, guaranteeing the rights of serfs and breaking down barriers between burghers and nobility, but as a properly paradoxical document, it also took several steps backward by making Polish kingship hereditary at a time when monarchies were being challenged all over Europe, and by identifying, against the secularizing tendency of its own and European history, Catholicism as the state religion. Polish nationalist movements of the nineteenth century explicitly sought to restore the dominance of the *szlachta* as well as the institution of the monarchy; as John Breuilly comments, "the political movement for the restoration of Poland can hardly be seen as particularly modern" (117). So far ahead of its time during the preceding several centuries, Poland was now, under the banner of modernity, retreating. Enlightened before the Enlightenment, Poland now began to be legitimist after the Revolution. Anachronistically modern in its golden age, Poland was now, at the beginning of modernity, anachronistically regressive.

Moreover, as a show of Polish independence, the philosophically rich Constitution provoked Catherine into attacking the Polish army, initiating a chain of events that led directly to the final partition. The Constitution demonstrates, then, a perfect "photographic negative" of Anderson's thesis, a direct relation within Polish nationalism between philosophical richness and political impotence, a relation that takes, among historians of Poland, the rhetorical form of "in spite of." "In spite of the fact that Poland was in ruins," one historian writes, "Polish thought continued to defend itself" (Lednicki 14). Or, in the words of *The Cambridge History of Poland,* "in spite of the political stagnation and the mutilation of the body politic, the intensity and universality of intellectual work increases more and more" (Reddaway et al. 125).

To recapitulate, post-Partition Poland precisely reverses all three of Anderson's "paradoxes": the nation was objectively ancient and subjectively recent; national identity was considered distinctive of Poles, and yet not exclusive of other (at least protonational) identities; and Polish nationalism was philosophically robust but politically impotent. In all three respects, Poland was genuinely paradoxical, and thus provides, it would seem, the best possible illustration of Anderson's contention that nationalism is structured as paradox; but it may be that the *properly* paradoxical character of Polish nationalism accounts for Poland's exclusion from Anderson's discussion. Anderson is concerned to articulate a coherent theory of nationalism, and true paradoxes must remain inimical to the theoretical enterprise. Poland is, then, both the ultimate nation-as-paradox and a kind of anti-nation, a negative of what a nation theoretically ought to be.

The peculiar relation of Poland to the theory of nationalism is confirmed by the calendar. By Anderson's calculations, the history of the limited sovereign community of the Polish nation occurred *before* the invention of nationalism. Nations were first conceived, he says, "towards the end of the eighteenth century," a date that has "not been seriously disputed except by nationalist ideologues in particular countries"—by which he certainly means Poland—and "nationalism" as an accepted term did not appear until a century later (*IC* 4). If nations were, as the experts contend, products of the Enlightenment, of pluralistic and revolutionary thinking that undermined the claims of divinely ordained dynasties, then Poland could not be a nation, for by the flowering of the Enlightenment, it was in coffins. Situated at the historical origin of republican political practice and of the very concept of the nation, Poland is rigorously excluded by the theory of nationalism that subsequently arose to explain the phenomenon. Poland is, in fact, as expendable and even intolerable to the theory of nationalism as it had been to nations themselves.

Anderson is merely typical in this respect, for Poland is in general conspicuous by its absence in recent theories of nationalism. It is entirely omitted from, or mentioned only as one of a series of examples in, such representative recent books as Liah Greenfield's *Nationalism: Five Roads to Modernity,* Miroslav Hroch's *Social Preconditions of National Revival in Europe,* Larry Diamond and Marc Plattner's *Nation-*

alism, Ethnic Conflict, and Democracy, Walker Connor's *Ethnonationalism: The Quest for Understanding,* Homi Bhabha's anthology *Nation and Narration,* William Pfaff's *The Wrath of Nations: Civilization and the Furies of Nationalism,* Ernest Gellner's *Nations and Nationalism,* Yael Tamir's *Liberal Nationalism,* and Michael Ignatieff's *Blood and Belonging: Journeys into the New Nationalism*—the last because, poignantly enough, Poland's reattainment of national autonomy preceded the more recent and fashionable revolutions of 1989; by the time Ignatieff got around to making his journeys, Poland was already and once again a depressing example of what Conrad, in "Poland Revisited" (1916), had called "the bitter vanity of old hopes" (*NLL* 170).

Nonetheless, in a familiar irony, the theory always seems to be drawn from the heart of Poland itself, as when Renan acknowledges the crucial role of suffering: "Where national memories are concerned, griefs are of more value than triumphs" ("WN" 19); or when Gellner claims that nations are "groups which *will* themselves to persist as communities" (53), and stresses the crucial role of high culture in this willing; or when Greenfield says at the conclusion to her study that "*nationalism is, fundamentally, a matter of dignity,*" and that "it gives people reason to be proud" (489). Poland is unmentioned in all three instances because, it seems, there is always something wrong with the *way* in which Poland exemplifies the theory, some incongruous element that frustrates the drive for clarity. For Renan, Poland may have had ample supply of grief, but may not, in its fractious disenfranchisement or its "anarchic" traditions, have evidenced the kind of "moral consciousness," centering on "the abdication of the individual to the advantage of the community," necessary to the legitimacy of a nation (20). For Gellner, *szlachta* high culture did not pervade the "entire population and not just elite minorities" in the way he considers definitive of true nations (55). Nor does Poland accommodate Gellner's "great, but valid, paradox": that nations "can be defined only in terms of the age of nationalism, rather than, as you might expect, the other way round" (55). Poland's prematurity also seems to disqualify it from Greenfield's consideration. She demonstrates that in most cases, the nationalist sentiment arises as the result of a crisis of identity excited by some traumatic encounter with an external form of power. This would seem to be the case with maximally traumatized Poland, and yet it is not, for Poland was a nation only when there was no external threat, and when there was a threat, Poland was a dream. For Greenfield, nationalism seems to be the only "road to modernity"; but while Poland had traveled that road—indeed it had blazed the trail—it remained, during Conrad's lifetime and beyond, rigorously unmodern. For Gellner and Greenfield, as for Anderson, Poland is unassimilable to the theory of nationalism, not because it fails to meet the criteria, but because it either meets them at the wrong time, or meets them and more. Geopolitically nonexistent, Poland is theoretically excessive.

When "the perennial Polish question" is actually considered in recent accounts of nationalism, the manner of its appearance suggests not its centrality but its aberrance, the dubious or paradoxical legitimacy of its nationalism and nationhood. The left-wing historian E. J. Hobsbawm points out in *Nations and Nationalism since 1780: Programme, Myth, Reality* that "most Polish-speaking peasants . . . did not yet feel themselves to be nationalist Poles," and that nineteenth-century Polish nationalism was largely grounded in religion, "a paradoxical cement for . . . modern nationalism" (44, 68). Poland eventually achieved statehood, he points out, not through the rippling effects of a widespread nationalist sentiment but because of a "combination of social and national demands" under the leadership of the socialist Pilsudski (125). Taken all around, he insists, the Polish "'nation' must not be confused with modern nationality" (74). Poland is also unsatisfactory when seen from the right. In a study of *Nationalism* first published in 1960, the conservative political theorist Elie Kedourie was if anything even more skeptical than Hobsbawm of Polish nationalism, pointing out once again the absence of nationalist feeling among Polish peasants, the lack of a "true" nation during the period of Polish statehood, and the rank opportunism of Polish nationalists who, at the conclusion of World War I, argued for boundaries based "on the historical principle, corrected by the linguistic wherever it works in our favour" (Namier, qtd. in Kedourie 116). Like Hobsbawm, Kedourie only mentions Poland to dismiss its claims to genuine, modern nationalism.

In short, Poland seems to have suffered a kind of theoretical partition, being divided among theories of nationalism, religious identity, class hegemony, political strategy, and other kinds of strategic maneuvering or abject victimization that are felt to be incompatible with proper nationalism.

Poland has, it seems, this effect on the theory of nationalism: it both excites and defeats it—and thus is rejected by it. Poland incites nationalist theory as it incited nationalism, but the benefits of this incitement do not extend to or rebound on Poland itself. In a comprehensive recent discussion of Polish nationalism, the distinguished Polish scholar Andrzej Walicki points out that while Poland was "an important catalyst in [the] process of national revival in Central and Eastern Europe . . . somewhat ironically, the results of this process made the notion of 'nation,' in its East-Central European usage, more and more dependent on ethnicity and language, thus undermining the special status of Poland and coming into conflict with the territorial claims of Polish patriots" ("PN"). Polish nationalists may have enabled others to think nationalistically, but when they themselves did so, they thought in ethnolinguistic terms; and when Poland itself was imagined in such terms, the result was a greatly diminished country, extending only over the territory inhabited by ethnic Poles. "Somewhat ironically," Polish nationalism benefited everyone but Poland.

Walicki's real point lies, however, deeper than this characteristically melancholy circumstance would suggest. He demonstrates that, because of the severance of nation from state, Polish nationalism was singularly unanchored and indeterminate. Members of a "stateless political nation," Poles were in a sense a weightless people, detached from the usual material, institutional, or linguistic sources of identity. While an emergent consciousness of "the nation" may have suggested that identity could be founded on something other than the state, statelessness created a series of obdurate questions. Was Poland a revolutionary or a reactionary nation? Did it belong to the autocratic or oriental East or to the democratic, liberal West? Was it entitled to exercise authority over the various nationalities it accounted part of itself, or was it a powerless but defiant victim of oppression? Was the national idea the product of ethnolinguistic national "feelings," or of a shared sense of history and political destiny? Other nations simply did not have to search for the answers to such questions: they were not as "free" as Poland. In the thin air of such freedom floated virtually every possible variety of nationalism, including virtually all the kinds that other nations, struggling with particular material circumstances pegged to their history, would subsequently, and laboriously, discover. Walicki enumerates many: in addition to a Romantic literary nationalism that prized terms such as "tradition" and "spirit," a number of political conceptions were also in play, including a "multicultural" conception, a more conservative "Unitarist" or "French" model that envisioned the polonization of all inhabitants of Poland, and a "federal" conception based on the restoration of the old Commonwealth.

Poland seems to represent a kind of Periodic Table of the elements of nationalism. It is necessary to keep this fact in mind as we ponder the peculiar relation of Poland to an academic theory of nationalism that cannot accommodate it. Walicki both criticizes and repeats this failure of accommodation in his four conclusions. First, he says, the example of Poland makes it "necessary to give up all attempts to divide European nationalisms into 'Western' and 'Eastern' types," for Poland is both. Instead, he suggests, we should distinguish between older nations with their own ruling class and continuous national history, and newly awakened nations whose national formation had been retarded. But this is hardly an improvement, for, once again, Poland is both.

Walicki's second conclusion concerns the role of class. He approves the Marxian linkage between nationalism and the transition from a closed to an open society, but points out that in Poland the "national class" was not the proletariat but the gentry. "Hence," he writes, "the vulgarly Marxist argument about the Polish gentry as a 'feudal' class, which . . . could not have been credited with a truly positive role in the emergence of the modern Polish nation is untenable even from the point of view of Marx's Marxism." The Polish gentry, Conrad's class, confuses the most fundamental distinction of traditional Marxist theory—that between the ruling class and the revolutionary class—by being both. In fact, it was Marx and Engels themselves who drew attention to this fact, writing that if "the words *Pole* and *revolutionary* have become identical," this is because the gentry had taken upon itself the burden of fighting for national independence, "an old democratic and working-class tenet" ("DP" 81; "WC" 99; see also Marx *The First International and After*). Just as Rousseau saw his views on the social contract reflected in the Polish monarchy, Marx and Engels recognized the Polish *szlachta* as the living form of communism.

Walicki's third point reaches even deeper into the contradictions of Polish nationalism. As we have seen, nationalism stands in a disputed logico-temporal relation to the nation. According to some, nations are products of nationalism; a work of "imagining" precedes the empirical fact, and nations are properly considered as "inventions." Walicki points out, however, that in Poland's case, the nation preceded nationalism. In fact, he continues, if we ask whether nationalism creates nations or vice versa, the answer issuing from Poland is both. Medieval Poland exemplifies the nation before nationalism, while the "noble nation" of the Polish-Lithuanian Commonwealth is "a perfect example of a successfully 'invented,' or 'imagined' national community."

At this point, Walicki's last conclusion—that "nationalism could manifest itself in an amazing variety of forms having nothing in common with ethnicity"—can come as no surprise. What may, however, be surprising is the poignant tenacity with which Walicki, like countless others, clings to the idea of a finally effective theoretical formulation that would institute Poland as a fully coherent conceptual-political entity. His last attempt to do so involves—what else?—a "typological distinction," this time between "civic" and "ethnic" nationalism; and yet—what else?—Poland turns out to be both. It is true that Polish national identity during the nineteenth century had been defined in such "civic" terms as fidelity to republican institutions, national values, or libertarian mission, but when Poland regained its autonomy after the Great War, the boundaries were drawn in large part on ethnic grounds. Poland today remains an "ethnic" as well as a "civic" entity.

At the heart of Poland's national darkness lies an extraordinary fact: Poland, while altogether unique in the history of nations, stands as a primary, even privileged, example of every possible theory of nationalism. Reflected in all nationalisms, Poland is an exemplary example, sustaining theory, all theory, any theory. However, the equally extraordinary consequence of this fact is that, like the most illuminating examples, Poland disconfirms by exceeding all theories of nationalism as well, since all theories are based on distinctions that should make such universal exemplification impossible. Thus, despite the universal applicability of Poland as theoretical template, it is also the one inadmissible example. As Waclaw Lednicki wrote during World War II, when Poland had disappeared once again, the "average Pole" "feels only one thing: that his world-outlook, in spite of his deep attachment to Western civilization, differs from that of the Western European, and that his opinion of his country, her past and present, is very unlike the opinion held by the non-Pole" (7).

Perhaps the chief obstacle to seeing post-Partition Poland as a model of nationalism—and the chief obstacle to Poland's regaining national autonomy—has already been indicated: the virtual ownership of national aspirations by a single estate, the remnants of the *szlachta* class. The political and cultural dominance of this class runs against the grain of modern nationalism, the arrival of which, Tom Nairn states, "was tied to the political baptism of the lower classes," whose enlightenment was solicited and valued by the middle class and the intellectual leadership (*Break-up of Britain* 41). This was not the case in Poland, where the lower classes were scarcely recognized by a nobility that regarded itself as the sole representative of "Poland." Priding itself on past glories, fundamentally impractical, given to outbursts against oppression, quixotically dedicated to severe Catholicism, to freedom, and to its own racial superiority, this class was responsible for Poland's reputation as "a peacock among nations," or even, in its own more megalomaniacal moods, as "a Christ among nations," a phrase even Apollo Korzeniowski used on occasion (Karl, *JC* 40). Flourishing alongside the notoriously arrogant vanity of this class was an equally notorious predilection for self-doubt and self-accusation, for many laid the blame for Poland's having become an imagined community on the imagining class itself. The unexampled freedom and autonomy of the gentry (unencumbered as it was by responsibility) had produced at the end of the eighteenth century a state of decay and disorganization that made Poland incapable of holding its own between two despots who each desired a "buffer state" between himself and the other. After the partitions, the cooperation of opportunistic Polish magnates was crucial to the smooth functioning of imperial administration. Defenders and mourners of Poland have always combined a defiant condemnation of aggression with a mortified awareness of the nobility's share of responsibility.

Thus, in *The Cambridge History of Poland*, W. F. J. Reddaway repeats Conrad's assertion that the First Partition was "an unpunished crime. In that crime, the Poles themselves had no immediate share. . . . The First Partition was wholly a foreign crime"—and also that the Polish nobility was guilty of "parochialism, faction, pride, intolerance and venality" (88). About the Second Partition, Reddaway is even more ambivalent, calling it a "pure aggression"—but one that, while "unrelieved by any generous trait in outer Europe, is darkened by the inner history of Poland," a chronicle of intra-Polish intrigue, cowardice, arrogance, and short-sighted opportunism that "made it impossible to declare that Poland was guiltless of her own destruction" (136). "The Polish 'nation', that is, such of the upper class as diplomatists were wont to meet in Warsaw, remained," Reddaway writes, "marked by 'extreme versatility,' 'inconsequence' and a 'turn to chicanery,' entangled in 'labyrinths of intrigue, faction and self-interest'" (139). In a recent history of Poland, Norman Davies brings the history of the *szlachta* forward into the nineteenth century:

> Of all the products of Polish life before the Partitions, the Polish nobility . . . might seem to have been the most discredited. . . . Their peacock pride in a supposedly exclusive ancestry was grotesquely unsuited to their miserable decline. Their social ideals of brotherly love and equality ill fitted their continuing support for serfdom. The political philosophy of their "Golden Freedom" resulted in common anarchy. . . . If, in Carlyle's cruel words, their noble Republic was "a beautifully phosphorescent rot-heap," then they were the parasites who swarmed upon it. (331)

It is this ethos of improvident, preposterous decadence that Ford Madox Ford sought to evoke when he claimed that Conrad was essentially "an aristo-royalist apologist" whose writing "wistfully tended towards the restoration of the Kingdom of Poland, with its irresponsible hierarchy of reckless and hypersophistically civilized nobility" (*PL* 65; qtd. in Fleishman viii).

Davies retrieves a charge often heard in the last days of the old kingdom when he introduces the subject of anarchy among the ruling class, sometimes referred to as "oligarchic" anarchy (Lednicki 13). As part of the evidence for this charge, the most conspicuous element of the Royal Republic, the *liberum veto* that enabled any member of the Diet to dissolve it and to nullify all its proceedings, was often invoked. Rousseau discussed it in a chapter titled "Specific Causes of Anarchy," and even *The Cambridge History* concedes that, because of the *liberum veto,* "Poland could neither be, nor appear to be, a rational European state" (94). "Brothers," the historian Bishop Naruszewicz told his contemporaries after the First Partition, "this anarchy has overpowered and ruined us, the evil began from us" (Reddaway et al. 127). As far as the Constitution goes, the introduction to *The Cambridge History* asserts that "Few can now doubt that the 'golden freedom' of the Polish squires was chaos thinly gilded, or that their pride in a constitution which as they held drew the best from monarchy, aristocracy and democracy, sprang from failure to comprehend any of the three" (xiii). When internal rot is coupled with the well-documented political crimes or blunders of the oligarchy, who cultivated disastrous alliances with despots on both sides that had the effect of inviting invasion and ultimately sanctioning partition, it would seem that the nation scarcely needed enemies to ensure its disappearance.

Whether through murder or suicide, Poland's identity seems staked on disappearance. In this respect, Poland exemplifies what Kedourie describes as "ideological politics," which, he says, first emerged at the time of the French Revolution (or rather, the time of the partitions). Characteristically, Kedourie says, the ideologist looks upon state and society "as a canvas which has to be wiped clean, so that his vision of justice, virtue, and happiness can be painted on this *tabula rasa,*" but "a further moment's reflection will lead one to see that the very attempt to wipe the canvas clean must entail arbitrariness, lawlessness, and violence on a stupendous scale." As a consequence, ideology is "necessarily and inevitably caught up in a perpetual disastrous and self-destructive tension between means and ends" (xiv). Of all political entities, partitioned Poland is most unmistakably evoked by the image of the *tabula rasa* created by violence—more so than France, which was profoundly altered but not eliminated by the Revolution—and thus stands as the very image of ideological politics. However, the full dimensions of the Polish example become apparent only when one considers the nation as a moral entity. Michnik's crystallization of the Polish self-description—"None of us has ever done anything wicked"—suggests how the nation's moral status, like its political-ideological status, is articulated in negative terms. Kedourie himself makes the crucial reference, to Kant's 1790 pamphlet on *Perpetual Peace,* which argues that peace will prevail when all states are republics regulating their citizens according to the categorical imperative. This imperative is, of course, famously empty, formal, a kind of wiping clean of the subject of moral freedom. Indeed, Jacques Lacan draws attention to the way in which "the Poles have always distinguished themselves by a remarkable resistance to the eclipses of Poland" as a worldly example of "the experience of the moral law," in which the subject is "no longer faced with any object" (57, 56). (Lacan's thinking edges even closer to the Polish experience when he claims that Kant's formalism is "completed" by the thought of de Sade, who grants to the other an infinite "right of enjoyment" over one's own body [58].) In this way, Poland, the *wiped-out* nation, is granted as compensation a claim to being the most thoroughly *wiped-clean* or *moral* nation in post-Partition times, a nation that does nothing wicked because it does nothing at all.

While Conrad does not discuss Poland's moral character directly in his fiction, his discourse on other subjects constitutes an indirect meditation on the nation. Take, for example, the Conradian dog. The most memorable canine appearance in Conrad occurs in *A Personal Record,* where Conrad devotes five lugubrious pages to an incident where his granduncle was reduced to killing and eating a "Lithuanian village dog," having been brought to this miserable state by a fervent "patriotic desire . . . kindled like a false beacon by a great man to lead astray the effort of a brave nation" (35). The great man in question is Napoleon, in whose Grand Army many Poles served against the Russians, in the faith that if the campaign were victorious, the Emperor would liberate Poland. Despite the heroic efforts of the Poles, the campaign was not successful, and the Grand Army retreated in defeat, battered, freezing, and, obviously, starving: the dog marks the pathos of Polish identification with the West. Dogs reappear often in *A Personal Record:* the Russian police officer charged with taking Conrad's mother from Tadeusz Bobrowski's home to continue her journey into exile despite her grave illness confides that "my trade is not fit for a dog"; Stephen Crane gives Conrad's son a dog, whose stoic tolerance of rough boyish displays of affection provokes a Conradian meditation on "the pain that may lurk in the very rewards of rigid self-command"; and Conrad recalls his youthful shock at hearing life at sea described as a "*métier de chien*" (67, 105, 122). In the form of "cur," dogs had, however, already made their mark on Conrad's fiction, through "Kurtz," through Allistoun's calling Donkin "a cur," and through the point of confusion that mars the first meeting between Marlow and Jim at the official inquiry where Jim persists in his mistaken belief that he has heard Marlow call him a cur. Can we articulate the system that regulates these appearances? Perhaps. For Conrad as for others, dogs stand loyally at the intersection of limitless fidelity and utter debasement, between fullness of being and a perfect zero. The possibility of such an intersection may, in fact, have been more immediately apparent to Poles (who were universally regarded, Edward Garnett notes, as "under dogs") than to others (qtd. in *NN* 169), and Conrad may well have formulated a tacit equation, construing not just dogs as the Poland of domestic animals, but Poland as the dog of Europe, an accursed nation whose history was a *métier de chien.*

If so, this would illuminate the peculiar moral challenge posed by Poland to the nations of Europe. With its clamorous protestations of allegiance to the ideals of the West, Poland laid claim, infinite claim, to Western sympathies; the impossibility of returning this fidelity would have represented a perpetual challenge to the magnanimity of the Western nation-states. Hélène Cixous, undoubtedly beset by French guilt over Napoleon's treatment of Poland, interrupts a meditation on the conditions of writing to assert, in the very voice of the West, that "we need dogs to understand this strange, ambivalent relation we have to love—hatred." The problem with dogs, she contends, is that they are "bundles of love. This infinite, complete, and limitless giving of love is exhausting for a human being. . . . We cannot cope with such an open, superhuman relation" (48). For Conrad, by contrast, superhuman relations constitute the truest test of character. In his work, to *abandon* a friend or ally is to treat him like a dog, rewarding fidelity with betrayal. Moreover, to *eat* or *be* a dog is to reach the lowest point of abjection. By contrast, to *love* or *assume responsibility for* a dog, like Captain Brierly of *Lord Jim* (who commits suicide after presiding over the inquiry, having first given instructions that his dog should be shut up to prevent it following him overboard), is to be faithful to fidelity even in its lowest forms, to extend affection, guardianship, and responsibility to those outcast from the political-symbolic order. Such humble and unreciprocated guardianship defines a certain ethical, superhuman principle within that order, one to which Conrad, like Poles generally, was responsive: he was recalled by a Polish acquaintance petting a puppy "for a long while with obvious pleasure" while repeating, "Doggy, doggy, doggy . . . you dirty dog!" (Najder, *CUFE* 157).

This somewhat quixotic distinction helps define the ethical dimension of the numerous acts of "identification" in Conrad's work between Marlow or some other figure, and those such as Kurtz, Jim, or Leggatt who find themselves in the dog's position. With an all-but-Polish sensitivity to the moral grandeur of abjection, the Slovenian philosopher Slavoj Žižek enables us to see the productive force of such identification, making the striking theoretical claim that, in fact, a passage through the zero point of symbolic suicide—a momentary identification with *the dog*—"is at work in *every* act worthy of this name" (*EYS* 44). Žižek argues that when the act is independent from the agent, when it is not something one accomplishes but rather something one "undergoes," it can radically transform the agent by suspending "the network of symbolic fictions which serve as a support to his daily life" (53). This transformation ensures that the act is not simply an ecstatic suicidal swoon, but rather, at its best, a fresh beginning for the polis. Thus, Žižek concludes, "a 'suicidal' gesture, an *act,* is at the very foundation of a new social link" (45). It is in such terms that the foundational agency, for nations and for the theory of nationalism, of Poland's partition—"assisted" though its suicide may have been—must be grasped. The forms of agency involved in mounting a doomed insurrection such as the one Apollo Korzeniowski led in 1863 must also be placed in this category, along with the creative work of his son.

POLONIZING THE NOVEL

Insofar as he believed in anything, Conrad believed in "the idea of nationhood," which he offered as "a definite first principle" to be opposed to the pronouncements of "extreme anarchists" (Karl, *CL,* 2:160). His knowledge of nationalism, or the national idea, did not take theoretical form, but it was no less knowledge for that. He did not "know" the theory of nationalism, but he knew what a theoretician would have to know, and have to manage, master, generalize, or simply forget in order to forge a theory. Take, for example, Benedict Anderson's suggestion that "the way the nation is imagined is ancestral." What Anderson means is that the genealogical family, with its store of "unremembered information and tropes of continuity," provides the most adequate model for the way in which people understand themselves as citizens of a modern, secular nation (secular despite the fact that some people—for example, Poles—"occasionally feel themselves to be under special divine guidance," he adds). By being "narrated" in the same way as the family, the nation acquires for its citizens the antiquity, naturalness, and "sense of fatality" that individuals attribute to their own heritage ("NN"). While such thoughts may never have occurred to Conrad, his early childhood constituted an uncompromising schooling in the linkage of personal genealogy and nation, and while his experience was necessarily limited, it in fact suggested both a tighter and a more spacious way of framing the question. As we have seen, Conrad registered not just the *similarity* of family and nation, father and Fatherland, but their near *identity,* and he did so at the moment of his father's funeral. Žižek's most Conradian intuition concerns precisely this act of finding a "metaphorical substitute" for the father. The Lacanian dictum of the "non-coincidence of symbolic and real father," he argues, implies that "some 'non-father' (maternal uncle, the supposed common ancestor . . .) is 'more father' than the (real) father" ("whereas," he adds, "the 'non-sublated' part of the father appears as the obscene, cruel and oddly impotent agency of the superego" [e.g., Kurtz]) (*TKN* 134). Conrad's "imagining" of the nation is radically paternal in this respect, and becomes so in the specific form of mourning.

Conrad's experience also afforded him a subtheoretical experience of the true parameters of mourning, enabling him fully to apprehend a spaciousness that its first theorist, Freud, only glimpsed. In his first approach to the subject, Freud distinguished between "mourning," in which the lost object is "introjected" or taken into the ego as a component of the self, and a more or less sterile and unproductive "melancholia," in which one engages in a long-term relation with the memory of the lost loved one, who is neither reconciled nor rejected (see "Mourning and Melancholia"). Freud seemed uncertain about this distinction, however, and in *The Ego and the Id,* written several years later, he softened it by suggesting that melancholia was simply a stage in the process or grieving that would optimally result in mourning. With his functional bipaternity, Conrad was able to mourn one father and settle into an ongoing, largely epistolary, quarrel that lasted well into his adulthood with another, a father figure who was by turns condescending, proud, concerned, generous, irritable, resentful, moralizing—the entire paternal range. (Certain passages from Bobrowski's letters seem intended for some anthology of parental exasperation: ". . . let us jointly consider if such expenditure on your behalf is and was possible, fair and worthy??? . . . a little more contrition would not be amiss and particularly a more thoughtful mode of behaviour. . . . and I, the victim of these absurdities, forgive you with all my heart, on condition, *that it is for the first and last time!!*" [Najder, *CPB* 40–42].) Conrad's particular experience of the loss of the father—and the discovery of the "substitute"—suggested, therefore, that the relation between mourning and melancholia might not be either a typological or a temporal distinction. One can do both; healthy and pathological, mature and immature forms of grief, might constitute a single, dynamically untheorizable complex.

Conrad's relation to the Fatherland was comparably ambivalent, marked on one side by emigration and various refusals to participate in Polish political activities, and on the other by professions of fidelity

and patriotism. As a writer whose growing fame led various organiza-
tions—the Anglo-Polish Society, the Polish Association, the Literary
Association of the Friends of Poland, the Relief Committee for War
Victims in Poland, and the Society of the Friends of Poland—to seek
his support, he remained aloof from such involvements by plead-
ing ill health, inability to speak in public, a limited circle of friends,
ignorance of contemporary Poland, and a general "dislike of 'social
work'" (see Najder, *CUFE* 267, 228–68 passim). At the same time,
however, he was increasingly candid about his Polish origins in various essays and prefaces, and took his family there in 1914 (only to
have war break out immediately after their arrival in Cracow). The
blurred quality of his relation to Poland can be focused by seeing in
it a repetition of the mourning-melancholia that marked his experience of paternity. In both instances, Conrad's personal experience
seems to be graspable by theory but in fact falls on both sides of
distinctions—family and nation, mourning and melancholia—that
theoreticians (Anderson and Freud) wish to maintain. It is this
double relation to theory, exemplifying and exceeding it, that characterizes Conrad's childhood experience. As such experience generally
provides a template for subsequent experience, we can hypothesize
that Conrad's adult life and works are "Polish" in this respect, and
that Poland functions as a structural principle of equivocation, a
"Polish question" that shapes and disturbs his sensibility regardless
of the ostensible subject of his work.

In this respect, it cannot be accidental that his work took the form
of fiction, the construction of imagined communities. For is not fiction itself one form of mourning for some real living substance that
it can only encrypt and memorialize? Might not a fictive memorial,
on the other hand, actually constitute an agent of death? Žižek argues
that the "symbolic order" in general possesses a "tremendous power
that tears apart what 'naturally' belongs together and is thus able to
subordinate the very reality of the life process to symbolic 'fictions'"
(*EYS* 52). Thus, the emergence of the symbolic order is marked by
the dominance of fiction over reality. His authorities in this respect
are Lacan and Hegel, who argue, he says, that "what we forget, when
we pursue our daily life, is that our human universe is nothing but

an embodiment of the radically inhuman 'abstract negativity,' of the abyss we experience when we face the 'night of the world'" (53). Hegel's discourse is unexpectedly evocative in this respect:

> The human being is this night, this empty nothing, that contains everything in its simplicity. . . . This night, the inner of nature, that exists here—pure self—in phantasmagorical presentations, is night all around it, here shoots a bloody head— there another white shape, suddenly here before it, and just so disappears. One catches sight of this night when one looks human beings in the eye—into a night that becomes awful. (*Realphilosophie* of 1805–06, qtd. in *EYS* 50)

What this strangely disjointed passage evokes for the reader of Conrad is a series of images clustering around this inner darkness, a string of "bloody heads" that includes, among others,

—the previously mentioned crushed head of *Almayer's Folly* ("There are his flesh and his bones, the nose, and the lips, and maybe his eyes, but nobody could tell the one from the other"), a sight that gives Almayer the feeling that "for many years he had been falling into a deep precipice . . . falling, falling, falling" (*AF* 98, 99)

—the head of James Wait, "vigorously modeled into deep shadows and shining lights—a head powerful and misshapen, with a tormented and flattened face—a face pathetic and brutal; the tragic, the mysterious, the repulsive mask of a nigger's soul" ("Yer nobody! Yer no one at all! . . . ye're a thing—a bloody thing!" Donkin tells him later on) (*NN* 11)

—the skulls drying on stakes beneath Kurtz's windows at the Inner Station, in particular "the first I had seen . . . black, dried, sunken, with closed eyelids . . . with the shrunken dry lips showing a narrow white line of the teeth" (*HD* 57)

—the face of Marlow himself after the explosion on board ship in "Youth," "no hair, no eyebrows, no eyelashes . . . my young mustache was burnt off . . . my face was black, one cheek laid open, my nose cut, and my chin bleeding" ("Y" 135)

—the body of Stevie, in *The Secret Agent,* after the explosion near the Greenwich Observatory, "Blown to small bits: limbs, gravel, clothing, bones, splinters—all mixed up together. I tell you they had to fetch a shovel to gather him up with" (*SA* 196)

—the head of the "secret sharer," at first apparently missing from a "headless corpse" and then seen as a "dimly pale oval" that gives the captain the sense that he is "faced by my own reflection in the depths of a somber and immense mirror" ("SS" 654, 658)

—the grotesque, "prodigiously old" head of Prince Roman, the one Polish patriot in Conrad's *oeuvre,* who possesses, to the narrator's immense and repeated consternation, a "deathlike pallor" ("P" 63)

—the head of Tom Lingard, which appears suddenly over the siderail of the grounded yacht in *The Rescue,* speaking to a fascinated Mrs. Travers of his obsessions and her present danger in a tale "as startling as the discovery of a new world" (*R* 138).

Perhaps the most phenomenal glimpse afforded by Conrad into the inner night would be the storm at sea, which rends all terrestrial realities, exposing their deep "fictionality."

The recurrence of such images in Conrad suggests that they had, on him, a powerfully stimulating and productive effect. But why? Could it be that they evoked, from a distance, the scene of his mourning, the genealogical nation? The connection seems at first improbable, but Žižek makes the connection between bloody heads and the nation by identifying the message of Hegel's passage as the "*ontological nullity of what we call 'reality'*" and by offering as a less bloody instance "the ethical-political arrangement of a given community." The identity of this community, he contends, is a function of certain symbolic rituals or "fictions." "The Fatherland as the cause for which we fight," he points out, "'is nowhere in reality,' but in spite of this, we cannot explain the very 'material' reality of fights and sufferings without reference to it" (*EYS* 52). Poland exemplifies this complex theoretical argument with tragic efficiency. The only way a patriot such as Apollo Korzeniowski could explain his life would be by reference to a Fatherland—or, as he preferred, Motherland—that could not be seen. His life, like that of patriots of other nations, only had meaning when situated within the historical destiny of this "fiction." One might feel that Poles occupied a privileged position with respect to patriotism because their nation was so manifestly and inescapably fictive, but, for Poland, fictiveness was a disaster, a special curse, in a way that it was not for others (although Shaw makes something of the same point about the richly inventive Irish imagination in *John Bull's Other Island*). What the example of Poland demonstrates, therefore, is that one cannot simply turn away from "reality" and towards "fiction" in the confident expectation that a redemptive meaning will be found there, for fiction registers, among other things, the fact of death or nonexistence.

Conrad is obsessively instructive on this point, for the loss of substance is repeatedly represented as origin and end of narrative action. The salutation at the end of *The Nigger* to the "crew of Shades" whom, he says in a letter, he hopes to have enshrined in a "decent edifice" could stand as the last, and as the first, word in Conrad's work as a whole (see *NN* 176). Characteristically, the course of his plots leads to death, diminishment, or desubstantiation of various kinds—*after* which narration begins as a restless, retrospective, but still inconclusive quest for meaning. "Jim looked at [Marlow], then turned away resolutely, as after a final parting," Conrad writes in *Lord Jim;* "And later on, many times, in distant parts of the world, Marlow showed himself willing to remember Jim, to remember him at length, in detail and audibly" (21). Conrad's major works not only end but begin in death and loss, when the subject to be narrated has become "fictive," a "Shade," an object of mourning. Early in his career, he developed the habit of informing his friends of the completion of a book with a mock funeral notice: "I regret to inform you of the death of Mr Kaspar Almayer, which occurred this morning at 3 o'clock"; "It is my painful duty to inform you of the sad death of Mr Peter Willems late of Rotterdam and Macassar" (*CL*, 1:153, 245).

Thus, while the Fatherland may be the best possible example of the ontological nullity or fictiveness of reality, Conrad is not simply a novelist of the nation, any more than he is a novelist of modernity: for him as for Poland, fictiveness is instinct with death. To understand Conrad's ambivalent relation to a term such as "the nation," we can recall Benedict Anderson's widely disseminated but undeveloped argument to the effect that the novel and the newspaper serve as the primary vehicles by which "print-capitalism" fashions a modern nation. In both instances, readers understand that their solitary reading experience is replicated by countless others who will remain anonymous to them, an "imagined community" of experience, information, and sensibility. As a contrast, Anderson mentions a celebrated literary work by a Filipino Indio, Francisco Balagtas's *Pinagdaanang Buhay ni Florante at ni Laura sa Cahariang Albania,* which dates from the mid-nineteenth century. Unlike Western novels, this text is clearly not meant to be read but to be sung aloud, as it is sprinkled with "quatrains simply to heighten the grandeur and sonority of [the] diction" (*IC* 28). Since it is the solitary yet collective experience of reading that builds nations, a text meant to be transmitted orally addresses some other, non-national community, a community that conceives of itself as a "face to face" collectivity. Thematically speaking, Conrad's works are manifestly modern and Western, speaking of heroism in difficult circumstances, adventures in strange lands, moral and physical testing, political intrigue, empire building, and cross-cultural intercourse. However, they are also distinguished for the "grandeur and sonority" of their diction, and in many instances constructed as tales told orally. In this respect, Conrad's works are both nationalist *and* non-nationalist.

This combination also helps us achieve a more precise understanding of what is generally taken as Conrad's "modernist" or "innovative" use of time. One of Anderson's most suggestive claims is that the modern novel creates a "modern" sense of time in which "a sociological organism [moves] calendrically through homogeneous, empty time"; and it is this image that most precisely expresses the idea of the nation, "conceived as a solid community moving steadily down (or up) history" (*IC* 26). In novelistic time, each citizen comprehends that all other citizens are on the same time line, and this assurance, imagined and imaginary though it is, helps to create the historically stable community of the nation. The contrast with Balagtas brings out this feature of the modern novel even more clearly. Balagtas's plot begins in the middle, and the complete story is presented through a series of "spoken flashbacks" as an "alternative to a straightforward single-file narrative." Characters are connected not by a narrative perspective that sees them from above and reports on their simultaneous activities, but "by their conversing voices." "In effect," Anderson concludes, "it never occurs to Balagtas to 'situate' his protagonists in 'society,' or to discuss them with his audience" (*IC* 29). Instead of steady, anonymous, simultaneous activity of the sort that would imply a society ("meanwhile, back at the ranch"), the non-national narrative has a dense mesh of encounters and conversations that imply no larger unit. Early readers of Conrad were vexed and fascinated by precisely this handling of time and society. As one Polish reviewer noted about *Lord Jim* in 1905, "reading it one sometimes gets the impression that the printer mixed up the pages of the manuscript and that what was supposed to be at the end, he placed in the middle, and moved the middle to the beginning" (Gomulicki 196). The proliferation of vehicles by which *Lord Jim* gets told ensures not only temporal displacements but constant fractures in the sense of "society" generated by the novel, which, in this respect, seems more closely modeled on Balagtas than on Henry James.

However, Conrad is not simply rewriting Balagtas, even in the novels such as *Almayer's Folly* that are set in that part of the world. To be sure, that text, with its slithering confusion of points of view, temporalities, and voices, seems non-nationalist in Anderson's sense; the reader is inducted into a world in which things happen over and over, and each time entirely differently. As a modern editor notes, "the cannon shot proclaiming the arrival of the Dutch which startles Nina and Babalatchi at the end of the first episode . . . is the shot heard by Abdulla and Reshid in the next chapter as they interrogate Taminah . . . and again, three chapters later, the shot that reaches Dain's ears as he waits in hiding downstream" (Berthoud xxviii–xxix). The weaving of voices, the shuttling of forward and backward movements, the use of spoken flashbacks, the jumbling of temporal occasions all militate against what Anderson describes as a "national imagination" (*IC* 30). At the same time, however, the reader is subjected to a pre-Marlovian narrative voice that can best be characterized as "not quite omniscient," in which the point of view of the character currently being narrated partially determines the tonality as well as the content of a narration that still manages to remain quasi-independent, superior, and therefore "social" and ultimately, if not quite national then at least decisively not local. This at least is how one might begin to describe the following passage, which represents a shared moment of intimacy, rare in Conrad, between mother and daughter:

> [Mrs. Almayer] wailed to herself softly, lamenting the lost possi-
> bilities of murder and mischief that could have fallen to her lot
> had she been mated with a congenial spirit. Nina bent down
> over Mrs. Almayer's slight form and scanned attentively, under
> the stars that had rushed out on the black sky and now hung
> breathless over that strange parting, her mother's shrivelled fea-
> tures, and looked close into the sunken eyes that could see into
> her own dark future by the light of a long and a painful experi-
> ence. Again she felt herself fascinated, as of old, by her mother's
> exalted mood and by the oracular certainty of expression which,
> together with her fits of violence, had contributed not a little
> to the reputation for witchcraft she enjoyed in the settlement.
> (*AF* 148–49)

An incongruous irony, something like a mordant sense of humor, plays over the account of the daughterly gaze. Where does this come from, what perspective does it articulate, what community does it speak for or from? While limiting itself to recording some version of the thoughts of Nina and her mother, the narration nevertheless establishes a rhetorical distance that implies a difference of evaluation, a difference of culture that is definite yet nonabsolute. A brief text Conrad wrote in 1895, printed as an "Author's Note" to the 1992 Oxford edition, is for the most part clumsy and obscure in its rhetoric, but still manages to express the Conradian difference from both the non-nationalist and the nationalist novel in a single, radical sentence: "And there is a bond between us and that humanity so far away" (lxi). The nature of that bond, which would have encountered resistance from both "us" and "that humanity" out there, could only be established by reference to a geopolitical community whose archetype is plainly Poland, a nation of undetermined boundaries and battered hopes: "For, their land—like ours—lies under the inscrutable eyes of the Most High. Their hearts—like ours—must endure the load of the gifts from Heaven: the curse of facts and the blessing of illusions, the bitterness of our wisdom and the deceptive consolation of our folly" (lxii).

Neither nationalist nor non-nationalist, then, but with elements of both, Conrad occupies a space that is comprehensive yet all his own. This paradox applies, as well, to his handling of what Anderson refers to as the last element of novelistic national imagining, that of boundedness. In the novel proper, he notes, we see "the movement of a solitary hero through a sociological landscape of a fixity that fuses the world inside the novel with the world outside. This picaresque *tour d'horison . . .* is nonetheless not a *tour du monde.* The horizon is clearly bounded" (*IC* 30). While the novel may encompass a vast range of situations, attitudes, values, class perspectives, events, and characters, its sociospatial limits work to make its elements *representative.* To an extent, Conrad's novels answer to this account, but it is the partial failure of their attempts to contain their multitudinous elements into a "society" that really indicates the singularity of his achievement. *Almayer's Folly* typifies the novels that followed in its failure to establish a representative society within its horizon. The action occurs within a tiny area, and yet the characters collected within that area—Arabs, a Siamese slave, Malays, Dutch colonialists, independent profiteers—cannot be said to typify a larger, much less a coherent, cultural group. As Berthoud notes about the novel's force fields, "Decisions taken in London and Amsterdam affect every household in Sambir. Captain Ford's steamer, owned by a Singapore merchant, brings news and cargo; Dutch naval frigates assert the presence of foreign authority; and the brig of a Balinese prince . . . appears, to disturb a desultory nationalism and to precipitate Almayer's final disintegration" (xx). Indeed, characters themselves do not even typify their own conditions: a weak, deluded, and mediocre man, Almayer, Berthoud points out, must not be seen as "a sample of a certain type of colonialism," a system to which he is altogether marginal (xxxii). Nor, in general, does the Conradian hero gather into himself elements of a sociopolitical totality. Marlow, we are told in *Heart of Darkness,* "did not represent his class;" he "was not typical." The men who are representative—Kurtz, to whose making all Europe contributed; Jim, who is so insistently designated as "one of us"; Nostromo, the man of the people and "our man"—do not found nations, they lose them, peeling off and becoming strictly individual, and then dead (*HD* 9).

The Secret Agent (1907) presents a more mature, and apparently more "modern" representation of a bounded, and so at least potentially national, society, but here again, through what have been taken to be "modern" techniques of temporal fracturing, simultaneity, and a mobile point of view, the nation is undone. This undoing is, moreover, the very subject of the novel, as the security of the capital city is threatened by agents of foreign governments and by a police system that mimics and feeds off the criminals it is supposed to eliminate. *The Secret Agent* lacks what Anderson calls "a solitary hero" representing some aspect of a national or nationalizable character. Each figure in the text takes a turn at being protagonist, fully occupying his fraction of the totality as if it were the totality itself. *The Secret Agent* was originally entitled *Verloc,* and Verloc occupies much of the book's attention, but in his "Author's Note," Conrad refers to "the story of Winnie Verloc" (41). The idiot Stevie is often identified as the "true hero" or "moral center" of the novel, but one cannot regard the moral intuitions of the mentally retarded as exemplary. From another point of view the most arresting figure is Chief Inspector Heat, who circulates among and mediates all classes of society from Sir Ethelred down to the anarchists. The book ends with none of these, however, but with the Professor, explosives strapped to his chest, walking through "the odious multitude of mankind . . . unsuspected and deadly, like a pest in the street full of men" (269). Conrad represents a bounded unit, but it *leaks,* hemorrhaging constantly, its "desultory nationalism" permeable to a host of nation-destroying influences. As he conceded in a letter, a universalizing "fraternity" "tends to weaken the national sentiment" (Jean-Aubry, 1:269 [8 February 1899]). Not fully or finally committed to either one, Conrad imagined limited aggregations of people that were yet not true societies, communities invaded by their Others, obscure bonds linking "us" with that humanity so far away.

Like novels, nations are bounded temporally as well as spatially, and both derive a very considerable portion of their identity and character from the point of origin. Regis Debray argues that nations, like earlier cultures, try to make themselves "sacred" by cultivating, in the national imagination, certain "anti-death processes," including the imagining of a "zero point" whose power is recuperable by a "ritual repetition" that signals the "defeat of the irreversibility of time" (27). In the service of the nation, another critic writes, the modern novel finds it necessary to appropriate this ancient practice, evoking a "background of spirituality and permanence" as "a contemporary, practical means of *creating* a people" (Brennan 50). Conrad's contribution to this aspect of the novel is characteristically idiosyncratic and, one might say, characteristically Polish. Perhaps more explicitly than any other modern novelist, he is preoccupied with deep time, but unlike novelists generally, he does not discover in the ancient past a foundational moment for any modern geopolitical entity, much less a stay against death.

Consider, as Conrad does, Singleton of the *Narcissus*, a "learned and savage patriarch, the incarnation of barbarian wisdom serene in the blasphemous turmoil of the world" (3). This lonely relic, this colossal figure, "old as Father time himself" and yet one of the "everlasting children of the mysterious sea," is as ripe a specimen as modern fiction can offer of a zero point of humanity, an origin in which the nation (in this case England) might take a legitimate pride (*NN* 15). As an antideath process, however, Singleton is singularly deficient, for his one insight, the proof of his hoary wisdom, is the recognition that for James Wait, as for himself, the end is near: he seems on equally intimate terms with the zero point of origin and the zero point of death. He is deficient, too, in the disconcerting way in which he conjoins immense old age and infantilism. Nor does he spawn a nation, or even a tradition. His successors are not, like him, children of the sea, but neither are they adults; they are simply "grown-up children of a discontented earth," children who eventually arrive at the filial observation that his oracular prediction of the death of James Wait "meant nothing" because, after all, everyone will die (15, 26). Singleton exemplifies, in complex ways, the inverted temporality of Conrad's imagination, which did not move from green youth to maturity to old age and death, but began with "Shades" and worked backwards. As he wrote in a letter while working on his first novel, "Everything is still chaos, but, slowly, ghosts are transformed into living flesh, floating vapours turn solid" (*CL*, 1:151).

The very image of tradition, Singleton produces nothing, and nothing claims him as its forebear. Indeed, the incoherence that will come to plague the *Narcissus* can be seen to operate in him, its most self-consistent crew member, from the very outset. He first appears in the narrative not as a representative crew member but as an aloof and superior dilettante, seen from a certain distance off by himself reading Bulwer-Lytton's "polished and so curiously insincere" novel *Pelham;* but as the narrative perspective closes in, he is revealed to be simply stupefied by the experience, moving his lips and drooling tobacco juice as he spells through the text "with slow labour" (3). Throughout, Singleton is actually the object of continual uncertainty as the crew try to decide whether he is ancient—authoritative, authentic, wise—or simply old. There is, in short, a luminous "origin" represented in the text in the person of Singleton, but elaborate pains are taken to cast doubt on his credentials as a forefather.

Conrad approaches a terrestrial time of origins in *Heart of Darkness,* where Marlow suggests that the Congo stands as a kind of ancestral kin to England, which "also . . . has been one of the dark places of the earth" (9). Marlow's listeners do not, at this moment, rouse themselves and propose a toast to the Queen because the origins Marlow invokes are not those a nation may wish to commemorate. Marlow's insight rather exposes the nation to an open-ended past, a past that contains not a proper beginning but an infinite possibility of post-Darwinian regression. Temporal boundaries in *Heart of Darkness* are as porous and indefinite as national borders in *The Secret Agent;* the community of the novel that models the nation is, in Conrad, *un*imaginable as a bounded community at all.

Timothy Brennan points out that two of the most eminent early theorists of the novel, Mikhail Bakhtin and Georg Lukács, both explain the genesis of the novel in terms of what Brennan calls the "undercurrents of nationalist thought," which emerge in periods "when large, incorporating dynastic realms are in the process of decline" (54). Brennan points out, however, that the specifically modern novel, the novel of European nationalism—the kind of novel, he claims, that Conrad wrote—"co-existed with the consolidation of empire," when "the world became Europe's 'little circle'" (55). Taken together, Bakhtin, Lukács, and Brennan represent a small collection of ways of understanding the relation of the novel to imperial or authoritarian structures: the novel can celebrate the dynamic process of their decomposition (Bakhtin); it can commemorate their passing (Lukács); or it can rejoice in their majestic power (Brennan). Brennan notwithstanding, Conrad does none of these. His stance with respect to the national-imperial project, whether English, Dutch, French, or American, is rigorously equivocal. He notes imperial self-delusion and inefficiency with a notorious and deflating indifference. "It appears the French had one of their wars going on thereabouts," Marlow comments about a French gunboat off the coast of Africa; "In the empty immensity of earth, sky, and water, there she was, incomprehensible, firing into a continent" (*HD* 17). He also, however, notes the more effective forms of imperial violence, cruelty, corruption, and hypocrisy without recording any pronounced or sustained moral outrage. And when he turns his attention to those indigenous cultures unlucky enough to live near large quantities of ivory, silver, spices, rubber, or anything else deemed essential to the imperial-capitalist mission, he cannot bring himself to represent them as organic, integrated, pristine, or even as objects of a liberal tolerance of difference. "Then we fought amongst ourselves and were happy," a Malay tells Almayer about the precolonial past; "now when we fight with you we can only die" (*AF* 206). Among the many shocks administered to the liberal sensibility by *Heart of Darkness* is the fact that the Congolese culture representing the "beginnings of the world" confusedly enthrones Kurtz as its deity and then plunders the country at his behest. The larger point, barely indicated here but easily demonstrable at length, is that, although he was, especially early in his career, obsessed with the *subjects* of native cultures, nations, and empires, Conrad sustains no settled *attitude* towards these subjects at all. One reason for this may be that, beneath a superficial exoticism, Conrad sensed a deeper affinity between peoples of a kind that closed the gap on which judgment normally depends. As Frederick Karl states, "one reason he found the Borneo area a spur to his imagination was its similarity to Poland. Borneo was an area of contention between Dutch and English imperialists, its people fought over by Arabs, Malays, and various piratical forces" (*JC* 243). Beholding the torpid and partitioned Other, Conrad saw much that was familiar.

The same can be said of his representation of racial difference. Perhaps the most alien feature of Conrad's work to an average European reader of the 1890s, for whom empire was an established fact, was not the setting of many of his books amidst the Others, but the equality of treatment allotted to all characters, as though absolutely nothing were at stake in noting racial differences. In Conrad's first book, the Siamese slave, the Arabs, and the Malays are just as "round," fully developed, reflective, and capable of significant agency as Almayer himself, and often somewhat more capable of responsibility and personal dignity. Moreover, they entertain a different view of race. According to most of the Europeans, racial difference signifies the difference between civilization and savagery; for the Malay characters, race is cultural, a matter of behavior and attitudes: whites lie and sentimentalize, and Malays don't. Almayer seems to regard whiteness as imposing a certain standard of behavior and entailing certain benefits, and he is not above thinking of Malays as racial inferiors; but he has married a Malay woman, and imagines, in his daydreams that race-consciousness could be suspended. If he could get rich and take his half-caste daughter to Europe, he dreams, her wealth and beauty would earn her universal admiration. Her declaration that "I am not of your race. Between your people and me there is . . . a barrier that nothing can remove," contributes a new thought to Almayer's limited stock (*AF* 179). Conrad seems capable of placing racist and nonracist thinking on the scale and finding them equal, just as he finds people of different races equal notwithstanding the many inequalities in their circumstances. He does not, for example, seem to regard as anything but fitting Lord Jim's offering his own life in return for having caused the death of Dain Waris. Kipling, who ought to have known, commented that the "purely human" attitude taken towards James Wait in *The Nigger* "does not fit in with the English mentality" (qtd. in Perłowski 163). Accused in a widely reprinted lecture by Chinua Achebe of being a "bloody racist"—subsequently altered to "thoroughgoing racist"—who, in *Heart of Darkness,* calls "the very humanity of black people into question," Conrad at the very least is not a simple racist, and by most measures is simply not a racist at all, surely not in a text that emphasizes "their humanity—like yours" (Achebe, "IA" 124, 126; for "thoroughgoing racist," see Achebe, "IOA" 257; Conrad, *HD* 38; see also Goonetilleke). In a passage he later apparently regretted because he edited it out of a subsequent printing of his essay, Achebe compared Conrad to a physician who poisons his patients, to slave traders, to Nazis who have "rightly been condemned for their perversions," and to Hitler himself ("IA" 125). But Hitler, if asked "what of all the things you've seen in life has made the greatest impression on you?" would probably not have responded, as Conrad did, "A certain woman. A Negress. It was in Africa. She was pacing up and down in front of the station building and was covered with beads, bracelets.... C'était la maîtresse du chef de la station" (Zagorska 218). It is possible that *Heart of Darkness* began as the story not of Kurtz, or of Marlow, or of the soul of Europe, but of this luminous African woman around whom various contingent others were arranged.

When Conrad does stereotype, it is, as often as not, the imperialists who are the targets: "the French had one of their wars going on thereabouts." Comments such as this have led some to represent Conrad as an indignant anti-imperialist. In a study of *Fiction and the Colonial Experience,* Jeffrey Meyers, later to write a biography of Conrad, contrasts racist imperial texts, such as those of the early Kipling, with "humanistic" colonial novels that register not firm moral certainties but "a universal fascination with the savage and the incomprehensible" that provides the basis for a more nuanced meditation on the "human lessons of previous colonial entanglements" (qtd. in Brennan 62). However, Conrad refuses this oddly phrased compliment, for his fascination is omnidirectional. Marlow finds Kurtz as "irresistibly fascinating" as Kurtz had found "the wilderness" (*HD* 57). "The French" in this book are as collectively savage as the Africans, and if Marlow feels a certain kinship with Kurtz, he also feels a powerful tug in the direction of his slain African helmsman: "for months I had him at my back—a help—an instrument. It was a kind of partnership. He steered for me—I had to look after him, I worried about his deficiencies, and thus a subtle bond had been created.... And the intimate profundity of that look he gave me when he received his hurt remains to this day in my memory—like a claim of distant kinship affirmed in a supreme moment" (51). He steered—like the battered helmsman of *Typhoon* who declares, in an exhausted fit of fidelity, "I can steer forever if nobody talks to me"; and like Singleton, whose greatest physical and moral feat, guiding the ship through a thirty-hour storm, is recorded in a single sentence: "He steered with care" (*T* 252; *NN* 55).

The point of such kinship in *Heart of Darkness* is not, or not only, to evoke, in a moment of piety and guilt, a fellow-feeling between the European and the native victim of the violence that attends imperial rapacity. Nor can it be reduced, as has the novel as a whole, to an assertion of the inner savagery of civilized man. Rather, the flow of identity between the two men is, from Marlow's point of view, unimpeded and unthematized; it is recorded but made to mean *nothing in particular*. It does, however, demonstrate once again a certain porosity or decomposition in the field of modern, imperial identity. Conrad does not found a nation or an empire because he represents the imperial encounter as one in which everyone on all sides is variously decomposed. The least fortunate die or are enslaved or exploited; the most fortunate are disconcerted by unsettling intuitions of "partnership" with people whom official ideology represents as subhuman. Even the sheltered Intended lives as a ghost in a world constructed by intentions she does not divine, much less control. Conrad may appear to inaugurate a certain tradition of fictional-imperial anthropology, but he lacks the anthropologist's distance. He must, therefore, be exempted from the company of those—including such latter-day fictionalists as Roland Barthes (Japan), Julia Kristeva (China), Claude Lévi-Strauss (Brazil), and others—who enclose, illuminate, or frame the Other as a "good object of knowledge, the docile body of difference." I have borrowed these phrases from Homi Bhabha, who seeks to cultivate a resistance to the terms of the West's earnest attention to its Others, to empower the Others to establish "[their] own institutional and oppositional discourse" (*LC* 31). Conrad himself represents a persistently fascinating (if not altogether "good") object of knowledge, a (not altogether "docile") body of difference, for Bhabha, Achebe, and other Others, who cannot fully repudiate Conrad any more than they can fully accept him as one of them.

I am contending that Conrad's Polish experience—the experience of dominating and being dominated, of being implicated in power on both sides—gave him singular access to a position that, for most people, would have seemed strictly impossible. For Conrad, no group was a priori more or less substantial or significant than any other, and the colonized life, however impoverished or alien it must appear to a European, was just as worthy of being represented as the colonizing one. His view was nonmoralistic in that, for him, virtue or significance had no proper home. At his best, he wrote without a dominant thematic insistence, as one who had no natural, exclusive, or overriding affiliation with either side of the great binaries of colonizer vs. colonized, or West vs. East. Conrad seems—but perhaps only seems—to occupy the chimerical and "unrepresentable" position Bhabha theorizes as the "Third Space of enunciation," a position of "hybridity" outside of and beneath the dualism of Same and Other, a nonposition founded on discontinuity, heterogeneity, and nonfixity as such, but one that, Bhabha claims, underlies all positive articulations of cultural difference (*LC* 37). If Conrad is not, in the end, docile with respect to this space, it is because he does not stand in the position of the in-between, that sliver of human potentiality dominated by gestures of sly mimicry and hybrid identity; he is, rather, in the comprehensive but incoherent position of being *both* Same and Other, a thoroughly English gentleman who was also an oppressed Pole.

I urge this view against that of Edward Said, who has recently depicted Conrad as an agent of what might be called "vulgar imperialism," "a man whose *Western* view of the non-Western world is so ingrained as to blind him to other histories, other cultures, other aspirations. All Conrad can see," Said asserts, "is a world totally dominated by the Atlantic West, in which every opposition to the West only confirms the West's wicked power" (*CI* xviii). This statement precedes and overshadows a more complex argument to the effect that Conrad had "two visions" of empire. In the first of these, Said says, Conrad "allows the old imperial enterprise full scope to play itself out conventionally," and leads, by routes unspecified, "if not to literal mass slaughter then certainly to rhetorical slaughter" (25). The second line of possibility leading out of Conrad, however, "shows [imperialism's] contingency, records its illusions and tremendous violence and waste," and even "permits his later readers"—although not, apparently, Conrad himself—"to imagine something other than an Africa carved up into dozens of European colonies" (26). In the end, Said returns to his initial point, that "Conrad could not grant the natives their freedom" or even concede that "Africa or South America could ever have had an independent history or culture," and so while Conrad is of two minds, one of them—the one obsessed with domination—dominates, and that one is Western and imperialist (30, xviii).

Said has, I think, avoided the implications of his own deepest insights by ignoring, in the interest of recovering a suppressed historical actuality, Conrad's own history or the history of Poland's suppression. He seems unable to imagine that Conrad was unprejudiced, or rather that his prejudices were anything out of the ordinary Western run. The "second vision" theory registers the resistances to this hypothesis within Conrad's work, but leaves these resistances unaccounted for, historically and psychologically orphaned. Said ignores the salient fact that Conrad on many occasions detailed a mighty "alternative" to "the West's wicked power": the East's equally wicked power. More to the point, Said fails to note the true source of Conrad's enduring power to disturb. In *Heart of Darkness,* two Europeans, Marlow and Kurtz, come to realize not only that other people had lives and cultures not totally controlled by imperialists, but, more troubling still, that those lives and cultures were, in unmappable ways and to an indeterminate extent, inescapably *continuous with their own.* The general question raised by this continuity is not whether the West was right or wrong to pursue an imperial mission or to enforce Western values and practices as a global norm on cultures who had every right to autonomy and self-determination. It is, rather, whether *anybody* has a life or culture or nation "of his own," a truly "independent history or culture."

Skeptical on this point, Conrad has no single opinion about empire; he does not *weigh in* on the subject at all. His perspective is unambivalently ambivalent: it is Polish. It is consistent with the perspective of the Polish (Lithuanian) philosopher, Emmanuel Levinas, who speaks of a "foreign interference in human causality." Levinas is exploring the "fission of the self" that occurs in "inspiration," a division that produces a kind of "stain," a linguistic "incoherence" or "delirium" that signifies the eruption, within the consciousness of the author, of the overriding ethical law (151, 186). Conrad's most "inspired" passages are perhaps the same ones Said is thinking of when he notes the "odd discrepancies" that litter Conradian narration (for example, the French "firing into a continent"), verbal peculiarities that leave the reader "with the acute sense that what he is presenting is not quite as it should be or appears to be" (*CI* 29). These discrepancies or interferences are, however, not only stylistic signals of an ethical imperative interrupting the reproduction of ideology. They are also traces of a specific political history—Poland's. Poles of Conrad's time both *had* a foreign interference, in the form of the states that had partitioned their nation, and *were* a foreign interference, in that they were Poles *in* Russia or Prussia, in the East or the West.

It is, however, Conrad's heroes who most conspicuously have and are foreign interferences. Most of the central figures of Conrad's work, including seamen, are foreigners to the element in which they find themselves. But this might be considered "simple" foreignness, the kind experienced by anybody outside his homeland. A distinctively Polish foreignness begins to emerge when we consider, for example, the unusual role played by narration in the composition of the Conradian hero. Kurtz "was just a name for me," Marlow says, suggesting at once his distance from a man he had never met and his intimacy, even his tentative identification, with him. So close is the affiliation between the narrator and those he narrates, so *constructive* is the narration itself, that the Conradian hero may be considered a kind of demonstration of the Lacanian dictum that, as Žižek puts it, "What the Other thinks I am is inscribed into the very heart of my own most intimate self-identity" (*TWN* 69). An inscribed Other, Kurtz is just a name for partitioned Poland—as Poland is a Kurtz among nations, so is Kurtz a Poland among men—but Poland is hard to find, and, finding it, you may also have found Russia. Thus, a man largely determined by, and contained within, another man's thought can still display an appetite whose immensity becomes virtually symbolic, as when Marlow writes, "You should have heard him say, 'My ivory.' . . . 'My intended, my ivory, my station, my river, my . . .' everything belonged to him" (49). Considered as a determined object of narration, Kurtz may be Polish; considered thematically, as a primitive autocrat, Kurtz stands in the "Russian" position. Indeed, if *all* Europe contributed to his making, then he must be in part Russian, and any affiliation with him must constitute an identification with the oppressor.

Marlow has a lot in common with Kurtz, not least this particular Polish-Russian ambivalence. In his omnivorous narrative productivity, he contains or "swallows" "all the men before him," but in other respects he is distinctively Polish. He owes his preeminence among Conrad's heroes to his status as the Other who thinks, the Other whose thought is inscribed in the identities of Kurtz and Lord Jim, and who is reciprocally determined by the thought of them. From the reader's point of view, Marlow *is* little more than his surprising partnerships and sympathies, which constitute—the insistent praise of single-mindedness and steadfastness, especially in those who steer, notwithstanding—the real distinctiveness of Conrad's sensibility. Marlow focuses one particular element of this sensibility, the capacity to identify or sympathize with those at the margins of human experience, even those who stand at opposite extremes, while retaining the sense that his "own" identity remains apart, discrete, integrated, unassimilated. As a creator, Conrad was conspicuous for the quality he attributes to Tom Lingard in *The Rescue,* an "implanted faculty of affection" (139). It is the perspective not of the citizen-captive of a partitioned nation, and certainly not of the oppressor, but of the Polish émigré adrift in the world.

The law in Poland is that freedom, agency, and value are elsewhere. For Kurtz, they are in the wilderness; for Marlow, they are in Kurtz. But the law has, in Conrad, a very long reach. Edward Said describes a curious feature of *Nostromo:* "the action at the beginning of the novel seems to wind its confused way forward until a hero appears who can dominate it in order to give it intention and method, whereas it eventually becomes apparent that the action has merely been searching for a hero (Nostromo or Gould) to own, to use, to enslave" (*B* 133). In Conrad's early works, the concept, the practice, the threat, the claim of slavery are, indeed, ubiquitous, functioning as the dominant trope of impotence. Malay society as Conrad represents it is a slaveholding society, but Conrad adds to this brute fact an ongoing narrative reintroduction of the term, as when the narrator of *Almayer's Folly* describes "[Almayer's daughter's] half-formed savage mind, the slave of her body—as her body was the slave of another's will" (116). Slavery is also a ready figure for power and agency themselves. The purest and most condensed expression of this paradox occurs in an obscure story, "Gaspar Ruiz" (1906), a tale of an "acquiescent soul" (6) who is pressed into service by the Republicans, the Royalists, and the Republicans again. Despite his initial indifference to all politics, Gaspar Ruiz eventually becomes an indispensable Royalist leader, in large measure because of the influence of his Royalist wife. The narrator, a Royalist officer telling the tale forty years later, emphasizes Ruiz's immense physical strength, and it is clear that his own power as a commander had owed much to his association with Ruiz, his "strong man." The forces of the King win the war, but it was not the King's force that decided the issue. Rather, it was the King's army, which is to say the army's strength, which is to say, ultimately, the strength of Gaspar Ruiz. However, Conrad is scrupulous to establish that Ruiz's strength is not fully or properly his own, but that of his wife, who had "poured half of her vengeful soul into the strong clay of that man, as you may pour intoxication, madness, poison into an empty cup" (52). Ruiz tells her that he is "your slave," and even that "You are my strength" (38, 39). Is Mrs. Ruiz, then, strong in herself, or has she, dressing and riding like a man and carrying a sword, merely appropriated her strength from her own powerful father or from some notion of manhood in general? "Gaspar Ruiz" expresses core Conradian insights, first that autonomy and will are concentrated in charismatic individuals, and second that they are functions of attribution by, or appropriation from, others. As Said suggests, the most expansive and complex representation of these insights is *Nostromo*, where the financier Holroyd's strength is appropriated from Charles Gould, whose strength derives from Holroyd's money and from the local effectiveness of Nostromo, the man regarded as "our man" by both the guileless Captain Mitchell and by the local people—the magisterial capataz who becomes, in an often repeated phrase, "the slave of the San Tomé silver." The setting may be "Costaguana," but the phenomenon is Polish.

The Conradian hero is both extraordinary and typical, alien and yet one of us, exotic and yet familiar. He is complicated in a particular way, made foreign to himself; in a word, he is polonized. In a (Conradian) world linked by waterways, where "this also . . . has been one of the dark places of the earth," everybody is implicitly foreign and displaced even when he is in his proper place. The all-European Kurtz, the all-human Wait, and the all-moral Lord Jim exemplify this Polish revelation about the human condition.

Conrad's heroes are Polish above all, however, in their "ontological nullity." In a preface to *The Nigger* addressed "To My Readers in America," Conrad notes that while the West Indian prototype of James Wait that he knew was an "imposter of some character," the figure of Wait he had created "is nothing: he is merely the centre of the ship's collective psychology and the pivot of the action" (*NN* 168). To what Conrad hero could such a description not apply? Some, such as Peter Willems of *An Outcast of the Islands* or Almayer, are simply neo*szlachta* idlers whose shabby marginality makes them capable of experiencing, without the necessity of ongoing responsibility for the business of the empire, extreme emotional states. The original of Heyst in *Victory* is recalled by Conrad in his "Author's Note" chiefly for a "detachment which . . . I cannot help thinking he had carried to excess." The fictional character Heyst is a kind of tailor's dummy on which, Conrad says, "I have fastened . . . many words heard on other men's lips and belonging to other men's less perfect, less pathetic moods." Even the more imposing figures can function as "nothing": Lord Jim is merely the center of a moral problem of responsibility; Kurtz is merely the center of the imperial encounter with the Other; Nostromo is merely the center of the struggle between the force of international capital and an emergent nationalist political movement. All are more significant for what goes on around them, including narration, than for what they are or do.

Especially given the subjects of Conrad's work—storms at sea, moral tests in difficult circumstances, strange doings in exotic locales—it is remarkable not just how little happens in his work, but how utterly given over to inertia that work is. One of the most illuminating sections of Frederick Karl's biography details, in text after text especially during the great period of 1899–1904, the many ways in which Conrad cultivated immobility, stasis, paralysis, the myriad forms of his inability to represent or imagine significant action. "We note, then," Karl writes, "a particular tone to Conrad's creativity in this period: its lack of thrust, its paucity or trivialization of movement" (*JC* 456). The plots of Conrad's works can indeed be reduced to almost nothing: a ship makes a voyage, with difficulties; a man inches upriver in a boat and then back, with difficulties, etc. The first four parts of *The Rescue,* the composition of which immediately preceded *The Nigger,* read like a sustained effort to create the most possible confusion and distress using the least possible quantity of incident. In this, as in other works, an inordinate amount of time is occupied by *waiting*—waiting for rivets, for Jimmy to die, for the storm to arrive, for the storm to exhaust itself and depart. Other modern novelists, including Gide, Mann, James, Proust, and Woolf, also seem to devalue action, at least in comparison to Fielding, Dickens, Clemens, or Tolstoi; but the torpor of Conrad's works has a peculiar and distinctive quality. According to Karl, this quality derives from the fact that Conrad is not, like his modernist contemporaries and immediate successors, a novelist of ideas, sensibility, or technique, but rather a novelist of memory. The stagnation that hangs over the Conradian narrative reflects no positive interest in exploring resources of novelistic interest other than action, but rather the fact that the action that constitutes the center of interest has already happened and must now be recalled, examined, commemorated, fertilized by meditation and narrative recounting. Karl does not make the further, more speculative claim that this commitment, or perhaps addiction, to memory was learned early, in Poland, with Poland itself constituting the very type of the memorable, of that which can *only* be apprehended through memory. The case can, however, be carried even further than this into the heart of Poland—a nation in which, for a patriot, action was obligatory to the precise extent that it was impossible—by considering Conradian inaction as an attempt to imagine, determine, and represent what Žižek identifies as the zero point at the core of all action. Conrad is, in other words, exploring the dark heart of agency itself, the nullity that inhabits and enables action in general, and this is why he can insist that his own modernity, like that of Wagner, Rodin, and Whistler, is based on an unswerving commitment to "nothing but action ... action of human beings that will bleed to a prick, and are moving in a visible world" (*CL*, 2:418).

Equally as remarkable as the general inertia of Conrad's adventure stories is the way in which the few instances of action "in a visible world" afforded by his texts disappear from the field of representation at the decisive moment. The murder of Verloc by his wife constitutes the drollest example of a vanishing that is characteristic of Conrad's rendering of action generally. Twenty-five pages into an elaborately rendered—an appallingly leisurely—account of a brief conversation between Mr. and Mrs. Verloc, Conrad at last approaches the deed itself. Responding to Verloc's amorous "Come here," Winnie approaches her husband, who is lying on the sofa. "Her right hand skimmed slightly the end of the table, and when she had passed on towards the sofa the carving knife had vanished without the slightest sound from the side of the dish." Lying on his back, waiting, Verloc

> saw partly on the ceiling a clenched hand holding a carving knife. It flickered up and down. Its movements were leisurely. They were leisurely enough for Mr Verloc to recognize the limb and the weapon.
>
> They were leisurely enough for him to take in the full meaning of the portent, and to taste the flavour of death rising in his gorge. His wife had gone raving mad—murdering mad. They were leisurely enough for the first paralysing effect of this discovery to pass away before a resolute determination to come out victorious from the ghastly struggle with that armed lunatic. They were leisurely enough for Mr Verloc to elaborate a plan of defence, involving a dash behind the table, and the felling of the woman to the ground with a heavy wooden chair. But they were not leisurely enough to allow Mr Verloc the time to move either hand or foot. The knife was already planted in his breast. (234)

Moments later, Winnie "was a woman enjoying her complete irresponsibility and endless leisure, almost in the manner of a corpse. She did not move, she did not think. Neither did the mortal envelope of the late Mr Verloc reposing on the sofa. Except for the fact that Mrs Verloc breathed these two would have been perfectly in accord" (235). Aided by the complicitous silence of knife and dish, the stabbing takes place through an unmarked agency in an unnarrated moment, a pause, a breath, after which the narrative resumes its complete but indifferent chronicle of events *chez* Verloc.

The single most famous act in Conrad's work, Jim's fateful leap from the deck of the *Patna*, the leap legible to many Polish readers as symbolic of Conrad's own emigration from "Patria," or Poland, simply does not occur as far as the reader is concerned. The narrative begins well after the leap, circles back to before the leap, progresses towards it, skips over the moment once again, returns to the official inquiry whose proceedings dance back and forth over the chasm of the event, eventually starts down the runway for good in chapter 9, and then, "'I had jumped . . .' he checked himself, averted his gaze . . . 'it seems,' he added" (68). (Many other Conradian heroes jump, it seems: Kurtz, James Wait [who actually slides, as a corpse, into the sea], the Secret Sharer [twice], Razumov. Conrad was drawn to jumping as a form of action that took the form of a gap.) Jim's second most famous act, offering himself up to be shot by Doramin, typifies the "symbolic suicides" committed by Kurtz, Wait, Nostromo, Haldin, Heyst, and Gaspar Ruiz as well (among a total of fifteen fictional suicides, by Karl's count), all of whom, if they do not exactly take their lives, are, like true Poles, implicated in the loss of them.

Even those more stolid and exaggeratedly British figures such as Singleton or Captain MacWhirr tend to inertia; they form a series with other Conradian characters who stay the course, submit to fate, steer with care, face head winds squarely, conceal a man hiding in their cabin, conceal their surrender of a man hidden in their closet, row for days. At the crucial moments, Conradian agency goes limp. His heroes arrive at a moment of choice—and they choose to submit to necessity or to the agency of another. Thus, Kipling noted, the "basic idea" of *Lord Jim* "is not [as it would be in an English novel] the inner drama of a man guilty of an offence and plagued by remorse," but rather the exploration of responsibility. "Conrad expresses the opinion that under certain circumstances the responsibility may be reduced to such an extent that it almost ceases to exist. Conrad is undoubtedly right," Kipling concluded, but "I would not encourage Conrad to expound his theory before any English jury" (Perłowski 163). An English jury would be disturbed at the missing elements in Conrad's accounts of nonheroes pursuing, through nonacts, their nonidentities in settings (Costaguana, Sambir, Patusan, Moscow, Borneo, the sea, the Inner Station, Sulaco, etc.) that can collectively be called the non-West or even the nonworld. His novels are structured, in a way essentially repugnant to the juridical mind, around a principle of negation that is not simply the other side of a positive center, but the center itself. Conrad is committed not to a definite principle of irresponsibility—Jim is haunted by the question of his own responsibility long after the "English jury" of the court of inquiry has finished with him—but rather to an idea (reflective of a "Polish" alienation from manifest authority) of *responsibility outside the positive law,* or, more generally, to a notion of *negative responsibility* to a negative law. Jim's crime can only be represented in such terms, as a *failure not to leap.*

Conrad thus represents a crisis of the center, of centrality itself. Another acute and sympathetic, but nonjudicial, reader of Conrad, E. M. Forster, commented that Conrad was "Obscure! Misty in the middle as well as at the edges, the secret cask of his genius contains a vapour rather than a jewel" (138). Conrad actually anticipated this insight by having the anonymous supernarrator of *Heart of Darkness* define Marlow's atypicality in terms of his narrative methods: while the yarns of most seamen "have a direct simplicity, the whole meaning of which lies within the shell of a cracked nut," in Marlow's tales, "the meaning of an episode was not inside like a kernel but outside, enveloping the tale which brought it out only as a glow brings out a haze, in the likeness of one of these misty halos that sometimes are made visible by the spectral illumination of moonshine" (5). Like other English seamen's tales, then, Marlow's contains an inside, a heart, but nothing is inside it, except for darkness. Marlow himself is a container of Kurtz, or rather of the story of Kurtz, the meaning of which lies "outside" of Kurtz—that is, in Marlow rather than in Kurtz himself—who is, as one critic has argued recently, "a character without a center, a faceless identity . . . hollow" (Galef 117).

While Conrad endlessly constructs forms of containment, of things within things (tales within tales, selves sharing selves, men within ships, Europeans within jungles, darkness within hearts or vice versa), he never places anything substantial at the very center.

This failure has become an endlessly repeated disappointment for critics looking for secrets. Terence Cave says of *Under Western Eyes* that there is "a blank in the center of the novel" (473); Malcolm Bradbury reports the discovery of a "big hole in the narrative of *The Secret Agent*," and not just in Verloc's chest (242); and Fredric Jameson notes the "hole at the center" of *Nostromo* where "political upheaval" should be, as well as the "empty slot in a system" occupied by the figure of Lord Jim, a system that "proves to have been the absent center of the narrative" (272, 243). One consequence of having speaking narrators is to introduce, as an effect of realism, lacunae and inconsistencies into the tales as they unfold. Ford Madox Ford describes another means of creating gaps in their collaborative novels, a means Conrad carried over into his own work: "One unalterable rule that we had for the rendering of conversations . . . was that no speech of one character should ever answer the speech that goes before it" (*JC* 200–201). What they sought, in other words, was to structure the conversation as a series of empty spaces or gaps to be negotiated by guesswork and supposition. This structure informs even those conversations where each utterance does appear to answer the one before it; it determines, in fact, the most famous conversation in all of Conrad, a passage that he and Ford reworked intensively together, Marlow's interview with the Intended: "'his goodness shone in every act [she says]. His example. . . .' 'True,' I said; 'his example too. Yes, his example. I forgot that'" (*HD* 75). The core of the conversation is not the utterances themselves but the holes or blank spots the utterances surround and peer down into. Even the locations of Conrad's narratives have a certain spotlike character, blankness constituting a mark of exotic substantiality more provocatively real than anything known and demarcated could be. In *Heart of Darkness*, Marlow recalls a protocolonialist boyhood fantasy about the Congo as "the biggest—the most blank" spot of all on the map of the world, "a white patch for a boy to dream gloriously over"—the very same dream that Conrad himself, as a proto-anticolonialist boy of nine, had dreamed when he had put his finger on a map of Africa, "the blankest of blank spaces on the earth's figured surface," and declared, "When I grow up I shall go *there*" (*HD* 11, 12; *PR* 13). Blankness accommodates varying desires, and the rule of Conradian containment is that everything has a center, and the center is empty.

What we are confronting in Conrad's heroes, his representation of agency, his fictional conversations, his settings, can most efficiently be characterized as *partition as a way of understanding the world.* Conrad seems to have been inspired by the spirit that moved one Pole, quoted anonymously in the *Cambridge History,* to speak with desolate precision of "the spot which remains Poland" (Reddaway et al. 153). Conrad's work constitutes, I am arguing, manifold reinventions of this spot, which confronted Conrad visually every time he looked at a piece of paper. Michael Fried astutely points out that "a particular fantasmatic relation to the blank page lies at the heart . . . of Conrad's fiction generally, and points out that acts of "erasure" (such as Jim's desire to begin with a clean slate, to leap from his leap) actually constitute meaning in Conrad rather than effacing it (199). But Fried leaves this symptomatic blankness, this obsessive smudging of a prior act of writing (represented, as it were, visually in the smudging of James Wait's name on the ship's roll), historically orphaned, when its proper home is clearly Poland, the blank origin of blank origins in Conrad. The Polish spirit affects even Conrad's Polish biographer, who begins his prodigiously detailed account by conceding that he is "conscious of several blank spots left" (Najder, *JC* viii). To be blunt, Poland is the missing term, the positive content of the holes in the center of Conrad's books. When Fredric Jameson, to take one prominent example, refers to Lord Jim as a placeholder, "an empty slot" that "proves to have been the absent center of the narrative," or when he sees in *Nostromo* a repression of politics, a smudging or displacement of history into caricature, melodrama, hyperconscious reflexivity, and "stylistic immanence," it is possible to fill in the blank with the name of Poland (243, 243, 275). (Indeed, Jameson nearly does this himself by referring to Jim as a "mere effect or pole of a larger signifying system" [243].) Doing so, we not only provide a bit of biographical amplitude to Conrad's texts, but we come closer to understanding the historical form taken by—or from—Poland. This historically specific form can, by a dialectical movement of the sort that Jameson has so powerfully plotted out, serve to confirm what

Žižek calls "the enigma of the status of the father in psychoanalytic theory": the fact, as Žižek sees it, that something (a man, a father) is "more present in [its] traces than in his direct physical presence" (*TKN* 134). The absence of Poland, and of politics in general, in Conrad's works, is "more X than X," more eloquently and passionately expressive of the reality of Poland than any concrete rendering of Poland could possibly be.

Partition, producing a sense of disjunction, of emptiness at the center, and thus of "irresponsibility," can be traced most clearly in Conrad's style. Critics of Conrad's style since Leavis have singled out for special abuse sentences such as the one in *Heart of Darkness* where Marlow reports that the stillness of the river "was the stillness of an implacable force brooding over an inscrutable intention" (36). But such passages should be considered not for their "tropical" lushness of effect, but aetiologically, as part of a "Polish" practice of privation, in which the referent is inaccessible even to language's most frantic efforts to grasp or render it. This passage in particular—a single paragraph nearly three pages long, interrupted only once—is the very heart of *Heart of Darkness* and one of the greatest descriptive passages in the English language. The manner of description is, however, decidedly un-English. "Going up that river was like travelling back to the earliest beginnings of the world," it begins;

> On silvery sandbanks hippos and alligators sunned themselves side by side. The broadening waters flowed through a mob of wooded islands. You lost your way on that river as you would in a desert and butted all day long against shoals trying to find the channel till you thought yourself bewitched and cut off for ever from everything you had known once—somewhere—far away—in another existence perhaps. There were moments when one's past came back to one, as it will sometimes when you have not a moment to spare to yourself; but it came in the shape of an unrestful and noisy dream remembered with wonder amongst the overwhelming realities of this strange world of plants and water and silence. And this stillness of life did not in the least resemble a peace. It was the stillness of an implacable force brooding over an inscrutable intention. (35–36)

Intensely specific with respect to the effect of the experience, the passage is scrupulously vague about the concrete particulars that provoke that effect. Beginning with hippos and alligators, the language rapidly "loses its way," invoking "everything you had known once—somewhere," "overwhelming realities," "plants," "water," before arriving at that implacable force, that inscrutable intention. As Marlow becomes uncoupled from himself, the language becomes uncoupled from its objects, partially emancipated from the task of recording specifics. The effect on Marlow, as on the reader, is paradoxical: on the one hand wholly concentrated in the moment, that is, in himself as a subject of this singular experience, Marlow is also exposed to a kind of flooding out of sympathy that permits him to recognize that the figures he observes on the shore, the "whirl of black limbs, a mass of hands clapping, of feet stamping, of bodies swaying, of eyes rolling" were "not inhuman. Well, you know that was the worst of it—this suspicion of their not being inhuman. It would come slowly to one" (37). In this unframed frame of mind, Marlow can think his way from this particular river to the origins of things, from himself to "one," and from the Inner Station to the heart of darkness—darkness as such, darkness of any and all kinds whatsoever.

No matter how disorienting a trip up the Congo must have been, it is Conrad's original and enduring sense of personal displacement that underwrites this passage. Nor are the effects of this sense confined to thematic preoccupations or narrative point of view. What might be called Conrad's "style" (which, especially in Conrad's case, cannot be isolated from theme, point of view, or indeed anything else) gives a persistently disquieting sense of elsewhereness—as in the following passage, which must have startled British readers accustomed to realism by its nearly hysterical rendering of what is, after all, mostly vegetation:

> In the middle of a shadowless square of moonlight, shining on a smooth and level expanse of young rice-shoots, a little shelter-hut perched on high posts, the pile of brushwood near by and the glowing embers of a fire with a man stretched before it, seemed very small and as if lost in the pale green iridescence reflected from the ground. On three sides of the clearing, ap-

pearing very far away in the deceptive light, the big trees of the forest, lashed together with manifold bonds by a mass of tangled creepers, looked down at the growing young life at their feet with the sombre resignation of giants that had lost faith in their strength. And in the midst of them the merciless creepers clung to the big trunks in cable-like coils, leaped from tree to tree, hung in thorny festoons from the lower boughs, and, sending slender tendrils on high to seek out the smallest branches, carried death to their victims in an exulting riot of silent destruction. (*AF* 165)

One cannot say what is being described here, things or the sense of things as they appear to someone. Judgments and rhetorical figures are constructed, but the responsible consciousness is nowhere to be seen. Indeed, it is imperfectly differentiated from the inhuman things it sees, for these things cling, leap, hang, carry death, prosecuting with fantastic energy their inscrutable intentions. The most inert item in the scene is "a man." With this single exception, everything else is alive with a sentience issuing from some unspecified source elsewhere; everything submits to a principle of being that is neither "its own" nor that of any other definite thing. On occasion, the displacements can achieve dizzying effects: "the sun, all red in a cloudless sky raked the yacht with a parting salvo of crimson rays that shattered themselves into sparks of fire upon the crystal and silver of the dinner-service, put a short flame into the blades of knives, and spread a rosy tint over the white of plates. A trail of purple, like a smear of blood on a blue shield, lay over the sea" (126). Consciousness and agency figure as "foreign interferences" in a wild prose that Levinas might call inspired, prose in which language struggles free from its "servitude towards the structures in which the *said* prevails" and aspires to a pure act of enunciation (153). Often praised for its "polish" or "purity," Conrad's style—especially his early style—is, in fact, marked by foreign interferences and for this reason constitutes a foreign interference in English literature. At its most polished, Conrad's style is most Polish.

It is tempting to think of Conrad's work as a fictive, nontheoretical working out of the Levinasian ethical imperative, a concentrated effort to produce an "anarchic" language that has liberated itself from the task of signification so that, like the ethical law, it cannot be derived from any particular knowledge of the world. But the text most clearly devoted to the subject of anarchy, *The Secret Agent,* is not easy to call "ethical" in any positive sense. The elaborate parallels drawn in that novel between the anarchism and official society, no matter how grimly inspired they may be, have a corrosive effect on any kind of ethical resolve or conviction. This novel in particular answers not so much to Levinas's ethics as to Jameson's account of dialectics, which Jameson insistently opposes to ethics, with its stark binary judgments. For Jameson, dialectical thinking renounces the untroubled clarity of ethical thought in order to invent "a space from which to think . . . two identical yet antagonistic features [for example, the anarchist underground and the police, progressive and reactionary forces, and so on] together all at once" (235). But can the system of total complicity and codependency represented in *The Secret Agent* be so confidently opposed to ethics? Wouldn't a truly dialectical approach seek to hold ethics in an unresolved dialectical suspension with its Other rather than attempt to eliminate or replace it? Such a metadialectical structure, in which an ethical energy would appear, but only in tension with or resistance to its opposite, informs Conrad's thought from the very beginning. My example is one of the most famous passages in Conrad, the beginning of the fourth chapter of *The Nigger,* which resumes narration after the ordeal of the storm:

> On men reprieved by its disdainful mercy, the immortal sea confers in its justice the full privilege of desired unrest. Through the perfect wisdom of its grace they are not permitted to meditate at ease upon the complicated and acrid savour of existence. They must without pause justify their life to the eternal pity that commands toil to be hard and unceasing . . . till the weary succession of nights and days tainted by the obstinate clamour of sages, demanding bliss and an empty heaven, is redeemed at last by the vast silence of pain and labour, by the dumb fear and the dumb courage of men obscure, forgetful, and enduring. (55)

The passage constitutes a monologic "missing" conversation in which adjective and noun, subject and predicate seem conjoined across an internal gap, an absent principle of mediation. A just sea, disdainful mercy, desired unrest, the privilege of unceasing labor, clamoring sages, empty heaven, an easeful mediation on the bitterness of life —every phrase is conflicted, every concept set against itself. "Ethics" —wisdom, justice, heaven, mercy—is "dialectically" confused with principles of pointless suffering, cruelty, inanity, and mere endurance.

What might be called the oxymoronic sensibility exhibited here achieves quieter but just as decisive expressions elsewhere: in, for example, the passage where the narrator notes James Wait's "unmanly lie," and adds, "But he stuck to it manfully"; or in the passage in *The Nigger* where Wait is described as "invulnerable in his promise of speedy corruption"; or where the narrator confides that "the secret and ardent desire of our hearts was the desire to beat him viciously with our fists about the head; and we handled him as tenderly as though he had been made of glass" (45, 29, 45); or in the juxtaposition between the "unbounded power of eloquence" in Kurtz's report to the International Society for the Suppression of Savage Customs and the handwritten scrawl Marlow finds at the bottom of the last page: "Exterminate all the brutes" (*HD* 50, 51); or in *Lord Jim,* where Marlow comments that Jim "was imprisoned within the very freedom of his power" (172); or in the power of silver, the "incorruptible metal" that serves as the protagonist of *Nostromo,* to enmesh its slaves in webs of corruption and idealistic self-delusion (245).

Writ large, such verbal and conceptual oxymorons can register as "comprehensive," even "universal," because they seem to exceed or shatter the limits of ordinary common sense. Unlike the Levinasian ethical imperative, however, Conrad's confusion of anarchy with the law, corruption with idealism, eloquence with extermination *can* be derived from knowledge about the world. It can be derived, in fact, from knowledge about Poland, where children become accustomed to thinking of their nation as an "elective monarchy," a "radical democracy among nobles," or, most tellingly, "an anarchy of laws." In fact, *The Cambridge History* displays the same oxymoronic feature; the very first sentence of volume 2, which covers the period from 1697 to the twentieth century, begins on a note of apparent pride that abruptly turns sour: "The year 1697 . . . is universally regarded as a landmark in the decline of Poland" (xiii). "In domestic disintegration and in foreign pressure," the text continues, "the long reign of Sigismund III, the first Swedish king of Poland (1587–1632), has a sad pre-eminence. . . . Poland's most dangerous enemies, however, were the laws and customs in which her squires embodied their victory over all other forces in Church and State" (xv). So distinctive of Poland is a kind of political-intellectual oxymoron that we cannot really call this feature of Conrad's style Conradian, as though it were the private stylistic property of an individual.

Conrad was, of course, both more and less than Polish. He seems to have drawn his inspiration not simply from being Polish but from being, at the time of composition, not-Polish, and from writing in a language not his own about people who were not his own, or rather, not exactly his own. Most students of Conrad's life agree with Jean-Aubry that his 1890 journey up the Congo on behalf of the Société Anonyme Belge pour le Commerce du Haut-Congo—in which he packed the well traveled but unfinished manuscript of *Almayer's Folly*—"killed Conrad the sailor and strengthened Conrad the novelist" (1:142). As Edward Garnett puts it, the trip "determined his transformation from a sailor to a writer." "In his early years at sea," Garnett recalls Conrad telling him, "he had 'not a thought in his head'. 'I was a perfect animal', [Conrad] reiterated." It was, Garnett speculates, "the sinister voice of the Congo" that "had swept away the generous illusions of his youth, and had left him gazing into the heart of an immense darkness" (qtd. in *HD* 195–96). But what actually happened? Many of Conrad's experiences are recorded in *Heart of Darkness,* but for part of the voyage, from November 1890 to January 1891, no account of any kind exists. "Gradually, as Korzeniowski penetrates deeper and deeper into the interior, getting closer to the core of affairs" Najder says, "he vanishes from sight," turning up, nobody knows exactly how, in Brussels towards the end of January 1891, his health permanently wrecked and a changed man in other respects as well, his letters and memoirs forever silent on this critical period (*JC* 139). Could the sight of colonial brutality and rapacity have transformed an animal, no matter how perfect, into one of the world's indispensable writers? Or is Marlow, in his meditation on the primordial river, indicating another factor, the alienation and return of "one's past"? Can we speculate that Conrad, during those obscure and unchronicled months, somehow found a way back, by way of a great and improbable—he would say "inconceivable"—loop, to his own grounding, a life he had done his best to leave behind him? Finding himself—once again—bereft of all external signs or confirmations of identity, Conrad may have recalled, or re-experienced, a life in which one's civic, national, linguistic, and historical past was no more than an "unrestful and noisy dream" with no material grounding or legal standing, a life in which the Motherland, as Apollo Korzeniowski calls it in a poem written for his wife, could only be found in "an abyss . . . For nowhere, nowhere can Poland be seen!" (qtd. in Najder, *JC* 12).

In the Congo, Conrad may have found that he could understand the experience of the mastered as his own, and could do so from the perspective of the master, which was also, at the moment, his own. This double identification informs Conrad's sense of things everywhere, but achieves nearly direct expression in the opening of the crucial early text that became *The Rescue.* Here, Conrad describes Malayan political culture in oxymoronically Polish terms, citing "their love of liberty, their fanatical devotion to their chiefs, their blind fidelity in friendship and hate," and expressing a fellow sufferer's regret at the prospect of their "unavoidable defeat"—at the hands of the Dutch and English, whose interests Conrad the seaman served (*R* 15). The Congo may have represented for Conrad, then, not only a decivilizing experience to which any European would be vulnerable in the proper circumstances, but something much more specific, personal, and powerful—Poland as a generalizable condition, Poland as a lost but recoverable land, Poland as a dimension of the Other, Poland as something one could neither escape nor forget. The single interruption in Marlow's description of the passage upriver to "the earliest beginnings of the world" is an interjection, which must be read as poignant and pointed rather than merely impatient or tension breaking, from one of his listeners: "Try to be civil, Marlow" (36).

*

As a writer, Conrad became a specialist in constructing circumstances of partial concealment, and even gave to Chief Inspector Heat of *The*

Secret Agent a worldly meditation on the radical undesirability of a full confession from Verloc:

> The turn this affair was taking meant the disclosure of many things—the laying waste of fields of knowledge, which, cultivated by a capable man, had a distinct value for the individual and for the society. It was sorry, sorry, meddling. It would leave Michaelis unscathed; it would drag to light the Professor's home industry; disorganize the whole system of supervision; make no end of a row in the papers, which, from that point of view, appeared to him by a sudden illumination as invariably written by fools for the reading of imbeciles. (196–97)

Despite the fact that the continued operation of anarchists in London makes England permeable to a host of foreign interferences, Heat persists in his belief that the very idea of complete and public confession represents a principle of stupidity, that intelligence and society as a whole flourish only in twilight.

This settled preference for shadows, which extended to a notorious diffidence toward the prospect of a fully independent Poland, ensured an uncertain reception in his homeland. Attacked by Poles early in his career for abandoning his country, Conrad still seemed to some Poles, years later, so vividly Polish that, as one of them put it, "*we* alone are in a position to understand him entirely and to feel what he expresses and what he suppresses, what he conceals and what he obscures with symbols" (Żeromski, qtd. in Fleishman 18–19). Others, feeling perhaps that outspoken British jingoism was an inappropriate disguise for a Polish sensibility, maintained, as Witold Gombrowicz wrote in 1935, that Conrad is "one of the most alien authors translated into our language" (Najder, *CUFE* 274). Interestingly, four years after this austere pronouncement, Gombrowicz himself faced a Conradian moment. In Venezuela in 1939 when Hitler invaded Poland, Gombrowicz boarded the ship that would take him back to Europe; but at the last moment, after the ropes were cast off, he dashed down the gangplank with his suitcases—and *leaped.* Conrad's Polish pertinence emerges in surprising places, a fact that leads some to define his Polishness *as* unplaceability, as a structure of secrecy. Thus, Jan Perłowski commented that while "his language and the subject-matter of his writings made him a stranger to us . . . through his emotions he inadvertently belonged to us: he was one of us in a specific way" (157–58). A Polish writer reviewing *Lord Jim* in 1905 confessed to being at first unable to find anything but English "eccentricity" in the book, but then "some voice inside me seemed to call out: 'And perhaps all this is just symbolic?' That ship doomed to sink . . . those travellers overcome with sleep and exhausted by religious ecstasy . . . those selfish men, who driven by greed for life escape from the ship they are responsible for . . . and particularly that basically noble-minded young man, a stray among scoundrels, who for the rest of his life suffers pangs of conscience that prey on his heart like the Promethean vulture. . . . Is it possible that the hidden meaning of it all is only such as it appears to English readers?" (Gomulicki 196). Another cited the "colonial" character of *Lord Jim* and commented, "Here the homeland extends over the entire globe" (Komornicka 193). A young Polish interviewer, dazzled by finding herself talking to "the greatest writer in England today," came to understand "that secret forces were at work in the soul of this *expatrié* Pole, and that his soul was ours, ours" (Dabrowski 196, 199).

Ours, or theirs? One of us, or one of them? A typical case, or an aberration? Some Poles may have felt that they, perhaps even they alone, could apprehend the soul of the man behind the façade of eccentricity. But the fact is that Conrad left Poland, or rather the spot where Poland had been, at the first possible opportunity in obedience to an imperative felt by virtually no other Pole. He went to sea.

TWO

To Go to Sea

AN UNRELATED EXISTENCE; OR,
THE LAW OF THE SEA

"There was no precedent," Conrad wrote three and a half decades later of his abrupt decision, at the age of sixteen, to leap not *from* but *to* a ship (*PR* 121). The man who administered his Master's examination in 1886 had offered the same assessment. "Not many of your nationality in our service, I should think," he commented; "I never remember meeting one.... Don't remember ever hearing of one. An inland people, aren't you?" (118). In 1917, Conrad would recall having met just one other Polish seaman, in the Sailor's Home in London, a man who "was slow-witted and indolent at sea"; but that was years later (Najder, *CUFE* 201). Conrad's resolution to leave Poland, perhaps for ever, to take a "standing jump out of his racial surroundings and associations" and embark upon a career for which nothing in his background had prepared him—a career chosen, for all he knew, by no other Pole, an altogether anti-Polish career—had plunged the tiny circle of adults charged with Conrad's upbringing into the deepest confusion and consternation (*PR* 121). Like other Poles, they were undoubtedly accustomed to thinking of the countries of Western Europe as the only place for émigrés. For his own part, Conrad was both absolutely convinced of the necessity of his "mysterious vocation" and, even in retrospect, mystified by its "somewhat exceptional psychology" (119). The most mysterious element of his decision was the fact that he was not attracted by any benefit or reward the sea might confer. As Karl writes, "His decision to depart lacked future definition; it was simply the decision itself" (*JC* 112); or, as Conrad put it, "I understood no more than the people who called upon me to explain myself" (*PR* 121). But he understood at least something that they did not, that he was not interested in entering the service of any of the partitioning nations, not even that of

Austria. "The truth is that what I had in view was not a naval career but the sea" (121).

*

Especially very late in life, Conrad often complained about being cast as a "Spinner of sea-yarns—master-mariner—seaman writer," claiming that his sea life "has about as much bearing on my literary existence, on my quality as a writer, as the enumeration of drawing-rooms that Thackeray frequented could have had on his gift as a great novelist." He declared to his friend Richard Curle in 1923 that "in the body of my work barely one-tenth is what may be called sea stuff" (Curle 147–48). And even in that one-tenth, the role of the sea is, he declared, strictly contingent. The "problem that faces" the crew of the *Narcissus,* he wrote to another friend in 1924, "is not a problem of the sea, it is merely a problem that has arisen on board a ship" (qtd. in *NN* 189). From one point of view, the justice of these complaints is immediately obvious. Conrad should not be classed with the authors of such books as *Two Years before the Mast, Captains Courageous, Mr. Midshipman Easy, Treasure Island,* or *Mutiny on the Bounty.* These tales of adventures written for boys may have provided a certain literary tradition into which Conrad could insert himself, as it were silently, without having to work out, step by anguished step, the programme of his incipient modernity. In their cryptic novelty, however, Conrad's works simply transcend this genre, which was already played out at the time he began writing, and demand to be read according to more demanding and sophisticated protocols. Conrad, this argument goes, is more comfortably lodged among such conquistadors of modernity as Freud, Nietzsche, Cézanne, Stravinsky, and Simmel than among Marryat, Cooper, Verne, Dana, Melville, and Stevenson. For Conrad, the sea is merely a convenient locale for the staging of dramas whose real import is moral, psychological, philosophical, or linguistic.

The claims of this chapter are, on the contrary, that the function of the Conradian sea vastly exceeds the scenic; that Conrad is a "seaman writer" even in much of the work that is not "sea stuff"; and finally, although this case will not be made in detail, that when he is not a seaman writer, he is no writer at all.

What could Conrad have meant by stressing a strangely phrased desire not for a particular kind of life but for "the sea," the sea itself? Why does he insist that he somehow had the sea "in view," as though he were not in Poland and as though one could actually see the sea in its totality or essence? (What, after all, can one ever see of the sea but a tiny portion of its surface, which is not truly "the sea," since the whole point about the sea is its invisible size, its vast depth and its beyond-the-horizon breadth?) What was it about the sea that summoned a Ukrainian youth? For Najder, Conrad simply wanted an opportunity to idle, "to taste a life of adventure and voyage without the hardships and rigors demanded by the calling" (*JC* 36). Most scholars agree, however, that the sea attracted Conrad chiefly as a negative of Poland, a country whose collective imagination was drawn not outwards but inwards to its deep interior woodlands as the site and symbol of national endurance so powerfully evoked by the historian Simon Schama in *Landscape and Memory*. "It was not so much the sea," Jean-Aubry writes, "it was a life in the open that he longed for with all the eagerness of a youth who had hitherto been physically and spiritually cramped and suffocated" (1:27). "He broke away from the world which was presented to him as dying and hurled himself into a whirl of life such as is conceived by a teenager," Perłowski says, "and thus Conrad cut himself off from his motherland" (168). Jocelyn Baines points out in his 1960 biography that the sea was the one thing in the world for which it was absolutely necessary to leave Poland (32). "To desire the sea was, then," Fleishman concludes, "equivalent to an absolute rejection of Poland" (11), and not just Poland, but his father's Poland in particular: "So he decided to reject Apollo's sacrificial legacy ('Be a *Pole!*')" (Meyers, *JC* 29). The certainty of these scholars contrasts impressively with Conrad's own enduring bafflement over his real motivations for taking up what he referred to in 1915 as "an unrelated existence" (*NLL* 145).

We cannot, of course, ignore the fact that Conrad had ample reason to leave. As the son of a political convict and a Russian citizen, he faced conscription into the Russian army for an extended period unless he could obtain citizenship elsewhere. Even apart from the spectre of military service, Conrad's prospects were bleak. Frequently interrupted by illness "of nervous origin," as Najder puts it, his schooling was very imperfect; he had few friends, no profession, and no property (*JC* 37). He was becoming expensive, and difficult to manage. Emigration recommended itself to him as it had to countless young Poles: to Chopin and Mickiewicz before him, to his near contemporaries Paderewski and Marie Curie, and, a bit later, to Guillaume Apollinaire, Lewis Namier, and Bronislaw Malinowski.

Still, it is difficult to give shape to a positive impulse to go not just *away* from Poland but *to* the sea. We might begin, however, by pressuring the phrase, "an unrelated existence." Like so many other Conradian formulae ("The horror! the horror!), this one is repeated. In the 1915 passage quoted above, it implies voluntary and decisive schism: "It was within those historical walls [of Cracow] that I began to understand things, form affections, lay up a store of memories and a fund of sensations with which I was to break violently by throwing myself into an unrelated existence" (*NLL* 145). But in *A Personal Record,* written in 1908–09, the phrase is enlisted to defend against the charges of desertion: "The fidelity to a special tradition may last through the events of an unrelated existence, following faithfully, too, the traced way of an inexplicable impulse" (36). Here, the phrase indicates an *apparent* disconnect sustained by invisible knots and hooks to a form of life that endures in secrecy. In this earlier passage, then, the leap to the sea actually continues, or translates, the "special tradition" of Poland, providing Conrad with an opportunity to be a Pole by other means than futile struggle against vastly superior force.

When approached from this angle, Conrad's "inland" youth seems idiosyncratically maritime in spirit. His father, we notice, translated Victor Hugo, including *Les Travailleurs de la mer* and some poems from *Flogging,* one of which, "Au peuple," concludes with the lines,

> The sea, like you People, foams and bursts forth;
> But it never fails. He, who from afar
> Wistfully looks out, waiting
> for the incoming tide . . . shall see it come!
>
> (qtd. in Najder, *JC* 25)

Apollo Korzeniowski, at least, had no difficulty constructing a Polish understanding of the sea. His son, meanwhile, pursued a characteristically Polish fascination with maps and geography, supplementing his reading of Polish poets with translations of the sea tales of Cooper and Marryat. But his chief distinction among his playmates was not his erudition, but his fertile faculty of invention. Thanks to the republication of an obscure record of a conversation with one of Conrad's boyhood acquaintances in Cracow, we have a snapshot of the artist at twelve or thirteen, already working out the details of an unrelated existence. "And in there, in a corner of the courtyard," the elderly former playmate of Conrad recalled, pointing to the place, "that strange boy told us . . . the most extraordinary stories. They were always of the sea and ships and far-away countries. . . . They were weird and fantastic almost beyond belief, but in the way he told them they seemed to us actual happenings. . . . And always they were about the sea" (Najder, *CUFE* 143).

In later years, Conrad was eloquently appreciative of the special traditions of the sea, of "the continuity of that sea-life into which I had stepped from outside" (*PR* 118). But one reason that he may have been able to take the step—and to take the next step, becoming a seaman writer, "without question, the greatest of all writers of sea fiction," as Tony Tanner says—was that there was, for him, a continuity, a relationship, between his related existence in Poland and the unrelated existence of the sea ("I" xvii). Conrad raises the issue of continuity in the very first of his surviving letters written as an adult, to Stefan Buszczynski, who had been, for a time, his guardian: "I always remember what you said when I was leaving Cracow," Conrad wrote; "'Remember'—you said—'wherever you may sail you are sailing towards Poland!'" (*CL,* 1:7–8). He raises it again, in a more purposeful and freighted way, in his account in *A Personal Record* of his Master's examination, where, he says, the examiner, a retired British sea captain, made him feel virtually "adopted. His experience was for me, too, as though he had been an ancestor . . . a professional ancestor, a sort of grandfather in the craft"—an improved ancestor, perhaps, who had useful wisdom to pass on, and who had eaten no dogs (118–19). As Conrad was to assert repeatedly, the sea was the place for ancestry, especially for a deep, if speculative, genealogical affiliation that reaches past the parental generation to the grandparental, and from there to the very beginnings of time. "If you would know the age of the earth," he writes in *The Mirror of the Sea*, "look upon the sea in a storm. The greyness of the whole immense surface, the wind furrows upon the faces of the waves . . . give to the sea in a gale an appearance of hoary age, lustreless, dull, without gleams, as though it had been created before light itself" (71). Singleton, of course, is an exemplary seaman in that he seems "colossal, very old; old as Father time himself . . . a lonely relic of a devoured and forgotten generation" (*NN* 14–15). Conrad apparently felt that he himself might be claimed by this earlier generation as "one of us," and confided that his refusal to embrace steam over sail would make of him, if he lived long enough, a kind of Singleton, "a bizarre relic of a dead barbarism, a sort of monstrous antiquity" (*PR* 117). Just as insistently, however, Conrad sees the sea as bestowing, or enforcing, an infinitely protracted minority. In the continuation of the passage about Singleton, this figure of phenomenal antiquity is described as a "child of time," and his fellow crewmen as "everlasting children of the mysterious sea" (*NN* 15). Speaking as a seaman, Conrad could imagine the sea, or at least the Mediterranean, as an inconceivably ancient site of infancy, a "cradle of oversea traffic," a "vast nursery in an old, old mansion where innumerable generations of his own people have learned to walk" (*MS* 148). "I say his own people," Conrad adds, "because, in a sense, all sailors belong to one family: all are descended from that adventurous and shaggy ancestor who, bestriding a shapeless log . . . accomplished the first coasting trip in a sheltered bay ringing with the admiring howls of his tribe" (148–49). Seamen form an ideal family without procreation. They have ancestors and grandparents but no parents; children themselves, they have no children—and, of course, no wives, sisters, or mothers. They do not pass through stages of life, but occupy the unchanging poles, as prolongations of the "childhood" of the race and anticipations of its extinction, the pre- and post-history of humanity. Meditating on them, one may experience a temporal extension of one's self-understanding by allowing a recognition of kinship, of a bond, of "their humanity—like yours."

We now have the rudiments of a more nuanced understanding of the possible relation Conrad may have sensed, if not fully understood, between Poland and the sea. Clearly, the sea represented a radically anti-Polish otherness, an escape from the memory and the promise of loss, and above all from the unendurable necessity of a brutally restricted existence. Just as clearly, the sea offered itself to Conrad as a compensation, not only of the political and historical loss *of* Poland but also, with its expanded network of pseudofamilial relations, of the personal losses he had suffered *in* Poland. (Hence the stress Conrad lays on the sense of being "adopted" by his examiner, a man who certifies Conrad's qualifications to join the "family" of mariners. Conrad, we might say, did not "go to sea" in this compensatory sense until he passed this examination and entered his majority.) At the same time, however, the antiquity of the sea and the voluntary yet hierarchical character of life at sea may have appeared to Conrad as a kind of translation of certain characteristics of traditional Poland. More pointedly, the exilic condition of life at sea may have seemed to the young Conrad a more honorable version of a familiar and humiliating privation. In "The Voyage," Washington Irving notes that "a wide sea voyage severs us at once. It makes us conscious of being cast loose from the secure anchorage of settled life and sent adrift upon a doubtful world. It interposes a gulph, not merely imaginary, but real, between us and our homes" (15–16). For Jameson, this "gulph" provides Conrad with a vantage point, a kind of crow's nest from which the "dreary prose of the world which is daily life in the universal factory called capitalism" may be viewed. The sea, Jameson argues, is a "privileged place of the strategy of containment" that drives politics underground by endowing events in the terrestrial "factory" with a quality of aesthetic totality (210). While Conrad may well have experienced the sea as a site of aesthetic emotion—speculative freedom, spectatorship, and reverie—he may also have discovered in it numerous points of connection to a very familiar politics. He may, that is, have understood the sea from the Polish point of view as radical Other, as compensation, and as a faithful continuation of Poland's special traditions, including the traditions of hierarchy and exile.

The character of the decision to go to sea itself is similarly complicated, for, appearances of free choice notwithstanding, his emigration to the sea was determined by two hard facts. First, the Poland Conrad left was not a dying but a dead nation, a nation under erasure whose traditions could *only* be continued under an assumed name. Second, Conrad, the orphaned son of convicts, could *only* affiliate himself with those to whom he was "unrelated." In one respect, then, the youthful Conrad went to sea in the spirit of radical autonomy, exercising an unconditioned capacity to undertake a project without precedent, to abandon all one's contexts and leap into an almost inconceivable future. In another, however, he made no true "choice" at all, but simply found a novel way of expressing his own inescapable personal and political impoverishment. No wonder he found his own impulse "inexplicable."

We can make both the Polish and the anti-Polish aspects of the sea even more explicit. Some of the peculiar emphases in Conrad's accounts of the sea can best be explained as dreamy versions of an ideal, emancipated Poland, a domain in which unmarked boundaries signified an unconquered immensity rather than a hole in the map of Europe. The sea, Giorgio Viola of *Nostromo* asserts, "knows nothing of kings and priests and tyrants. . . . The spirit of liberty is upon the waters" (281). At sea, Conrad discovered, in sharp and welcome contrast to the obsessive politicality of Poland, the category of the universal, a form of life, which, it was traditionally believed, was created directly by God, who ruled with an infinite and unmediated justice: in the words of the Psalmist, "The sea is His, and He made it." "Who else can heave its tides and appoint its bounds?" one nineteenth-century essayist asks; "Who else can urge its mighty waves to madness with the breath and wings of the tempest, and then speak to it again in a master's accents and bid it be still? . . . Majestic Ocean! Glorious Sea! No created being rules thee or made thee" (Greenwood). Ruled by God alone, the sea is the reconciler of contradictions, the accomplice of human liberty and, as Conrad suggests, the ally of humanity in general. "Water," Conrad writes in a well known passage, "is friendly to man. The ocean, a part of Nature farthest removed in the unchangeableness and majesty of its might from the spirit of mankind, has ever been a friend to the enterprising nations of the earth. And of all the elements this is the one to which men have always been prone to trust themselves, as if its immensity held a reward as vast as itself" (*MS* 101). It takes a certain effort to see how complex this rhapsodic monologue actually is. Initially implying a commonality among its overgeneralized terms—water, man, Nature—the passage then specifies that the ocean, while friendly and natural, is radically unlike man, and that its quasi-divine favor is concentrated on "enterprising" (that is, imperial, trading, Western) nations, nations that scour the planet in search of vast "reward." As a domain of primordial liberty friendly to Western interests, the sea is explicitly depoliticized and then implicitly repoliticized in terms that recall the "Western" countenance of Poland.

If only that were all. But the effort to make the sea almost Polish in its essential condition of freedom entails projecting into its depths other features of Poland as well, including self-betrayal and identification with its oppressors. Thus, a few pages after celebrating water's friendliness to man, Conrad finds himself thinking other thoughts: "The ocean has the conscienceless temper of a savage autocrat spoiled by much adulation. . . . If not always in the hot mood to smash, he is always stealthily ready for a drowning. The most amazing wonder of the deep is its unfathomable cruelty" (*MS* 137). Unfathomable? The sea's cruelty would, perhaps, have been unfathomable if it did not so closely resemble, at least in Conrad's rhetoric, another autocrat closer to home. The sea, as he nearly states in a passage written in 1918, is virtually a watery Russia:

> And then, what is this sea, the subject of so many apostrophes in verse and prose addressed to its greatness . . . ? The sea is uncertain, arbitrary, featureless, and violent. Except when helped by the varied majesty of the sky, there is something inane in its serenity and something stupid in its wrath, which is endless, boundless, persistent, and futile—a grey, hoary thing raging like an old ogre uncertain of its prey. Its very immensity is wearisome. . . . a devouring enigma of space. (*NLL* 184)

To go to sea, then, is hardly to leave home, for the sea is a kind of Russia *sans* czars. In fact, when Conrad wished, in "Autocracy and War" (1905), to present Russia as a colossal, undifferentiated, and "inhuman" figure of immense force but little brain, he could do no better than to appropriate features proper to the sea, likening Russia to a "dreaded and strange apparition . . . something not of this world, partaking of a ravenous ghoul, of a blind Djinn grown up from a cloud, and of the Old Man of the Sea" (*NLL* 89).

Furthermore, when he wanted, in *Under Western Eyes* (1911), to define "the mark of Russian autocracy and of Russian revolt"—the "spirit of Russia" en toto—he could think of no better word than "cynicism," which makes "freedom look like a form of debauch, and the Christian virtues appear actually indecent" (*UWE* 105). In its indifference to distinctions, cynicism equalizes the unequal, replacing a wall with a mirror. In "the cynicism of oppression and revolt" that is Russia, "virtues themselves fester into crimes" (329). A few years earlier, Conrad had devoted some thought to cynicism in another context, deploying it as the key term in the narrative of his maritime coming-of-age in *The Mirror of the Sea* (1906). There, he claimed that his "initiation" into the life of the sea was complete only after he had witnessed, during a rescue operation, an instance of the "cynical indifference of the sea to the merits of human suffering and courage": "In a moment, before we shoved off, I had looked coolly at the life of my choice. Its illusions were gone, but its fascination remained. I had become a seaman at last" (*MS* 141, 142). He "became a seaman," that is, as opposed to being merely a man at sea, when he recognized in the sea, his *chosen* existence, the same leveling and indifferent cynicism he would use to define "the spirit of Russia," as well as the same unprincipled destructiveness he had attributed to Russia in "Autocracy and War," written just a few months earlier. "Initiation"—the completion of his leap to the sea—occurs when he recognizes that he has freely positioned himself in the very scene of autocracy from which he had fled.

The sea could not be recognizably Polish if it were not also Russian; it could not serve as an ideal Poland without also mirroring an actual Poland. This is why the sea, like Poland, is shown to obey an oxymoronic imperative dictating that every feature attributed to it be matched and canceled by its opposite. Is water friendly to man? Absolutely; and the sea "has never been friendly to man." Is the sea unchangeable and faithful? Unquestionably; and it is the "unstable element itself . . . Faithful to no race after the manner of the kindly earth . . . the ocean has no compassion, no faith, no law, no memory" (*MS* 135). Conrad is not simply saying that the sea is friendly one moment and unfriendly the next, but something far more interesting. Through contradictory but unqualified assertions, he claims that the sea is friendly and unfriendly, constant and inconstant, faithful and unfaithful. The integrity of one quality is not compromised or negated by the coexistence of its opposite. Inconceivable though they may seem, and irrational though they may be, such oxymorons exhibit a certain regularity that is crucial to Conrad's cognitive and expressive style. Conrad even describes himself in terms that mirror those he applies to the sea, writing in 1918, "I am always myself. I am a man of formed character. Certain conclusions remain immovably fixed in my mind, but I am no slave to prejudices and formulas, and I shall never be. My attitude . . . will, within limits, be always changing—not because I am unstable or unprincipled but because I am free" (Jean-Aubry, 2:204). Even at this late date, Conrad could still have recognized himself in the "mirror of the sea."

The gloomy irony that passes for humor in Conrad should be considered an instance of this predisposition to mirrors. So, too, should the "cynical" or "nihilistic" negations, alternating with the most pious affirmations, that characterize his representation of politics. The phrase "material interests" in *Nostromo* exhibits the entire range. Charles Gould first uses the phrase to indicate the force at work in the stabilization of Costaguana: material interests, he says, "impose the conditions on which alone they can continue to exist"; thus, money making can be justified because the order and stability it demands "must be shared with an oppressed people" (69). At the end, Dr. Monygham takes up the phrase once again, but applies to it precisely the opposite predicates, predicates drawn, as it were, from the inconstant sea: "There is no peace and no rest in the development of material interests. They have their law, and their justice. But it is founded on expediency, and is inhuman; it is without rectitude, without the continuity and the force that can be found only in a moral principle" (406). Jameson discovers this dynamic, expressive of the dialectic of capitalism, within the phrase itself, in which, he says, "the whole drama of value and abstraction is concentrated." "If it is 'material,'" he writes, "then it is . . . at one with simple selfishness and egoism; if it can be isolated as an 'interest,' that is an abstractable value, then it is no longer material. . . . But to be able to conceive of the specificity of capitalism would be to hold both these incommensurable and irreconcilable things in your mind at once, in the unity of a single impossible thought" (278). To the extent that *Nostromo* concerns the destiny of material interests, it qualifies as a tale of capitalism; but to the extent that it is about the phenomenon of "unthinkability," it is also, as its subtitle asserts, "A Tale of the Seaboard."

Conrad may have settled upon the conventional phrase, "the mirror of the sea," because mirror-images are visual oxymorons, unlike likenesses of the objects they reflect. The mirror thus "explains" the sea's constant inconstancy. If greedy or ambitious men have seen the sea as friendly to their interests, this is because the mirror faithfully reflects all gazes; but if the sea "has never adopted the cause of its masters," as Conrad says in "Initiation," this is because all causes are alien to its nature: the "vast dreams of dominion and power" that would-be masters of the sea have pursued on the sea's surface "have passed like images reflected from a mirror, leaving no record upon the mysterious face of the sea" (*MS* 135–36). Like a mirror, or like mirroring in general, the sea is "immemorial" in its synthesis of primordiality and radical ephemerality.

Also like a mirror, the sea is not master of itself. Assertions of autocracy notwithstanding, the sea, in Conrad's account, is more ruled than ruling. Unmastered by its masters, the sea is also unmastered by itself. At its most autocratic, the sea does not behave as an independently maddened volume of water but as the will-less, passive instrument of the winds. Only when ruled by the "Rulers of East and West" does the sea master its masters, the ships and the men who sail them. If we look, in *The Mirror of the Sea*, for a "Russian" principle of autocracy, our search must lead us to the air, or rather to the agitation of the air, or rather to the profound darkness that results from the agitation of the air. It is, above all, darkness by which autocracy is exercised during that most autocratic of events, the storm at sea, when sailors become polonized in that they have nothing to see: "To see! to see!—this is the craving of the sailor, as of the rest of blind humanity. To have his path made clear for him is the aspiration of every human being in our beclouded and tempestuous existence" (*MS* 87). The East and West winds go about their business differently but to the same end of crippling vision. The "great autocrat" the "King of the West" "does not say to the seaman, 'You shall be blind'; it restricts merely the range of his vision and raises the dread of land within his breast" (87, 83–84). An Easterly gale "puts your eyes out, puts them out completely, makes you feel blind for life upon a lee-shore" (98). Even fresh winds frustrate the craving for sight. A fresh Easterly wind on the North Atlantic, for example, stalls a homeward voyage and if it does not blind you, "augment[s] the power of your eyesight [only] that you should see better the perfect humiliation, the hopeless character of your captivity" (97). Conrad learned about occluded visibility, in a symbolic and metaphorical sense in Poland, and in a literal sense at sea. In both instances, darkness was the agent of partition. "What we have divided we have divided," the King of the West says to his Eastern "brother" (92). Conrad, the retired master mariner and retired Pole, confesses in *The Mirror* that he has at last become resigned to the autocracy of the West Wind, "too much moulded to his sway to nurse now any idea of rebellion in my heart" (99).

What is the living original, and what the mere inert image, of autocracy? Can autocrats rule on behalf of other autocrats; can they rule by intermediary autocrats? Can one autocrat rule another? Are we looking—when we can see at all—at a general autocracy distributed evenly throughout the sea-wind field? Where, exactly, is the mirror placed, and which way is it facing?

Such questions, almost frivolously speculative considering the heinousness of autocracy itself, become more aggravated at every turn, nowhere more so than when Conrad tries to define the sea as unique and absolutely self-identical, like nothing else on earth. Surely, Conrad presumes, the sea is like nothing else on earth, but he is constrained from saying the only sentence that would express its singularity, "The sea is the sea," much less "The sea is like the sea," because to do so would express nothing at all. It would also be untrue, since, as a mirror, the sea is actually *like* those things that are unlike the sea and therefore *unlike* itself. The sea is like nothing else precisely because it is, in a certain respect, like anything else. Such recognitions were not available to Conrad in abstract form, but we can track their force as it mars his various efforts to move beyond tautology, to define the sea by implicit comparison with its Others, such as terrestrial autocrats. His accounts are marred because any comparison, while making the sea "real" or "understandable," works against the original premise of the sea's uniqueness. When the sea and Russia swap attributes—timelessness, stupidity, cynicism, indifference to humanity, immensity, and so on—the status and even, in a sense, the *location*, of the sea swims. Representation itself becomes subjected to the law of the sea: that everything floats in an unbounded, unmarked, indefinite, and reflective medium.

In general, *The Mirror of the Sea* proceeds by corrupted opposition, as Conrad attempts to contrast the sea to its Others—the land, the seamen, and above all the ship. As the refrain running through "Initiation" asserts, "Ships are all right." Against the cynical indifference of the sea, the ship "makes its appeal to a seaman by the faithfulness of her life" (*MS* 130). The love that men give to ships is, Conrad asserts, "profoundly different from the love men feel for every other work of their hands . . . The pride of skill, the pride of responsibility, the pride of endurance there may be, but otherwise it is a disinterested sentiment." The sea, by a contrast that could not be more extreme, has "no generosity. No display of manly qualities—courage, hardihood, endurance, faithfulness—has ever been known to touch its irresponsible consciousness of power" (*MS* 137). Unlawful in itself, the sea cannot command duty from a seaman because "it is too great and too elusive to be embraced and taken to a human breast. All that a guileless or guileful seaman knows of it is its hostility, its exaction of toil as endless as its ever-renewed horizons." No; what commands the seaman's devotion and respect is "something that in his eyes has a body, a character, a fascination, and almost a soul—it is his ship" (*NLL* 191). The ship—he even says at one point—"this ship, our ship, the ship we serve, is the moral symbol of our life" (*NLL* 188). The sea exacts what we might call *pure* toil—toil *pour* toil—while the ship exacts a *purified* toil—a *purposive* toil, a *moral* toil, a *redeeming* toil.

The absolute distinctness of the ship can barely be sustained in the unsystematic and heterodox discourse of *The Mirror of the Sea.* When subjected to the pressures engendered by a narrative of complex and violent action, the very idea of "ship" becomes destabilized, even disintegrated. In one of the best known passages of *The Nigger,* the ship is deployed as a figure for the island nation of England, which greets the *Narcissus* at the end of its journey as a mirror of its ideal self:

> alone in the midst of waters, like a mighty ship bestarred with vigilant lights—a ship carrying the burden of millions of lives—a ship freighted with dross and with jewels, with gold and with steel. She towered up immense and strong, guarding priceless traditions and untold suffering, sheltering glorious memories and base forgetfulness, ignoble virtues and splendid transgressions. A great ship! . . . A ship mother of fleets and nations! The great flagship of the race; stronger than the storms! and anchored in the open sea. (100–101)

The *Narcissus* comes home to mother, its own mother and the mother of entire fleets, whole nations—of humanity itself! The sentence ratchets upward from the tiny ship through the nation, all the way to the human race and beyond, in a passage that constitutes a general hymn to everything, troubled only by a persistent oxymoronic stain ("ignoble virtues . . . splendid transgressions"), and by the impracticability of anchoring "in the open sea." The passage itself is conspicuously unanchored, drifting from entity to entity, with each serving as a metaphor for all.

The ship is a mere point of salience in a homogeneous cosmic colloid, one node of a general system of mediation that can accommodate, it seems, all differences. Within this system, qualities and values float ambiguously, forming only provisional and temporary attachments, but attaching, potentially, to anything. The ship mediates between earth and sea, "alive" only while under sail but driven exclusively by land interests that are "forgotten" in the open waters. As a larger ship, England is dignified, even glorified; but as a parcel of land, it is simply a representative of the impure, polyglot, and "sordid earth" that takes possession of the *Narcissus* at the end of her journey (102). This ambivalence is retained as the ship becomes, in the rhetoric of the narration, a kind of asteroid, "a fragment detached from the earth," pursuing its course "lonely and swift like a small planet" through a universal sea; and even as it becomes a tiny planet: "Our little world went on its curved and unswerving path" (18, 63). Presented as an exemplary site of structural and moral integrity in contrast to the sea, the ship mirrors and is mirrored by the island, the nation, the moon, and the earth. Even the crew must be included in this system. The full formulation of the pronouncement that ships are all right was given by Singleton: "Ships are all right. It is the men in them!" (*NN* 14). In *The Mirror of the Sea*, Conrad retrieves this sentiment, attributing it to "an elderly seaman," and repeats it several times to indicate the crisp distinction between ships and the inconstant men who operate them (128). Ships, as Conrad says in his own voice, "are not exactly what men make them" and must be considered as things apart—apparently forgetting an earlier affirmation, the mirror-image of the first, that "ships are what men make them: this is a pronouncement of sailor wisdom, and, no doubt, in the main it is true" (134, 16).

In search of something that remains itself, something uncompromised by mirroring, some distinction that holds, we come at last to the opposition of cynical sea and simple seamen, whose aspirations the sea mocks, whose hopes it crushes, whose doubts it aggravates, and whose survival it imperils. The sea, we might wish to think, is an element, a thing of nature, while the crew constitutes an ordered, traditional, society. But Conrad does not simply draw attention to the iron routine of sea life, or to the clarity of its command structure; he refers specifically to "the autocratic realm of the ship" (*MS* 17). Captain Allistoun of the *Narcissus* cuts an especially impressive figure: "He, the ruler of that minute world, seldom descended from the Olympian heights of his poop. Below him—at his feet, so to speak—common mortals led their busy and insignificant lives" (*NN* 19). Allistoun's majesty may appear to reflect an analogy between the captain and the sovereign, but Allistoun's subjects, unlike Victoria's, do not enjoy parliamentary democracy or indeed any other guarantees of political rights. (The folly of such a mutinous notion is emphasized repeatedly in *Mr. Midshipman Easy,* a primary source of Conrad's earliest ideas about sea life.) Allistoun's power is more closely modeled on the autocracy of the sea than on the restricted authority of the English monarch. Conrad actually takes considerable pains to make this distinction by making the repellent, subhuman Donkin the spokesman not for socialism, as some have argued, but for the values of traditional English liberalism: the rights of man, the dignity of the individual, and the solidarity of labor. With his "filthy eloquence," Donkin insistently registers the fact that the ship's officers possess a species of power that would be intolerable on English soil. For making this political argument on board ship, Donkin is virtually flung to the land by the narrator at the end. "Let the earth and the sea each have its own," the narrator declares, placing Donkin and Allistoun on opposite sides of the shoreline (107). This simplifying gesture only points up, however, the complexity of Allistoun's position. As an English *captain,* he is a man of the (autocratic) sea; as an *English* captain, he is affiliated with both the protective sovereign and the mutinous Donkin. The exemplary Allistoun cannot be sheltered from contamination by any of his Others, on land or sea. Even at the point of death, the simplest of seaman is complicated. Singleton, a forgetfully sanguine narrator says at the very end, has "no doubt taken with him the long record of his faithful work [and perhaps a few of the dandified novels he cherishes] into the peaceful depths of an hospitable sea" (107). Singleton himself thinks of this event in rather different terms, regarding the sea as "an immensity tormented and blind, moaning and furious, that claimed all the days of his tenacious life, and, when life was over, would claim the worn-out body of its slave" (61). Even more troubling than this thought might be the fact that, on arrival, he will share a grave with James Wait, and will do so because they both belong to the sea. "You can't help him," Singleton had told the fascinated crew; "die he must. . . . The sea will have her own" (80). Picturing his end, Singleton aligns himself with his Other.

Clearly, rigorous systematic thought is not Conrad's long suit, but his very failure to keep his categories clean, a failure learned from long study of the mirror of the sea, produces not only the shimmering uncertainty that generates ongoing debate about the true meaning of his texts, but also the "transitional" status on which much of his importance in literary history depends. If, in an adaptation of Baudelaire's account of modernity in "The Painter of Modern Life," the premodern is to be distinguished from the modern in terms of the difference between, on the one hand, a stable object world, a view of language that assumes the primacy of reference and the crucial function in narrative of moral testing, and, on the other, rhetorical "flow," an unstable and "aesthetic" world of words, the ephemerality of appearances, and the indeterminacy of moral concepts, then Conrad stands at the water's edge. He does not pass gracefully from one to the other, spanning the troubled waters of the fin de siècle by beginning as a realist and ending as a modernist. (If anything, he progresses backwards, with his early novels from *The Nigger* to *The Secret Agent* suggesting the energies of an incipient modernism, and his work from *Under Western Eyes* on [*Chance, An Arrow of Gold, The Rover, Victory,* the last parts of *The Rescue*] belonging to an "earlier" era. The two parts of *Lord Jim* condense this regressive movement, with the first part constituting "an intricate and prototextual search for the 'truth'" and the second, a linear "paradigm of romance as such" [Jameson 207].) In his greatest works—*The Nigger of the "Narcissus," Heart of Darkness, Lord Jim, The Secret Agent*—Conrad effects an uncertain transition by dialectically exemplifying both modes, without apparent uncertainty or confusion, without feeling the need for resolution, in much the same way that an elastic Marlow in *Heart of Darkness* attaches his sympathies to both colonizers and colonized, Europeans and "savages." While Conrad insists "theoretically" on the premises of a premodern realism—his Arnoldian goal, above all, is to make you *see*—his actual fictive-rhetorical practice can only be grasped as sign and instance of the new era.

Alternating frequent encomiums on "the clearness, precision, and beauty" of the "technical language" of seafaring with extravagant rhetorical fantasias, *The Mirror of the Sea* is the most exposed text in this regard (13). A semitheoretical text comprised of reminiscence and reflection, *The Mirror* divides the experience of sea life into a number of categories ("Landfalls and Departures," "Overdue and Missing," "Initiation," "Rulers of East and West," and so on), within which Conrad elaborates further distinctions, as between kinds of winds, ship and sea, ships and men. *The Mirror* is rarely discussed by literary critics, despite the occasionally voiced suspicion that the book occupies a privileged place as the only direct frontal approach to the sea in the *oeuvre* of this eminent "seaman writer." When it is taken up, it is characteristically mined for passages that demonstrate the badness of Conrad's style and the tendency of Conrad to overwhelm substance with rhetoric. Gombrowicz took this approach in 1935, claiming that *The Mirror* revealed as no other book Conrad's tendency to grandiloquence, and the immense gap that lay between mere humanity—in this case, Conrad's rather paltry reminiscences themselves—and a style that inflates everything into "cosmic truths." The very greatness of the style aggravates the littleness of his material: "Perhaps in no other book," Gombrowicz wrote, "is his mastery of style so fully displayed—a style able to turn modest recollections into a great paean. And nowhere else can we perceive more clearly the entire poverty of the style. . . . And dazzled but unconvinced—as if only brushed by the wing of some enormous bird . . . we close the book in admiration" (276).

Gombrowicz misses the feature of *The Mirror* that I want to emphasize because he takes the subject of the book to be "modest recollections," and not the sea. The immediate cause of the extravagant display of stylistic mannerisms, I argue, is not a mere habit of writerly self-indulgence, but the deep itself: the sea is the *great fact* that *cannot be described*. A thing both monumental in its nature and changeable in its appearances, the sea necessitates a thoroughgoing figurality that virtually trumpets its own failure to provide an exact description. Rendering the actuality of the sea—the sea itself, not human life on board ship—must be an exercise in style, like painting a still life with a larger and much more violent subject. Conrad has chosen the one subject available to him that compelled figurative excess, but it is this very excessiveness that constitutes the sea's literal truth. Contrary to deep-laid cognitive habits, one cannot translate the figures that describe the sea into a cleaner, sparer, or more precise literality: tropes constitute the only form of language truly proper to the sea, which summons forth style with the same imperativity as it had summoned the young Conrad. For a writer, then, an excessive and irresponsible style, a style that defies the rule of representation, constitutes the law of the sea.

This writerly law provides a bewildering counter to the more philosophical "law" that is occasionally hauled up from the depths as a demonstration that nature, in the form of the mighty equilibrium of the sea, exists untouched by the contingency and disorder of human affairs. In *Le Contrat naturel* (1990), the French philosopher Michel Serres trawls for this norm, inferring the principles of an ideal civil or social law from the sea, or rather from the conditions of life at sea. Current conceptions of civil law, he complains, reflect only a Cartesian "mastery" over the natural world that has proven to be disastrous. But the fact that there can be no escape from a ship imposes on all crew members a "divine courtesy." Everyone on board a ship spontaneously forms a harmonious collective, aware that "they condemn their bark to shipwreck if they come to blows amongst themselves, if they attack the internal adversary." At sea, "the social contract comes to them directly from nature" (13). For too long, Serres argues, we have conceived of governors as administrators of a purely civil law, an exclusively social contract. Political leaders in today's global culture "must get out of the social sciences, streets, and city walls . . . [they must] emerge from the social contract and invent a new natural contract by reinstating the word *nature* with its original meaning of the conditions in which we are born—or in which tomorrow we ought to be reborn" (16). Serres concludes with an appeal to "a global law that requires us to love humanity" (20). But has he noticed that the "nature" from which this global law is supposedly derived is a violent and inhuman force, a "grey, hoary thing raging like an ogre" as Conrad puts it, that will, at the slightest break in communal harmony—or even without such a break—destroy seagoing society, manners and all, literally without a thought? Serres's "natural contract" is drawn against rather than from nature: no natural principle is reflected in it. As a consequence, his understanding of nature, law, human beings, and their relations suffers, it must be said, from a certain shallowness. Crystallized in the bond of men confronting a feared adversary, Serres's natural law is the theoretical equivalent of boys' adventure stories.

Without rejecting this view, just as he does not altogether reject the conventions of the adventure story, Conrad strikes deeper by treating the sea not as threatening depth alone but also as surface, as mirror. To get at the difference immediately, we can compare the two figures in whom, in Serres and Conrad, the social contract converges. For Serres, the central figure, the pivot in the conversion of nature into culture, is the pilot, who reads the sea and the winds, making constant adjustments "so that finally a course is steered amidst the set of constraints." Determined directly and entirely by nature, the conduct of the pilot provides a salutary model for "the art of governing people politically" on "the worldwide ship" (15). As we saw in the last chapter, Conrad has a special feeling for those who steer, but for him the crucial figure is the captain, precisely because the captain's authority mirrors both the social contract, with its concern for community, rights, and the principles of justice, and the violence of the law of nature as exhibited by the sea. For Conrad, the captain must not only confront but deploy the "internal adversary," a malign form of sheer power that defines all at once the law of nature, the nature of the threat, and the nature of his authority. In short, Conrad understands what has been withheld from Serres, that a civil code or social contract that came "directly from nature" would bear a relation with autocracy as well as Arcadia.

Thus, throughout the meandering chapters of *The Mirror*, Conrad approaches, in the modes of the garrulous raconteur and the untroubled moralist, the question of the relation of the law to crime, a relation Žižek represents as the best example of the more general "problem of identity" (*TKN* 33). Žižek outlines two approaches to this problem, each derived from readings of Hegel. In the first, "traditional" reading, crime is reduced to "a passing moment of the law's mediated identity-with-itself," a thoroughly controlled phase, aspect, or incident in the essentially undisturbed reign of law. In this view, a multitude of perversions, aggressions, and transgressions is negated by the "cul-de-sac" of a normalizing, regulating, universal law that enables the "pacific coexistence of subjects" (30). The second reading, preferred by Žižek because it is more "refined," proceeds by a "negation of the negation" (31, 30). In this reading, "universal law itself is nothing but universalized crime": the majesty of the law constitutes an "absolute crime" that renders all individual transgressions "mere particular crimes" by comparison, and the law becomes an incident in the undisturbed reign of crime (33). In the terms of this second reading, "one can say [or at least Žižek does say] that law divides itself necessarily into an 'appeasing' law and a 'mad' law: the opposition between the law and its transgressions repeats itself inside (in Hegelese: is 'reflected into') the law itself" (30). Thus, the law finally coincides with its opposite, frustrating efforts to name it or to assign it predicates. Ultimately, Žižek concludes, "identity is the surplus which cannot be captured by predicates ... identity-with-itself is *nothing but* this impossibility of predicates" (36).

We seem to be confronting in Žižek a more theoretically rigorous

approach to the problem Conrad was wrestling with in his description of the sea, with its internal and external mirrors, its dissolving
distinctions, its "mad" and "appeasing" faces, its predicate-exceeding
instabilities. Certain of Žižek's terms appear, in fact, to have been
drawn directly from Conrad's sea. For example, Žižek connects the
"split" in the law to a split in the subject, between the "subject of the
enunciated" (S1) and the "subject of the enunciation" (S2), with
the former representing the law in its "neutral, pacifying and solemn
side," and the latter, an obscene or mischievous "excess" within the
subject that refuses to be reduced to the symbolic mandate (*TKN*
233). Precisely such a distinction governs Conrad's portraits of the
West and East winds, with the West Wind pictured as "a poet seated
upon a throne—magnificent, simple, barbarous, pensive, impulsive,
changeable, unfathomable—but when you understand him, always
the same"; and the East, as "a subtle and cruel adventurer without a
notion of honour or fair play," malicious, diabolical, ingenious (*MS*
82, 94). But there are other such distinctions in Conrad, many others.
To Conrad, life at sea, life governed by the law of nature, is insistently
organized around the S1-S2 distinction. The epigrammatic judgment
that ships are all right, it's the men in 'em, places ships in the position
of a law commanding universal respect in contrast to the inconstant
and flawed S2s who man them. By the same criterion that separates
the ship from the crew, the seamen who are all right can be distinguished from those who aren't. Also by the same criterion, some qualities of those who are all right are all right (being a wise master), and
others (autocratic rule) aren't. Further, some qualities of those who
are not all right are all right (recognition of individual rights), and
some aren't (whining, laziness, mutiny). If we turn back to the ship,
we can see parts that are all right because they are not reducible to
what men have made and parts that aren't because they are what men
have made. As a thinker, Conrad seems compulsively drawn to things
that resist clear thinking, things such as reflections, in which he discovers everywhere the opposition of the regularizing law and its
excessive, obscene Other. If anything, Conrad's nontheoretical distinctions between men, ship, sea, wind, are more "refined," more in-
ternally detailed, more fractal-like than Žižek's because they never
stop: "the law" and "criminality" can be posited in any external or

internal mirroring, and the mirrorings extend theoretically to infinity.

James Wait, whose very surname is split between command and a proper name, represents an importation of this dialectic into the domain of the human. Appearing on board ship as the tardiest, tallest, blackest, and most generally imposing member of the crew, a man in comparison with whom the others—who spontaneously stand "behind him in a body"—seem diminished specimens, Wait is almost immediately shown, through a famous midsentence reversal, to be constituted as an internal mirror: "He held his head up in the glare of the lamp—a head vigorously modeled into deep shadows and shining lights—a head powerful and [the break] misshapen, with a tormented and flattened fact—a face pathetic and brutal; the tragic, the mysterious, the repulsive mask of a nigger's soul" (10, 11). The effect on the crew of his shamming a sickness from which he actually dies, and insisting that he is well when he is clearly ill, is only superficially to throw them into doubt concerning the status of his health. Nor would it be fully adequate to the doubt he generates to say that he drives a wedge between S1 and S2, although he does that. What he does is to promulgate among the crew a comprehensive and global doubt about everything. As an ill man, and even as a black man, he commands the crew's solicitude; as a shamming man, he solicits their violent and vengeful contempt and, perhaps, their envy. He awakens in the crew both a whettened sense of justice and their own repressed excess, but his most truly subversive effect is to cleave and complicate the law itself. By caring for, rescuing, and defending him, the crew obey *a* law, but not *the* law. They are faithful to a law of solidarity and compassion, but unfaithful to a law prescribing honesty, obedience, and work. "Work," Conrad says, quoting Leonardo, "is the law" (*NLL* 194), but he fails to add what *The Nigger* makes plain—that work is not the only law, that other laws compete with it, and that obedience to one may entail dereliction with respect to others. The impossibility of abiding by all lawful laws at once constitutes the "unlawful" aspect of the law, a factor that makes even the most law-abiding seamen criminals to an undetermined extent. Wait, as Žižek might say, spreads a general doubt about what can and cannot be "captured by predicates." The crew cherish him as "our Jimmy" (a formulation

Žižek might translate as "our Thing," or "the object within the subject"), but they berate and abuse him as well. They claim him as one of themselves at their peril, since their survival depends upon their fidelity to work and captain; but they reject him at their peril, too, since rejection implies an "inhuman" and certainly un-English slavery to a univocal and absolute principle of authority.

The real difference between Conrad and Žižek, however, is not simply that the seaman writer triumphantly "outrefines" the postmodern philosopher, but rather that, even while proliferating refinements, Conrad refuses to accept the general principle of refinement at all. Despite the multitude of internal reflections discoverable by analysis, Conrad insists on the integrity of—the absence of internal reflection in—his terms. As we have already begun to see, the means by which he does so typically suggest a failure of rigor, lapses of memory. At the beginning of *The Nigger,* for example, the narrator notes that "The sea and the earth are unfaithful to their children"; but the book concludes with the pacific pronouncement, "Let the earth and the sea each have its own" (15, 107). Conrad seems constantly to have forgotten, to stake everything on a flat declaration that contradicts an equally unequivocal pronouncement made elsewhere in the same text, sometimes even in the same sentence. This gesture is, I would argue, not simply careless, or simple at all, but directly inspired and determined by the unchanging ephemerality of the "mirror of the sea," in which it appears as nothing less than a law of nature. Because he viewed the sea not as a theoretician but as a seaman writer, Conrad did not have to choose between the "naive" negation in which the sea opposed the ship, the men, the countries of the earth, and the more "refined" negation of the negation in which these oppositions were reflected into the sea itself. With edifying and picturesque anecdotes about concrete things, Conrad managed to maintain both views at once, adhering to each, at the moment of enunciation, with unquestioning conviction.

The volume Conrad was writing virtually at the same time as *The Mirror, The Secret Agent,* is his most thoroughly urban novel, and concerns the sea not at all. It does, however, concern the law, and the powerfully curious intimacy shared by its representatives and its enemies. "Like to like," the Professor reflects on the relation between criminals and the police. "The terrorist and the policeman both come from the same basket. Revolution, legality—counter moves in the same game; forms of idleness at bottom identical" (94). This is a species of recognition Conrad never permitted himself in *The Mirror*, perhaps because he held a greater respect for the majesty of the sea than he did for that of the civil law, but the Professor's comments represent a general insight into the nature of the law and legality that applies equally well to his actual treatment of the sea. In *The Secret Agent*, oxymoron and contradiction collapse into a homogeneous irony, and the truth of the sea is disclosed in the streets of the metropolitan center.

At sea, Conrad did not discover general truths in particular circumstances, nor did he fabricate abstract statements of contingent facts. He discovered, in certain specifics of life at sea, a way of understanding and representing certain specifics of his Polish experience. By the time he went to sea, Conrad was accustomed, as a Pole, to thinking implicitly in terms of mirroring whenever the question of Poland's being essentially an Eastern or a Western polity was raised, or whenever the conversation turned to Polish "self-betrayal." In Poland, where the imagined community of the nation was constituted either as its partitioning enemies or its (unsympathetic) allies, mirroring could only function as an element in the local ideology of defeat, disorder, humiliation, and pathos. Poland could only exist as a reflection, either of its oppressors or its betters. The sea mirrored Poland, particularly with respect to mirroring, but did so in an altogether more promising context. For Conrad, the sea emancipated reflection from its Polish matrix. He discovered at sea a form of reflection become universal even as it was anchored to specific traditions of freedom, duty, tradition, heroism—and literature. In Poland, the image-concept of mirroring provided an abstract form for Poland's historical and political destitution, its substantive unreality. At sea, the mirror gave concrete form to the sea's literal reality.

As a seaman writer, Conrad retained the realist's ambition to do justice to the visible world as well as the Pole's sense of a pervasive and underlying unreality. This was, to be sure, a difficult project, one that virtually compelled the periodic forgetting of positions formerly taken, arguments made with conviction and good faith—and even compelled the forgetting of his forgetting, so he could continue if not with a clean conscience at least with a conscience whose disquiet could not be precisely located. This, at least, is how one might read passages in Conrad's letters that give an account of his deepest convictions, such as the one addressed to Cunninghame Graham on 8 February 1899, which concludes that "Man is a vicious animal. His viciousness must be organised. Crime is a necessary condition of organised existence. Society is fundamentally criminal. . . . everyday worries make us forget the cruel truth. It's fortunate" (*CL*, 2:160–61 [translated from original French by editor]). Nine months later he wrote to Edward Garnett—in the midst of his period of greatest accomplishment, with *The Nigger, Heart of Darkness,* and "Youth" finished, and *Lord Jim* going well—describing his writerly anguish:

> I am writing—it is true—but this is only piling crime upon crime: every line is odious like a bad action. I mean odious to me—though my morality is gone to the dogs. I am like a man who has lost his gods. My efforts seem unrelated to anything in heaven and everything under heaven is impalpable to the touch like shapes of mist. . . . All is illusion—the words written, the mind at which they are aimed, the truth they are intended to express, the hands that will hold the paper, the eyes that will glance at the lines. Every image floats vaguely in a sea of doubt—and the doubt itself is lost in an unexpected universe of incertitudes. (*CL*, 2:198)

Conrad seems to be struggling here with the growing recognition that his particular provenance as a writer is the faithful rendering of unreality. The traditional vocabulary in which he phrases this struggle— "gods," "heaven," "illusion"—cannot do justice to his task, which can perhaps be more accurately described oxymoronically as giving a countenance to negativity, or as converting the impossibility of presentation into the presentation of impossibility. The one formulation in Conrad's letter that is truly adequate to the task is the last sentence, where images, including the hallucinatory image of the anonymous reader, are said to float vaguely in a sea of doubt. Here the sea is momentarily recognized as the proper metaphor or medium of doubt before being diffused ambiguously throughout a universe not of doubt, which is, after all, a stable cognitive position, but of "unexpected" incertitudes, in the midst of which one cannot even know whether or not one doubts. The sea, to anticipate the next chapter, stands at the margin between the unreality of Poland and the reality of "images"—the gateway, for Conrad, to literature, and the gateway, for literature, to modernism. "Initiated" during a rescue *from* the sea, Conrad himself was rescued *by* the sea.

RESCUE

> ... my mysterious vocation was so strong that my very wild oats
> had to be sown at sea.
>
> —Conrad, *A Personal Record*

Conrad spent much of his life in need of rescue. At one time or another, most of his friends and relatives were called upon to save him in various ways. At a crucial point in his writing career, in March 1896, just as he was deciding to give up the sea, Conrad began his third book, to which he gave the awkward but personally resonant title of "The Rescuer. A Tale of Narrow Waters." He planned to spend a year writing it, but soon found himself suffering through the first of the bouts of writerly depression that would, like the gout that afflicted his writing hand, cripple him throughout his career. Writing to Garnett on 13 April 1896, he offered to "cut, slash, erase, destroy; spit, trample, jump, wipe my feet on that MS" if Garnett found any fault with it (*CL*, 1:273). Four months later, he resumed this line of discourse, saying that "The Rescuer" promised to be "a strange and repulsive hybrid, fit only to be stoned, jumped upon, defiled and then held up to ridicule as a proof of my ineptitude" (*CL*, 1:296). Between these two letters, Conrad began *The Nigger of the "Narcissus,"* in which the fate he envisioned for his manuscript is dispensed to "that consummate artist" Donkin, who is described in a protracted ecstasy of revulsion, looking "cuffed, kicked, rolled in the mud; he looked as if he had been scratched, spat upon, pelted with unmentionable filth" (61, 5). Conrad's creative confidence was clearly at a low ebb, particularly with respect to "The Rescuer." *The Nigger* was, in fact, the first of many such interruptions. Citing, in his "Author's Note," a "general difficulty in the handling of the subject," he began to break off work on the project regularly, turning to other, more manageable tasks—even entertaining the thought of another sea command through much of 1898—without ever abandoning it altogether (*R* 10). His rationale to himself was the thought, "That thing can wait" (*R* 11).

The thing waited while Conrad had his career. Among the projects undertaken specifically as a relief from the strain and frustration of this unwritable book were *The Nigger of the "Narcissus," Youth, Heart of Darkness, Lord Jim,* and *Nostromo.* All of Conrad's major works were written as it were within "The Rescuer," on which he toiled intermittently for parts of twenty-three out of his twenty-nine years of writing. More than two decades years after beginning it, and frankly describing himself as "played out," he returned decisively to the scene of the crime, finally publishing in 1920 *The Rescue: a Romance of the Shallows,* including an "Author's Note" that voiced the hope that "They Who had Waited" bore him no grudge (12).

What was this "general difficulty"? Why was the subject so obdurate that it could not be handled, and so compelling that it could not be abandoned? Why did he doubt his powers while working on "The Rescuer," and experience "a certain sort of mastery" only when doing something else (*R* 11)? What is the book *about?* His letters speak of a sense of wonder that the manuscript is getting itself written despite a kind of vacuum in the area of traditionally defined content. "I am writing the *R*[*escue*]! I am writing! I am harassed with anxieties but the thing comes out! Nothing decisive [he concedes] has happened yet" (*CL,* 1:429). In another mood, he reports that the text grossly "spreads itself, more and more shallow, over innumerable pages . . . *I know* there are no ideas. Only a few types and some obscure incidents upon a dismal coast" (*CL,* 2:31). These are accurate assessments. The narrative begins, or rather fails to begin, with Tom Lingard's brig stranded in calm waters. At the same time, a British yacht has run aground in shallow waters miles away. Some on the yacht have set out for help, and have discovered Lingard's brig. Lingard is disinclined to respond to their appeal because the request comes at a critical moment in a struggle between rival native groups for the local "kingdom," a struggle in which Lingard has been participating on behalf of the deposed rajah, Hassim. Still, he agrees to go to the aid of the yacht. Part 2 details the background to Lingard's involvement in Wajo politics. In part 3, Lingard boards the yacht and offers his assistance, but the owner, suspecting him of profiteering, rejects the offer. Hassim arrives in a boat with his sister Immada. Everybody contemplates each other. Mrs. Travers shows herself to be more sympathetic than her husband to Lingard. She and Lingard converse at length. Mr. Travers and another European go ashore and are taken into custody by natives. Mrs. Travers is upset. Lingard is disconcerted. We are about at page 200, and, indeed, there are no ideas and nothing decisive has happened.

No précis and no quotations can adequately convey the almost perversely "incompetent" effect of such pointlessly prolonged paralysis. Ultramodernist in that it goes a long way towards realizing the Flaubertian dream of a novel "about nothing," the text also seems afflicted by a premodernist, and even preliterary helplessness: "Alas no one can help me," Conrad writes Garnett; "In the matter of R. I have lost all sense of form and I can't see *images*" (*CL*, 2:66). The entire project simultaneously flourishes and flounders. He writes to Arthur Quiller-Couch: "I am now struggling with a book—a mass of verbiage with some dim idea so well lost in it that I, even I have a long time ago lost sight of it. . . . I write, I write and the wretched thing doesn't move an inch" (*CL*, 2:78). To another friend, he complains about "the wretched novel which seems to have no end and whose beginning I declare I've forgotten" (*CL*, 2:162). Like the stalled brig, the stranded yacht, the unresolved encounters, the suspended Wajo counter-revolution—like all of these, the novel, the career, and the author himself are going nowhere. Everything is in urgent need of rescue.

The letters testify to a multifaceted sense of *loss:* he has lost a sense of form, he has lost images, he has lost the guiding idea, he has forgotten the beginning. And yet the writing continues. Perhaps we could speculate that what Conrad has misplaced is an awareness of the positive relation between loss or forgetting and work, his work. This misplacement becomes especially striking in light of the fact that this last letter, in which he says he is writing his novel despite having forgotten the beginning, was written on the very same day—8 February 1899—as the one quoted earlier in which he expressed a qualified gratitude for the fact that "everyday worries make us forget the cruel truth" of the fundamental criminality of society so that we can live and work. Somewhere between these two letters, Conrad seems to have forgotten forgetting, to have mislaid the recognition that work proceeds only after an erasure of the truth, or perhaps that work itself is such an erasure, such a forgetting.

A forgetting of what? What was it that simply had to be recognized, and then, by an equally powerful imperative, had to be forgotten? Is "the criminality of organized society" the final or most adequate formulation, or is Conrad gesturing here towards some more comprehensive statement that resists formalization? If so, the resistance may be centered not just in the illogicality of specific oxymorons referring to society and crime, but in a more general indistinguishability or indifference between the terms of common oppositions, an indifference that would, if brought into sharp focus, paralyze language and orderly thought. What is in question here is not so much a settled philosophical conviction, a "cynical" attitude that might make someone too depressed to function, as it is a subphilosophical and even subarticulate intuition about the relation of intelligible discourse to the "world" that discourse maps. Conrad seems to sense that his work constitutes a respectful but determined approach to a general or "universal" phenomenon of which individual oxymorons are a trace or symptom, a *denegation* in the Freudian sense of a recognition and a denial. He grasps, that is, that his work *solicits* an intuition of the identity of unlike things such as "society" and "crime" that could be fully embraced only at the cost of his capacity to work or produce at all.

Conrad's work constitutes a continual calculation of distance from this—what to call it?—source, origin, navel, prime meridian, mine, mint, destructive element, explosive device, Inner Station. His work can in fact be ranked according to the distance it maintains from this thing, this place, with his greatest work approaching some optimal point so that it is stimulated into articulate anxiety—not so near as to be strangled but not so far away that discourse becomes garrulous and untroubled. What makes *The Rescue* fascinating in terms of Conrad's career is that the portion written early on, the manuscript of "The Rescuer" that extends well into part 4, is a signal instance of the former, while the end-of-career additions and modifications to the manuscript that resulted in the published text exemplify, like many of Conrad's other late works, the latter. *The Rescue* contains, then, both bad early Conrad and bad late Conrad. In the early going, Conrad found that he could write endlessly and with an immense sense of urgency, and yet fail almost spectacularly in the most basic narrative task of creating "characters" and moving the action along. In the more professionally competent conclusion to the novel, he constructed action—maneuverings take place, urgent messages are sent, people are killed in an explosion, things come to a head—but the action is as slack and uninteresting in its own way as the inaction of the first parts had been in its.

One of *The Rescue*'s primary sources of interest lies, then, in the modes of its failure, particularly its early failure, which inhibited but eventually yielded to his career as a master of the English language, a major figure in world literature, a pivotal artist in the transition to modernism. This career waited for Conrad to muddle through "The Rescuer," a project that then waited while Conrad discovered himself, first through the luminous figure of James Wait and then through Marlow, Kurtz, Lord Jim, Nostromo, and the others, all the while making the heroines—the Floras, Ritas, Freyas and Lenas that populate his last work—wait. (As an unbuttoned Marlow comments in *Chance* (1913), women "are not made for attack. Wait they must" [222].)

What was it in "The Rescuer" that both stimulated and forestalled Conrad's discovery of his project? It was, I argue, a misrecognition of the proximate cause of his writing—the sea. Conrad was under the impression that he was writing stories about life lived near the sea, on the sea, or across the sea, stories about adventurers, colonial hangers-on, or "that humanity so far away," as he put it in the "Author's Note" to *Almayer's Folly*. But just as he really entered into his career as a seaman when he passed his Master's examination (and was "adopted" by his examiner), so he truly entered into his career as a writer—*his* career—only when he began to engage directly not with the people he had known in the Malayan Archipelago, but with the sea. I do not mean only that Conrad found in life at sea an opportunity for speculative freedom and extension unknown to him in Poland, although that was certainly true—as is the proposition Tony

Tanner advances, that Conrad invented for British writing the "imaginative interaction with the awesome totality of the sea" ("I" xviii). Rather, I am arguing that the capacity Conrad discovered in the sea to mirror those things to which it was also opposed and to reflect into itself the entire relation, provided him with a powerful model of such general concepts as the essential likeness of unlike things, the permeability of distinctions, the migration of identity as things become attached to or affiliated with their Others, the confusion of vision. All of this had been experienced in Poland under the general title of (political, historical, and personal) defeat. But the sea provided him with experience and with a literary tradition centered on adventure, keensightedness, and heroic accomplishment, a literary tradition of clear images that is, as it were, made for illustration. Within this "innocent" tradition, Conrad could recast and redeem his blighted experience of darkness and confusion by way of a meditation on the sea itself, a surface so reflective and so vast that it cannot be reduced to images, cannot be properly seen.

So when he complains, with respect to "The Rescuer," that he has lost all sense of form and "can't see *images*," he is actually, unbeknownst to and even in spite of himself, approaching his own genius as a writer. In one of his letters, he complains about a feeling whose cultivation would prove to be his signal distinction. In the throes of his struggles with "The Rescuer," he writes to Garnett on 29 March 1898, that he "cannot even write letters," not even "the most commonplace note. I seem to have lost all *sense* of style and yet I am haunted, mercilessly haunted by the *necessity* of style. "And," he adds, "that story I can't write weaves itself into all I see, into all I speak, into all I think, into the lines of every book I try to read" (*CL*, 2:50). The shadow, the dubious double, of Conrad's unprecedented technical mastery, suprarealistic intensity, and extraordinary penetration, is the suspicion that he is simply incapable of *achieving* the commonplace, of writing—for example—an ordinary letter or of managing the basic techniques of narration. In fact, at this moment, Conrad is being guided away from a career as a writer of pseudotraditional literary exotica and more or less inept attempts at adventure tales, and towards a career as a writer of major importance in the global history of fiction. The sea is the subject and center of the story Conrad "can't write," the story that nevertheless suffuses itself into the story he did write about Tom Lingard, Mr. and Mrs. Travers, Carter, Hassim, Immada, Belarab, Jaffir, d'Alcacer, Tengga, Shaw, Daman, etc.

While Conrad's previous novels had been set near water, Lingard is the first Conradian hero truly to be a man of the sea. "He had grown on [the sea]," Lingard reflected; "he had lived with it; it had enticed him away from home; on it his thoughts had expanded and his hand had found work to do. It had suggested endeavour, it had made him owner and commander of the finest brig afloat" (*R* 112). The emphasis on what the sea had made of Lingard must be understood as a compulsive literalization rather than a figure of speech, for Lingard is, clumsily to be sure, identified with the sea in numerous ways, and refers to it as if to some essence of his troubled identity. "'Remember you are very far from home,'" he tells the yacht people, "'while I, here, I am where I belong. And I belong where I am. I am just Tom Lingard, no more, no less, wherever I happen to be, and—you may ask—' A sweep of his hand along the western horizon entrusted with perfect confidence the remainder of his speech to the dumb testimony of the sea" (107). This obsessive if unfocused concern on Lingard's part about what, exactly, he is constitutes a tic, a point of paradoxical consistency in his character. He is who he is because he is where he is, but he is who he is wherever he happens to be because, presumably, wherever he is, he is at sea, and on this point, he could—as the strangely tormented phrasing of the final clause suggests—entrust the wordless sea itself to speak for him.

The immediate source of the confusion in the image of Lingard is, however, the sea's gift, the brig. The extraordinary relation between "The Man and the Brig" (the title of part 1) dominates the opening of the novel. "He was proud of his brig," Conrad says in introducing Lingard, "and proud of what she represented.

> She represented a run of luck on the Victorian goldfields;
> his sagacious moderation; long days of planning, of loving care
> in building; the great joy of his youth, the incomparable free-
> dom of the seas; a perfect because a wandering home; his in-
> dependence, his love—and his anxiety. He had often heard
> men say that Tom Lingard cared for nothing on earth but
> for his brig—and in his thoughts he would smilingly correct

the statement by adding that he cared for nothing *living* but the brig.

> To him she was as full of life as the great world. He felt her live in every motion, in every roll, in every sway of her tapering masts. . . . To him she was always precious—like old love; always desirable—like a strange woman; always tender—like a mother; always faithful—like the favourite daughter of a man's heart. (20)

Always, whatever the case, female. The formulae of Lingard's affection have a nautical naiveté that reveals, with pre-Freudian candor, the displacements and deformations of his desire. "He was aware," Conrad says, *un*aware of the risibility of his hero's single-mindedness,

> that his little vessel could give him something not to be had from anybody or anything in the world; something specially his own. The dependence of that solid man of bone and muscle on that obedient thing of wood and iron, acquired from that feeling the mysterious dignity of love. She—the craft—had all the qualities of a living thing. . . . He—the man—was the inspirer of that thing that to him seemed the most perfect of its kind. His will was its will, his thought was its impulse, his breath was the breath of its existence. He felt all this confusedly, without ever shaping this feeling into the soundless formulas of thought. To him she was unique and dear, this brig of three hundred and fourteen tons register—a kingdom! (21)

He felt it very confusedly indeed, confusing himself—his will, his thought, his "breath," his youth, his history, his home, his luck, his accomplishments, Woman, Riches, Power—with his brig. But he is not *altogether* confused. "Lingard's love for his brig," the reader is assured,

> was a man's love . . . Every flutter of the sails flew down from aloft along that taut leeches, to enter his heart in a sense of acute delight; and the gentle murmur of water alongside . . . was to him more precious and inspiring than the soft whisper of tender words would have been to another man. It was in such moments that he lived intensely, in a flush of strong feeling that

made him long to press his little vessel to his breast. She was his perfect world full of trustful joy. (54–55)

Conrad (or Lingard) seems to have mastered the clichés of love, but to have misapprehended their customary object. Aiming at an expression of fullness, richness, and health, Conrad has instead produced a tableau of perversion, an aggregation of symptoms, a brig fetish. Nor is this fetish peculiar to Lingard. In his own voice, Conrad suavely praises the ship as a woman in *The Mirror,* assuring the reader that if a sailor, in his exasperation, ever "went so far as to touch his ship, it would be lightly, as a hand may, without sin, be laid in the way of kindness on a woman" (136).

What definite concept, what story that cannot be told, has woven itself into these passages in *The Rescue?* The issue often seems to be the relation between the ideal and immaterial being of a person and the material world. Lingard, we are told by a narrator struggling with the conventions of description, seems "as if made of wood and built into the ship's frame"; the brig is "his strength" (25, 189). While seeming to provide a concrete expression of Lingard's essence, such descriptions also leave him theoretically vulnerable if he should ever leave his brig. Lingard understands this perfectly. "When I am on board her," he says, "the brig and I are one"; but, "If I lost her I would have no standing room on the earth for my feet. You don't understand this. You can't," he tells Mrs. Travers, who does not pretend to (190, 191). Once, when he leaves the brig, "It seemed to him that he was saying good-bye to all the world, that he was taking a last leave of his own self" (196). Conrad is groping here for some way of articulating a dimension of identity that has no proper name because it has no proper place. What Lingard thinks of as "the brig" takes in a wide sweep from the innermost to the outermost. An internal principle of individuation, the brig also denotes a worldly *place* where Lingard can "stand," where he can be himself, at home. It translates Lingard, or the Lingard idea, into material terms as a fabricated thing, a product of will, craft, and intention. It expresses the particular sort of being he is, and determines the thrust of his being outward, its force, direction, and extension. Moreover, the brig inflects the objects of that self-extension, connecting them to himself *as* himself. Necessarily, the brig is sexualized, but it is not just a material girl, for its sexuality is only part of a more general principle of connectedness and relation, a principle of mirroring by which Lingard discovers tokens and confirmations of himself in the world, and of the world in himself. The brig is the first and primary such mirror, but as the narrative proceeds, others are disclosed. "The adventurer held fast to his adventure," the narrator says, "which made him in his own sight exactly what he was" (185). Conrad's imperfect command of the vernacular actually serves him here and elsewhere as he attempts not just to portray another "weak ego" such as Almayer or Peter Willems, but to pose the anxious question of what constitutes a human identity, what principle might ground a person in an "oceanic" world.

In the end, the brig does not seem to be the answer, for *The Rescue* documents not just Lingard's obsession with his brig, but also the failure of the brig to contain or channel all of his energies, or to provide a fully adequate home for his every desire. This failure is especially pronounced in the area of "man's love," where the narrative charts a progress from an untroubled solitude to a more problematic awakening to others. At the beginning, the "foreign" peculiarity of Conrad's phrasing suggests that the asceticism of life at sea is actually saturated by a loosely organized and diffuse sexuality that requires no object for its fulfillment. The mate Shaw appears on deck wearing a pith hat that gives him "the aspect of a phenomenal and animated mushroom," an all-but-phallic servant of his captain, who is, by strange coincidence, known throughout the region as "Red-Eyed Tom" (17, 20). Shaw's very virility suggests the redundancy of women: he stands with "his stout arms crossed on his breast—upon which they showed like two thick lumps of raw flesh" (17), and yet the incompleteness of a monosexual world is signaled immediately. The first words spoken are Shaw's, to a canary: "Dicky, poor Dick"; and the immobility of the brig suggests a certain "aim-inhibited" quality that is both unnatural and undesirable (18). Everything changes, however, with the news of the stranded yacht carrying, among others, Mrs. Travers, who interrupts the silent self-sufficiency of a sexuality whose burden to this point had been carried not by acts or even feelings, but by narration. Then Lingard meets Mrs. Travers, the wind picks up, and he begins to be anxious about what would happen if he left his brig.

Within the story that Conrad wrote about political maneuvers in the Malay Archipelago, then, is another story that couldn't get written but did produce a series of symptomatic formations. It is this secondary shadow-story that we must try to read, even at the risk of overemphasizing details at the expense of the most immediately legible features of the finished narrative. The unwritten story concerns a man whose desire befalls him, wrenching him from a perfect narcissistic security and sending him out into the wide world, the world of Wajo and women. However, as the flashback that constitutes part 2 reveals, and as Lingard's agitated exchanges with Mrs. Travers confirm, the real problem, and the one that betrays the true lineaments of Conrad's difficulties, is subtler: it is that Lingard's desire had already befallen him, his self-sufficiency had already been compromised, long before Mrs. Travers and the prospect of adult heterosexuality had appeared on the horizon. Part 2 details Lingard's commitment to the deposed rajah, Hassim, who had saved Lingard's life and now depends on Lingard's help to win the tiny "kingdom" that is rightfully his. Eminently coherent within the literary conventions of the adventure story, Lingard's heroic reciprocity becomes strictly unaccountable as he tells the story to a bewildered Mrs. Travers. He simply cannot clarify his relation to Hassim to her husband, he tells her, because "'There are things I could not tell him. I couldn't explain—I couldn't—not to him—to no man—to no man in the world. . . . Not to myself,' he ended as if in a dream" (133). Why, Mrs. Travers wonders, would Lingard risk his life backing a fugitive chief with eight followers? When Lingard suggests, "A kingdom," she asks pointedly, "Not for yourself?" (138). He responds by telling his tale, in which, to her, "The heroic quality of the feelings concealed what was disproportionate and absurd in that gratitude, in that friendship, in that inexplicable devotion" (138). And then Mrs. Travers is granted a glimpse of what was to become the germ of Conrad's career, the obsession with identity, the restless search for an object adequate to an intense but inchoate feeling, the oxymoronic asymmetry between a diminished worldly status and an exalted emotional state:

> It struck her that there was a great passion in all this, the
> beauty of an implanted faculty of affection that had found itself,
> its immediate need of an object and the way of expansion; a
> tenderness expressed violently; a tenderness that could only
> be satisfied by backing human beings against their own
> destiny. . . .
>
> What of it that the narrator was only a roving seaman; the
> kingdom of the jungle, the men of the forest, the lives obscure!
> That simple soul was possessed by the greatness of the idea;
> there was nothing sordid in its flaming impulses. (139)

The key to Lingard, and to Conrad's conception of character at this
time, is precisely this unwilled "possession" by some redeeming
"idea" that structures one's identity in default of some internal principle of structuration. "Appropriation" would be an inappropriate
term for this possession in the absence of any indication within the
text that Lingard has ever been truly autonomous or self-determined,
or that the idea or whatever it is that does the structuring intends or
wills its action at all. If Lingard is not his own man, he has not been
overwhelmed by some other, superior consciousness. He simply finds
himself "outside" himself, first in his brig, then in the bond with Hassim, then in Mrs. Travers. Meeting her does not introduce complexity
into Lingard's world, but merely aggravates a crisis of self-possession
that had begun long before.

In the subtheoretical system Conrad is developing, the man-brig
bond is primary, followed by the male-male bond, and then the male-
female bond, which is thematized as an exciting but finally a doleful
necessity. This is not a progression from immaturity to maturity, for
as we have seen, the love of the brig was already a man's love. Nor,
clearly, does it represent a process of sublimation from the carnal to
the symbolic—just the opposite. Nor does Lingard fall out of the
ideal and into the "sordid." What the text actually figures is a series
of relationships that gradually impose on Lingard the knowledge of
his own heteronomy, the awareness that heteronomy is the only thing
he has that is his own. The man-brig relation idealizes and sublimates
this truth, since the brig, although cast as "his strength," can plausibly
be conceived as a possession, almost a work of art, and the instrument
of his will. Hassim, by contrast, is not a possession. With the relation

to Hassim, moreover, the element of profit is brought more sharply into focus. The brig is, of course, the means by which Lingard makes his way and his money, but the mercantile aspect of Lingard's activities is unstressed. The "kingdom" at stake in Hassim's struggles, while not "for" Lingard, still must be counted an advantage for him. With the bond to Hassim, then, Lingard's claim to self-mastery is subverted as the prospect of worldly gain is heightened. Lastly, the force that draws Lingard to Mrs. Travers not only compels him to act against his own judgment and interests, but is directly implicated in values and practices he explicitly disavows—desire, interest, secrecy, even the priority of racial solidarity over a pledge of honor.

Hassim has in common with Mrs. Travers a direct line to Lingard's most private thoughts. At one point a Malay tells Lingard that Hassim has "perfect knowledge of Tuan's [Lingard's] mind as we all know." Lingard becomes enraged: "A new power had come into the world, had possessed itself of human speech, had imparted to it a sinister irony of allusion. To be told that someone had 'a perfect knowledge of his mind' startled him and made him wince. It made him aware that now he did not know his mind himself—that it seemed impossible for him ever to regain that knowledge" (177). Having acknowledged Hassim's infiltration of his mind, he is in no position to dispute other claims, and when Mrs. Travers declares that "There is not, I verily believe, a single thought or act of [Lingard's] life that I don't know," he can only mutter, "It's true—it's true" (197). A complex, deep, and charismatic man, Lingard is obscure only to himself; he is completely transparent to acquaintances from other cultures and to people he has met just the day before. A man of action, his particular genius is, and has always been, to reflect. Long before the events of this narrative, when he was on his brig, innocently cultivating his man's love, Lingard was "off his brig," decentered. The events represented in this text do not produce or change this fact; they simply disclose it.

Mirroring is a universal principle in *The Rescue,* one that acts not just as a steady undertow against the tide of Lingard's desire, but also as a factor of complication within the various figures to whom he becomes attached. Hassim, for example, is reflected not only by his ally Lingard, but by his ever-present sister Immada, who dresses "practically in man's clothes" and characteristically stands with her brother "side by side, and with twined arms" (63, 81). Observing Immada closely for the first time, Mrs. Travers is stunned into proclaiming, "Why, it's a girl!" (120). She might have added, "just like me," for Mrs. Travers herself replays Immada's sexual overdetermination in modern dress, boasting of her strength and courage and explicitly disowning a conventional feminine passivity. In other words, while Immada mirrors her brother as part of a single identity, Mrs. Travers reflects sexual difference into herself. They meet as two women standing at the poles of the evolutionary time line, with Mrs. Travers "assert[ing] herself before the girl of olive face and raven locks with the maturity of perfection, with the superiority of the flower over the leaf, of the phrase that contains a thought over the cry that can only express an emotion. Immense spaces and countless centuries stretched between them: and she looked at her as when one looks into one's own heart with absorbed curiosity, with still wonder, with an immense compassion" (121). In this early effort to unthink modernity, to imagine a continuum between "primitive" and "advanced" cultures, Conrad already senses that a psychic movement of identification can overcome temporal and cultural difference.

What rescues *The Rescue* from sentimentality is the keenly observed fact that identification also disarticulates those whose alienation it expresses, and devastates those who are its objects. The narrative concludes with an explosion that kills Hassim and Immada and, by destroying Lingard's stock of gunpowder and guns, renders him irrelevant to Wajo politics. The yacht people, including Mrs. Travers, sail away unharmed, leaving Lingard isolated on his brig. All those engaged in mirroring in any way are either desolate or dead, while the unreflective Europeans and the natives who had taken Hassim's kingdom are untouched. At this point, Conrad is capable of imagining a human character as a hall of mirrors, but incapable of imagining a structure or function of identification that will issue in anything other than disaster.

But the gloom settling over the conclusion only partially accounts for the dissatisfaction experienced by *The Rescue*'s few readers, most of whom surely begin to feel uneasy right from the start. The impression the book leaves of mysterious incompetence has, in the end, little to do with the fate of the characters. Nor does it reflect Conrad's literary inexperience, which may actually have permitted a certain kind of ungainly precision in the articulation of concepts and sensations alien to the Victorian novel. The persistent sense of a mistake doggedly pursued can, I believe, be traced to a single factor: Conrad has misconceived his subject. He thought he was writing a book about King Tom, Rajah Laut, a "disinterested adventurer," "a man of high mind and of pure heart [who laid] the foundation of a flourishing state on the ideas of pity and justice,"a man who was master of himself and of his brig (15). But his true subject was the sea. The man-brig, man-man, man-woman, woman-woman identifications so laboriously constructed throughout the book constitute lesions in the characters (and leaks in the brig), but they are, as Conrad eventually discovered in *The Mirror of the Sea,* proper to the sea. In *The Rescue,* Conrad has isolated what he would eventually announce as the law of the sea, the power to reflect things that are apparently opposed to it and to reflect the opposition into itself; but he has misconceived this law as a feature of human character, thereby normalizing it and limiting its force while making the affected characters incoherent. He was, in short, wise to abandon this project, to make it wait until his gift was depleted, the sea of his inspiration becalmed, and he could devote to it the attenuated energies it deserved.

IDENTIFICATION AT THE MOUTH OF THE RIVER

The first text undertaken as a rescue from "The Rescuer," *The Nigger of the "Narcissus,"* constitutes a dramatic advance. In it, James Wait serves not just as a charismatic hero but as a universal mirror in whom everyone sees himself. Singleton sees the man who will die; Donkin, the man who shams; Belfast, the potential convert; Allistoun, the test of authority. "The Rescuer" took place at sea, but was not about the sea. *The Nigger,* by contrast, is a sea book, and Wait is a true seaman, a human instance or form of the sea ("The sea will have her own"), a figure whose incoherence seems to be raised to the level of a principle, and whose radical inconsistency blocks any understanding of him as a mere "character," a plausible or realistic representation of a person. Kurtz is just barely a character in this respect, Lord Jim and Nostromo are more so (hence their dullness relative to their predecessors), but in all these cases the unconventional element of their presentation derives from their capacity to reflect the probing, questioning, identificatory gaze of some ordinary Marlow or other. The advance of *The Nigger* lies in the recognition, which will be more fully articulated in *The Mirror of the Sea*, that this capacity to reflect indifferently whatever stands before it belongs to the sea, and while certain human beings can possess it, in doing so they appropriate a function that is not properly human, an attribute that makes them strange, if compelling. Mirroring, *The Nigger* suggests, takes one out of the human community, or at least out of the community of statistically ordinary, conventional adulthood.

In the riptide of this "advanced" emphasis on the sea comes a certain kind of regression. While *The Rescue* seemed to allegorize a process of sexual awakening as Lingard shifted his allegiances from his brig to Mrs. Travers (if only to return in defeat to his brig), *The Nigger* remains within a pre-mature, monosexual world, a world in which to be "one of us" was to be, first of all, male. Not content simply to have an all-male crew, Conrad insists on their minority as "everlasting children of the mysterious sea." Even the ancient Singleton is "a child of time, a lonely relic of a devoured and forgotten generation" who has grown prodigiously old without ever having reached maturity, "with his childlike impulses and his man's passions already dead within his tattooed breast" (15). This is the first of Conrad's books to advance by regression, and one of the very first instances of the "modernist" cultivation of the primordial or primitive that would subsequently assume the form of a fascination with African masks, Neolithic cave paintings, ethnology, mythology, "archaic" psychic formations, and antiquated verse forms. In *The Nigger*, Conrad points the way down and back, all the way to a psychosocial formation that had, as it were, not yet discovered sexuality, much less steam engines.

According to Tony Tanner, the monosexuality of sea fiction severely limits its subject-matter and emotional range. There are relationships—"The Secret Sharer" in particular is "one of the most extraordinary relationships between men at sea ever imagined and analysed"—but "there is, as it were, no occasion for desire." "No women, no desire," Tanner writes; "this lack puts a constraint on sea narrative" (xiv). Such a judgment coordinates with Conrad's reputed inability to handle the subject of sex, but what Tanner misses is the particular way in which sexuality is routed among men at sea, and in Conrad's stories of men at sea in particular. Conrad exulted in the absence of women in one of his stories, declaring in a letter to Garnett that "the Secret Sharer between you and me, is *it*. Eh? No damned tricks with girls there" (qtd. in Meyers, *JC* 264). In Conrad's best work, women are consistently associated with the kind of imaginative restriction that Tanner says afflicts all fiction that renounces women. Moreover, in Conrad, it is women who display the "moody, metaphysical brooding" that Tanner claims as the peculiar temptation of seaman writers bereft of relationships and thus of the natural material for stories. Conradian women dream, or brood, or scheme, but they do not imagine. They are, in general, literalists of a separate world constituted of wishes or illusions, which they treat as hard facts. Their routinized, predictable circle of preoccupations and fantasies may, from one point of view, improve upon the "sordid" world of actuality, but does not really impinge upon it. They are, in Marlow's often cited phrase, "out of it." The most fully realized expression of this incomplete state of realization is the shadowy Intended of Kurtz, who insists on hearing in Marlow's bitterly ambivalent remarks a glowing account of her enlightened fiancé, a great man and great moralist. The stolid, depressed Winnie Verloc of *The Secret Agent* is equally representative of Conradian womanhood in her troubled repetition of the suspicion that "Things don't bear too much looking into." What they share is a dogged insistence, however disturbed, on the truth of their own fictions. They simply close their eyes to the "visible universe" Conrad mentions at the beginning of the crucial preface to *The Nigger* (145). It is no use trying to make them see, much less experience, a "latent feeling of fellowship" or a "subtle but invincible conviction of solidarity" (145, 146). They do not engage in such fusions, even with each other. Out of it they are, and out of it they remain.

Conrad is not insensitive to or disrespectful of a biological imperative to propagate, but his enthusiasm for this imperative is decidedly restrained. As a young Marlow declares in "Youth," "A sailor has no business with a wife—I say" (121). A more mature, presumably less passionate Marlow partially recants in the 1913 novel *Chance*, where he gives a weary and moralistic endorsement of what seems to be heterosexuality:

> Pairing off is the fate of mankind. And if two beings thrown together, mutually attracted, resist the necessity, fail in understanding and voluntarily stop short of the—the embrace, in the noblest meaning of the word, then they are committing a sin against life, the call of which is simple. Perhaps sacred. And the punishment of it is an invasion of complexity, a tormenting, forcibly tortuous involution of feelings. (338)

It is difficult to avoid the conclusion that, for Conrad, the ideal society was achieved at sea, where men could live a life of duty and yet evade altogether the duty to "embrace." But does this mean that a sailor has no business with sex? Tanner would say that it does, but sexuality can discover, or be discovered in, alternate channels. As Lingard's eroticized relation with his brig demonstrates, a principle of sexual division can structure almost any relationship, almost any entity. When, for example, Conrad speaks about nautical terminology in *The Mirror of the Sea*, he praises, in effect, its masculinity—its "severe technicality," "resolute sound," "brevity and seamanlike ring" (14, 15). An anchor, for example, is not "cast," but "let go." Seaman's language is in fact very like an anchor, Conrad asserts, in that it is perfectly adopted for its purpose by long experience, and must be protected against certain forms of quasi-feminine "degradation" that threaten it. "To take a liberty with technical language," he writes, is to produce an "affectation," to violate "the clearness, precision, and beauty of perfected speech," by introducing false and frivolous—in a word, feminine—notions into the simple, rough, and honest world of the seaman (13).

As Conrad develops the example, however, the vulnerability of the seaman and his language becomes more rather than less pronounced:

> Look at the anchors hanging from the cat-heads of a big ship! How tiny they are in proportion to the great size of the hull! Were they made of gold they would look like trinkets, like ornamental toys, no bigger in proportion than a jewelled drop in a woman's ear. (*MS* 13)

The anchor is figuralized and feminized in the very passage that extols a disintoxicated clarity and definiteness. The anchor is, in fact, a strange but revealing choice as an analogue to the "masculinity" of language, for of all the ship's equipment, it is the most closely associated with the land. "The anchor and the land are indissolubly connected," he asserts; and "directly [the ship] is clear of the narrow seas, heading out into the world with nothing solid to speak of between her and the South Pole, the anchors are got in and the cables disappear from the deck"—until the ship reaches its destination, a landmass peopled with grasping and graspable women, and they are let go once again. The anchor is the representative, the secret agent, of the land on board ship. In this respect, it seems curious, almost a sign of negligence or even of a very covert effeminacy, that "from first to last the seaman's thoughts are very much concerned with his anchors" (15). The sailor's preoccupation with his anchors mirrors Conrad's apparently unwilled tendency to figurality, and both constitute specimens of complexity that are at least adjacent to the "tortuous involution of feelings" that, Conrad says, accompanies the rejection of heterosexual coitus. Both the children of the sea and their chronicler and advocate run a structural risk of inversion.

We can see in the anchor the hinge of a sexual difference that structures Conrad's thinking about life at sea not despite but because of the absence of women. In a monosexual and presumptively ascetic environment, Conrad's sexual imagination becomes extravagant, complex, and rich; he becomes capable of conceiving of satisfactions unthinkable with a woman in the vicinity. Thus, in the "Author's Note" to *The Mirror,* Conrad describes as a "love story" his life at sea:

> Subjugated but never unmanned I surrendered my being to that passion which various and great like life itself had also its periods of wonderful serenity which even a fickle mistress can give sometimes on her soothed breast, full of wiles, full of fury, and yet capable of an enchanting sweetness. And if anybody suggests that this must be the lyric illusion of an old, romantic heart, I can answer that for twenty years I had lived like a hermit with my passion! (xxxiv)

Conrad confined his romanticism to the sea, the figurative mistress that did not disturb his hermit's passionate solitude. In another passage in *The Mirror,* he describes his relations with his first mate: "The bond between us was the ship; and therein a ship, though she has female attributes and is loved very unreasonably, is different from a woman" (19)—different, and better, because while a woman provokes jealousy, a ship inspires bonding. In a third passage, Conrad envisions the construction of a ship "by men whose hands launch her upon the water, and that other men shall learn to know with an intimacy surpassing the intimacy of man with man, to love with a love nearly as great as that of man for woman, and often as blind in its infatuated disregard of defects" (58). Here again, the ship is not quite a woman, but the difference enables solidarity between givers and receivers, and saves some men, some of the time, from being completely blind.

Unable to handle sex when people are involved, Conrad is unable to avoid it when he boards a ship. The young commander of "The Shadow-Line" recalls the almost unbearably intense sensation of "putting my foot on her deck for the first time," and receiving "the feeling of deep physical satisfaction," a thrillingly tactile confirmation of his intuition of "how much of a seaman I was, in heart, in mind, and, as it were, physically—a man exclusively of sea and ships; the sea the only world that counted, and the ships the test of manliness, of temperament, of courage and fidelity—and of love" (50, 40). Such experiences are not always legible as displacements or translations of the "simple" (heterosexual) "embrace." Immediately after boarding his ship, the young captain comes upon "two seamen, busy cleaning the steering gear, with the reflected ripples of light running playfully up their bent backs . . . unaware of me and of the almost affectionate glance I threw at them in passing towards the companion-way of the cabin" (50–51). Conrad records his own first contact with an English ship with a hedonist's appreciation of nuance: "my companion in the dinghy was urging me to 'shove off—push hard'; and when I bore against the smooth flank of the first English ship I ever touched in my life, I felt it already throbbing under my open palm" (*PR* 137).

Tanner insists that "there is, affectively, effectually, no sexual desire" in sea stories, and especially that "no trace of homosexuality seems ever to be found in this genre" (xiii). But this is true, if it is, only in a limited, literal sense, for the monosexuality of sea life infuses into the most banal incidents and phrases the possibility of a coded homosexual message, especially to readers alert to such signals. Whaling stories, with their harpoons, sperm whales, and "Thar he blows!" seem especially ripe for such interpretations. An 1839 precursor to Melville, J. N. Reynolds's altogether naive "Mocha Dick," describes the pursuit of a whale by two small boats in a way that permits a homosexual encounter to flicker in and out of focus:

> "Now, my fine fellows," I exclaimed, in triumph, "now we'll show them our stern—only spring! Stand ready, harpooner, but don't dart, till I give the word."
> "Carry me on, and his name's *Dennis!*" cried the boat-steerer, in a confident tone. (55)

Moby-Dick itself begins with Ishmael sharing a bed with Queequeg, and Conrad's beloved Marryat includes in *Mr. Midshipman Easy* an account of an extended joke in which a "diplomat" finds himself on board ship wearing a woman's petticoats.

Conrad almost eschews disguise altogether in describing the liberation of nonstandard sexuality at sea. He begins his breakthrough text with a scene in which the newly recruited crew gathers on the deck of the *Narcissus,* socializing before the first roll is called, the night before they sail.

> A little fellow, called Craik and nicknamed Belfast, abused the ship violently, romancing on principle, just to give the new hands something to think over. Archie, sitting aslant on his sea-chest, kept his knees out of the way, and pushed the needle steadily through a white patch in a pair of blue trousers. Men in black jackets and stand-up collars, mixed with men bare-footed, bare-armed, with coloured shirts open on hairy chests, pushed against one another in the middle of the forecastle. The group swayed, reeled, turning upon itself with the motion of a scrimmage, in a haze of tobacco smoke. . . . Two young giants with smooth, baby faces—two Scandinavians—helped each other to spread their bedding, silent and smiling placidly at the tempest of good-humoured and meaningless curses. (2)

These Norwegians are an intriguing couple; a couple of pages later, they are seen sitting "on a chest side by side, alike and placid, resembling a pair of love-birds on a perch" (4). Indeed, the entire ship couples up. The boatswain and the carpenter "sat together with crossed arms; two men friendly, powerful, and deep-chested … Couples tramped backwards and forwards. … Fellows with shirts open wide on sunburnt breasts," and so on (19).

We are given only the sketchiest accounts of the subjects of conversation during these shipboard rambles. One subject is "impossible stories about admirals"—but what would such stories be about? Bravery? Daring? Wisdom? Would these qualify as "impossible"; or would an "impossible" story have to concern some lapse, some breach in the dignity of the admiralty? But what kind of breach? Another subject of conversation is "the characteristics of a gentleman" (19). On this subject, "Dirty" Knowles presents himself as an authority, because he "had seen some of their pants"—thin at the backsides, from sitting in offices. This engages the full attention of "the strolling couples," and of "a man, bending over a wash-tub … with the soap-suds flecking his wet arms." Then, "at some opinion of dirty Knowles, delivered with an air of supernatural cunning, a ripple of laughter ran along, rose like a wave, burst with a startling roar. They stamped with both feet; they turned their shouting faces to the sky; many, spluttering, slapped their thighs; while one or two, bent double, gasped, hugging themselves with both arms like men in pain. The carpenter and the boatswain, without changing their attitude, shook with laughter where they sat" (20). This passage, manifestly intended as a portrayal of the dreamtime of the sea, the innocent fellowship of the deck, also solicits an altogether different interpretation, of life at sea as a floating bathhouse where ribald stories of closeted admirals and gentlemen with secrets circulate freely.

Later in life, Conrad commented on the satisfaction he had derived from showing English sailors that a gentleman from the Ukraine—a man who, according to one who sailed with him, "was always dressed like a dandy" at sea—could sail as well as they (qtd. in Karl, *JC* 256). But in his work, Conrad consistently associates gentlemen with homosexuality. "Gentleman" Jones of *Victory* is plainly, even caricaturally, homosexual—he despises women, keeps a paid lover, wears makeup, and troubles Heyst with insinuations about their common "tastes" (*V* 312). In his "Author's Note" to *Victory*, Conrad almost concedes that he shares or at least understands those tastes, commenting, not quite cryptically enough for disguise, that he will "say nothing as to the origins of [Jones's] mentality because I don't intend to make any damaging admissions." "Gentleman" Brown arrives at the end of *Lord Jim* to assert a similar connection of "'common experience'" to Jim, making a "'sickening suggestion of common guilt, of secret knowledge that was like a bond of their minds and of their hearts'" (*LJ* 235). Marlow, whose report of the encounter this is, would understand such an appeal intuitively, for his relation to Jim had begun in a feeling of undefined arousal. Jim was, he had told his listeners, "a youngster of the sort you like to see about you," the sort "whose appearance claims the fellowship of these illusions you had thought gone out, extinct, cold, and which, as if rekindled at the approach of another flame, give a flutter deep, deep down somewhere, give a flutter of light . . . of heat!" This passage introduces a Marlovian reflection on the illusions that attend the "glorious indefiniteness" of a life at sea, and from there to a meditation on commonality (78):

> Hadn't we all commenced with the same desire, ended with the same knowledge, carried the memory of the same cherished glamour through the sordid days of imprecation? What wonder that when some heavy prod gets home the feeling is found to be close; that besides the fellowship of the craft there is felt the strength of a wider feeling—the feeling that binds a man to a child. (79)

Beginning with the "sameness" of the romantic illusions fostered by the sea, Marlow moves, in the space of two rapid and complex sentences, through the sordid, ending in the pederastic.

What might seem an unnecessarily sordid reading of the final few phrases is made somewhat less speculative by the phrasing of a letter to John Galsworthy from March 1899, at the same time Conrad was working on *Lord Jim*, in which Conrad praises Henry James's most explicitly "homosexual" story concerning the feeling that binds a man to a child, "The Pupil." Here, Conrad says, is "where the underlying feeling of the man [James]—his really wide sympathy—is seen nearer the surface" (*CL*, 2:134). His praise of Proust for "enlarging, as it were, the general experience of mankind by bringing to it something that has not been recorded before" is also structured by the notion of a wideness achieved by bringing something hitherto suppressed to the surface, where it can enlarge itself ("PC" 105). Conrad is, as we have already seen, powerfully attracted by widenesses—by Kurtz's infinite appetites, by the sea generally, and, as Said contends, by the "chasm between words saying and words meaning," a gap which "was widened, not lessened, by a talent for words written" (*WTC* 90). The wideness of wideness includes, I am claiming, the implications of Marlow's comments on Jim and Conrad's on Proust—the man-child relation as conducted by a gentleman. For Conrad goes on to praise James as "the most civilised of modern writers"; and in *Lord Jim*, he makes a point of insisting on the mutual gentility of Marlow and Jim. "Don't you believe me?" Jim cries after he finishes explaining to Marlow why he had leaped. "I swear! . . . Of course I wouldn't have talked to you about all this if you had not been a gentleman. I ought to have known . . . I am—I am—a gentleman, too" (80). On the level of plot, *Lord Jim* begins with a situation of moral ambivalence climaxed by Jim's leap from a ship that did not, after all, sink. On a deeper level, on which the relation between Jim and Marlow is the true subject, it is the moral ambivalence of a disavowed homosexual attraction that drives the narrative on. The true germ of *Lord Jim* may, in fact, have been such a deeply personal disavowal, for which Conrad labored to construct an objective correlative by reworking official and journalistic accounts of an officer's culpable leap from the *Jeddah* (see *LJ* 309–44).

It is crucial that this wideness remain close to, but not precisely at the surface. When it does surface, when the gentlemen arrive from the sea to claim you as one of them (as though the sea were the only place they could exist without persecution, the only place where one could be a gentleman without also being a scoundrel), death and destruction follow. Perhaps in order to forestall this possibility, Marlow sends Jim away from him, arranging for Jim to work for a friend of his. Though older than Marlow, this friend is equally appreciative of what he describes in a letter to Marlow as "Jim's perfections": "For one thing," the friend writes, "Jim kept his freshness in the climate. Had he been a girl—my friend wrote—one could have said he was blooming—blooming modestly" (113). Nor is he the only one to notice. The engineer on the *Patna* shows up in the new place and behaves "familiarly" to Jim: "he would wink at me in a respectful manner," Jim writes to Marlow, "as much as to say, 'We know what we know.' Infernally fawning and familiar—and that sort of thing . . . the fellow had the cheek to say, 'Well, Mr. James'—I was called Mr. James [Henry?] there as if I had been the son—here we are together once more. . . . Don't you be uneasy, sir,' the engineer had continued, 'I know a gentleman when I see one, and I know how a gentleman feels.'" Jim abruptly leaves his employer to be rid not just of this dark familiar, but also of the employer himself, departing after an incident in which "He began to chaff me in his kindly way . . . I believe he liked me. . . . I know he liked me. That's what made it so hard. Such a splendid man! That morning he slipped his hand under my arm. . . . He, too, was familiar with me" (115). Jim does not rest until he finds a refuge deep upriver, where he marries a native girl and serves the community honorably until the arrival of the terminal gentleman, the one who insists on bringing everything up to the surface, converting uneasiness into inescapable knowledge. "Explicitness," Conrad wrote near the end of his life, "is fatal to the glamour of all artistic work"— including the "work" of being a gentleman (qtd. in *HD* 232).

According to Eve Kosofsky Sedgwick, the question of how much explicitness is too much is always on the table. In *Between Men*, Sedgwick describes a range of homosocial relations of reciprocity, exchange, rivalry, and support that work, in general, to insure the dominance of men over women. Conrad virtually begins his literary career with a homosocial exchange. Years ago, the reader is told in one of the nested flashbacks that substitute for forward movement at the beginning of *Almayer's Folly*, Lingard had captured a Malay girl; and then, some years later—"Lingard, having been brought often in contact with Almayer in the course of business, took a sudden and, to the onlookers, a rather inexplicable fancy to the young man," and employed him as a clerk to "'do all my quill-driving for me.' . . . Months slipped by, and Lingard's friendship seemed to increase. Often pacing the deck with Almayer, when the faint night breeze, heavy with aromatic exhalations of the islands, shoved the brig gently along under the peaceful and sparkling sky, did the old seaman open his heart to his entranced listener" (*AF* 9). Clearly, Lingard and Almayer are sailing pretty close to the rocks here. As Sedgwick explains, a homosexual short-circuiting of desire would threaten the dominance that homosociality is intended to secure. By displacing women altogether, homosexual relations actually permit women to run free, weakening the entire system. Cultural homophobia registers this danger, and the exchange of women solves it. This at least is one way of accounting for Lingard's abrupt directive to an astonished Almayer to "marry his adopted daughter" (10). Conrad's other early books seem to search for the right formula for the homosocial transaction. Despite her forcefulness and autonomy, Mrs. Travers occupies the position of the exchangeable female in *The Rescue;* and, in an innovation, a feminized James Wait—"our Jimmy," "Jimmy darlint"—assumes this function in the homosocial community of *The Nigger.* Only in *Heart of Darkness* does Conrad construct a "perfect" Sedgwickian triangle between Kurtz, Marlow, and the Intended.

As the uncertain relations between Almayer and Lingard indicate, the homosocial system runs the constant risk of an excessive explicitness. Sedgwick attributes this risk to the fact that homosexual feelings and expressions are not clearly demarcated, but rather constitute "arbitrarily defined segments" of a larger homosocial continuum (*EC* 185). The point of distinction is impossible to determine in advance or in theory, and so the system, so massively effective in most of its operations, is afflicted with a pervasive "homosexual panic," an anxiety proper to ordinary male entitlement about whether a given gesture, feeling, thought, or desire crosses the line, the "shadow-line" that separates, and fails to separate, the one from the other. "True, he had made that last stride," Marlow says of Kurtz; "he had stepped over the edge, while I had been permitted to draw back my hesitating foot. And perhaps in this is the whole difference; perhaps all the wisdom, and all truth, and all sincerity, are just compressed into that inappreciable moment of time in which we step over the threshold of the invisible" (*HD* 69).

If affective relations are experienced as most dangerously transgressive deep upriver, the fellowship of the sea, with its wide feelings and trackless expanses, is almost entirely untroubled in this regard. If we were to imagine a Conradian psychotopography, we would place homosexual panic, the anxiety over where the line is drawn, at the *mouth of the river,* which would serve as an indistinct, often unlocatable, but decisive boundary between a valorized homosociality and a reprobated homosexuality. Conrad is fascinated by mouths of rivers, by the unmarked transition between river and sea. *Heart of Darkness* begins and ends on the Thames in the contemplation of its flowing out to the sea, to the ends of the earth, and into the heart of an immense darkness. Less well known is the fact that the status of Lingard, Conrad's first literary creation, derives from his privileged knowledge of a river mouth. "That was it! He had discovered a river!" and the river had supplied him with the raw materials—"gutta-percha and rattans, pearl shells and birds' nests, wax and gum-dammar"—that had provided him his fortune (*AF* 7, 8). Everything—about Lingard, about *Almayer's Folly,* and hence about Conrad—comes from the secret mouth of the river. Even when he wasn't writing about river mouths, Conrad compulsively reproduced figures of secrecy and enclosure, including not only "Almayer's Folly" (the structure designed to hold the gold that would supposedly arrive from the interior), Jimmy Wait's cabin, all ships, Kurtz's Inner Station, Central America, Central Africa, Central London, and Lord Jim's upriver sanctuary, but also and more revealingly, such hiding places as Razumov's closet in *Under Western Eyes* and the captain's cabin in "The Secret Sharer." This list of enclosures, interiorities, and centralities might even include such powerful sites of value as Nostromo's secret cache, and the Greenwich Observatory of *The Secret Agent.* Frederick Karl argues that Conrad's material "suggests a squirreling away of data, the construction of holes and burrows in his mind where he could secrete details, his imagination as a kind of castle keep or treasure trove," and suggests that "in his stress on secret routes and disguised openings he had sought out the very opposite of ocean and sea" (*JC* 248). I am claiming, by contrast, that Conrad's fascination with such inner fastnesses *mirrors* his fascination with the sea.

The river's mouth connects not only the open sea and the Inner Station, but the topographical setting of Conrad's work with its mode of presentation. As Edward Said argued in 1983, Conrad wrote fiction "great for its presentation, not only for what it was representing" (*WTC* 90). Typically, Said points out, Conrad presents an oral rather than a written narrative, an account that is contested by others. One consequence of this is that the question of "the presentation of narrative" assumes an extraordinary salience: technique virtually replaces traditionally defined content. By emphasizing the figure of the river's mouth, or, more generally, of the mouth, I am trying to preserve, but at the same time to reorient such aspects of content as setting and thematics, and to enable these to flow, as the river flows to the sea, into the domain of technique. Many of Conrad's references to the orality of his narratives confirm such complex interconnectedness. In the 1920 "Author's Note" to *A Set of Six* (1908), Conrad assures the reader (in a style Said characterizes as that of "Everyone's Favorite Old Novelist") of the authenticity of his work, pointing out that one of the stories in the collection was "based on a suggestion gathered on warm human lips. . . . I have put the story into the mouth of a young man" (*WTC* 109; ix). In the "Author's Note" to *Victory* he recalls the original of Heyst as a man with whom he "became very friendly for a time and I would not like to expose him to unpleasant [but unspecified] suspicions . . . he had charmed me. . . . I have fastened on to him many words heard on other men's lips and belonging to other men's less perfect, less pathetic moods." The lips of Marlow himself attract notice. The narrator of *Lord Jim* relates that "with the very first word uttered Marlow's body, extended at rest in the seat, would become very still, as though his spirit had winged its way back into the lapse of time and were speaking through his lips from the past" (21). To stress speech while ignoring the literality, and even the evocative figurality, of the mouth, as Said does, is to suppress a bodiliness that Conrad insists on, and thus to miss a crucial, if disorderly, component of his meaning as well as of his technique.

The most disconcerting mouth in Conrad is that of Kayerts of "An Outpost of Progress," a story of two men living alone in the wilderness. Having killed his partner, Kayerts hangs himself, and is discovered "putting out a swollen tongue at his Managing Director," who comes upon the body (110). The most memorable mouth in Conrad belongs to Kurtz. Before their meeting, Marlow declares that "of all his gifts the one that stood out preeminently, that carried with it a sense of real presence, was his ability to talk. . . . A voice. He was very little more than a voice" (*HD* 48). In fact, however, it is Marlow himself who is little more than a voice; Kurtz is emphatically a mouth. "I saw him open his mouth wide," Marlow reports; "—it gave him a weirdly voracious aspect as though he had wanted to swallow all the air, all the earth, all the men before him" (59). *Heart of Darkness* is not just an oral narrative but a narrative of orality in which Kurtz's omnivorousness ("My Intended, my station, my career, my ideas"), his "imperialist" drive to appropriate, is channeled through the mouth (67). More immediately, Kurtz's mouth, the organ of eloquence and voracity, serves as the eroto-imperial-linguistic site of affiliation with Marlow. Interestingly, this point was noted by one of Conrad's more earnest critics of the 1950s, Robert F. Haugh, who cast Marlow as "a brother to Kurtz, identified with him in the climax of the story, impelled by the powerful attraction of the man—or demon—to something in himself, to search him out in the darkness. He must follow his demon to the nether regions," Haugh continued, gesturing ambiguously upriver, "to the heart of darkness, take the talisman from his lips, and return to the city." This talisman is "too dark for the Intended. It is not too dark for Marlow, though, nor for others with totems powerful enough to withstand its evil energies." What this "talisman" might be or how it found its way into Kurtz's mouth, Haugh leaves to the imagination, assuring his readers that Kurtz "defines the mortal condition, and in his last moment of vision he sees all the scheme of the universe; and we share it in a moment of tragic exaltation" (*HD* 242).

Miming Kurtz's own "thrilling eloquence," such phrases void and avoid any other possible uses of the mouth, restricting its functions to the verbal-symbolic. They represent a persistent gesture in what might be called humanistic or orthodox Conrad criticism, a gesture of disavowal by which "darkness" is noticed but negated, transfigured into an aspect of traditional heroism on the one hand or narratological craft on the other. Ian Watt, for example, enjoyed for many years a reputation as one of the greatest of Conrad's critics, in part, perhaps, because the terms of his praise of Conrad coordinated so well with a traditional way of construing greatness itself. Watt's Conrad is a man of wide experience who discovered powerful new ways of communicating that experience through masterly innovations in literary form. Disdaining any reading of Conrad that begins or ends in "the unconscious," Watt never ventures further upriver than the Outer Station of Conrad's genius, where one can still wear immaculate white clothing and keep one's—and Conrad's—books in apple-pie order, like those of the accountant by whom Marlow is so dazzled. For Watt, Marlow is confronted with a challenge essentially the same as that which faces Bunyan's Christian: he "must determine whether wilderness and darkness have an invincible power over man's moral being" (*CNC* 232). Of course, the issue is decided in favor of affirmation. "Neither Conrad nor Marlow," Watt concludes, "stands for the position that darkness is irresistible; their attitude, rather, is to enjoin us to defend ourselves in full knowledge of the difficulties to which we have been blinded by the illusions of civilisation" (253).

Nowhere does Watt concede the possibility of a fugitive current of libidinal energy, much less desire, flowing between the two men. Indeed, so thoroughly banished is the transgressive body that it might well be thought to represent, for Watt, the "darkness" itself. But like Haugh, Watt stands uneasily at the river's mouth, policing a boundary that does not exist in any comfortingly visible or material form, by raising possibilities and then trying to contain them. This, at least, is how one might read his comment that Marlow's behavior towards Kurtz, including the "lie" to the Intended, "can reasonably be explained primarily as the result of commitments over which he had little control"—followed by his assurance that these commitments are *not* uncontrolled because they are driven by unconscious forces, but uncontrolled because he has pledged his word to the Russian "harlequin" to protect Kurtz's reputation (*CNC* 241). Watt's refusal to consider the unconscious, the libidinal, the bodily, the desiring aspects of Marlow's account and Conrad's art stands aloof from both the easy acceptances of the sea and the anguished sense of criminality and taboo upriver.

Watt's rigorously superficial interpretive style has gone out of style, but it is interesting to compare it to another style seeking to replace it. In *Rich and Strange: Gender, History, Modernism* (1991), Marianne DeKoven consistently cites Watt approvingly, even while apparently arguing along altogether different lines. For DeKoven,

Conrad is not about the testing and strengthening of "man's moral being," but the subversion of the patriarchy by the cultivation of the disruptive feminine. Instead of "wilderness and darkness," Africa is a Mother to the European imagination. The sea is enveloping and maternal, and the trip upriver is a "vaginal passage," a revisitation of the maternal womb. In general, she claims, Conrad's work supersedes premodernist, patriarchal narrative with the same perfunctory efficiency with which the pilgrims bury the body of Kurtz "in a muddy hole" (*HD* 69). Her opponents on this issue are not Watt, Haugh, or other patriarchs, but those feminist critics who claim that, by feminizing the dark continent as a passive object of exploration, Conrad perpetuates the old order. Between Watt, DeKoven, and her opponents, there would seem to be little common ground. In fact, there is a wide expanse, for they share the conviction that the issue is knowledge and self-improvement, and is centered in *what Marlow learns.* Watt claims that Marlow learns to defend himself against illusions; DeKoven insists that "Marlow learns that all European imperialism is a corruption of the masculine ideal" (125); others argue that Marlow learns other lessons; but throughout the field of Conrad criticism, Marlow—and the reader—learns something.

The history of his reception testifies that Conrad solicits the warmest appreciation from those careful readers who approach a literary text as a "descent to the underworld," a character-testing exercise in which one risks doubt and despair and emerges triumphantly with a hardened certainty and tempered values. Such critics count Conrad as one of them, and he is; in many of his programmatic statements, and in *Heart of Darkness* in particular, he endorses the values and virtues of simplicity, fidelity, hard work, and solidarity over their opposites: subtlety, cynicism, sloth, despair. But his genius also flows out of this wide and ancient river, out to the sea, and from there into other rivers, where the issue is not knowledge or virtue at all, but identity, and especially identification. In traditional Conrad criticism, the use of this term is consistent with that of Paul Ricoeur, who argues in *Oneself as Another* (1992) that identification, an "otherness assumed as one's own," can be compared to the way in which we might value, for example, a "cause." "An element of loyalty is thus incorporated into character," Ricoeur says, "making it turn toward fidelity, hence toward maintaining the self" (121). Ricoeur could have adduced in support of his account numerous moments in Conrad's work, in which identification often entails a strenuous loyalty to the Other. As psychoanalytic theorists since Freud have deployed the term, however, identification refers to something else, to primitive psychic gestures that might even precede desire, and a fortiori, fidelity, principles, causes. On this account, the identificatory incorporation of the Other into the self works not to solidify but to disaggregate or disarticulate the subject, making it structurally complex, inconsistent with itself. Evidence for such a process can be found in Conrad, too, in the way in which the identificatory impulse of Marlow, for example, is drawn to figures on the margin, figures who represent failures of repression, fortitude, or moral resolve. Identification seeks out such figures, we can speculate, because it is itself just such a failure, a lesion in the bounded character. A Conradian understanding of identification would preserve both senses of the term, and would grasp together as a single act or process the commitments to which we are bound on principle and those to which we find ourselves bound in ways anterior to, beneath, or even contrary to principles. Such an identification, the kind represented in *Heart of Darkness*, *Lord Jim*, or "The Secret Sharer," can best be understood as a conscious "seconding" or confirmation of a commitment that one had already entered into without knowing it. Having signed on to command a steamer, explore the wilderness, and do some civilizing "work," Marlow finds himself engaged in the same business as Kurtz, and as the Manager of the Central Station tells him, "The same people who sent him specially also recommended you" (*HD* 28). In *Lord Jim*, Marlow's interest in the moral ambivalence of Jim's decision to jump ship derives perhaps from the moral ambivalence of his own "wide" feelings. And in "The Secret Sharer," the young captain on his first command feels the untested fragility of his own authority before his convicted double arrives to embody it. Identification is experienced in all these works as a recognition of what one is, or had been all along, a fresh complexity in one's being that, from another point of view, adds nothing to what one had thought simple just a moment before.

A comprehensive approach to identification as both an unwilled and a willed mental act enables us not only to understand Conrad's narratives, but also to understand the interrelatedness of apparently dissimilar concepts in other domains. The "categorical imperative" can be seen as one philosophical attempt to imagine an "automatic" identificatory process or function that equates and binds a person to Others, "the unconscious" might be another, and "class consciousness" (at least in some of its formulations) a third. These very different terms all refer to ways in which the self is structured, individuated, or maintained at the cost of being implicated in or determined by others. They all indicate modes of identification that take place at the threshold of the invisible, the undefined mouth of the river, where identity is established and demarcated (self/Other, river/sea, erotic/symbolic, libidinal/cognitive) but where nothing is discrete or exempt from the currents of the other.

How far out, and how far in, does the river's mouth extend? In complex circumstances, it is very difficult to say: you may be in or out of the mouth without realizing it. In truth, is not the very source of the river just the innermost reach of the sea, or the expanse of the ocean just the widest point of the river? Can any form of identification rigorously exclude others when identification itself constitutes a compromise of the boundary? The male-male identification proper to the sea takes the forms of work, duty, and hierarchy; it is an "innocent" fellowship, which, as we have seen, is not *altogether* innocent. It includes the homoerotic, but codes it as a common violation of a weak prohibition. Upriver, identification takes on a darker coloration, which is still, perhaps, not *altogether* unenlightened by the "civilizing mission" of Europe. As Conrad wrote in a letter, "the criminality of inefficiency and pure selfishness when tackling the civilizing work in Africa is a justifiable idea"—as though inefficiency rather than the "work" itself constituted the crime, and as though criminality might be either a justifiable idea for a narrative, or just plain justifiable, given its "civilizing" end (*CL*, 2:139–40).

Heart of Darkness discourages any trust in the rigor of distinctions by depicting a finely graded sequence of attachments to Kurtz, from the undisturbed accountant at the Outer Station, who notes of Kurtz only that "He is a very remarkable person" who sends in vast quantities of ivory, all the way to the Russian "harlequin," the helpless slave of Kurtz and the "spirit of adventure" who greets Marlow at the Inner Station (22, 55). Even at the Inner Station, the sea is not forgotten. Impressed by the fact that Marlow is a "brother seaman," the Russian tells Marlow that Kurtz forced open, widened, or as he puts it, "enlarged my mind" with his discourse, and perhaps by other means (62, 63).

> They had come together unavoidably [Marlow reflects, still thinking of the sea], like two ships becalmed near each other, and lay rubbing sides at last. I suppose Kurtz wanted an audience because on a certain occasion, when encamped in the forest, they had talked all night, or more probably Kurtz had talked. "We talked of everything," he said quite transported at the recollection. "I forgot there was such a thing as sleep. The night did not seem to last an hour. Everything! Everything! . . . Of love too." "Ah, he talked to you of love!" I said much amused. "It isn't what you think," he cried almost passionately. "It was in general. He made me see things—things." (55)

His mind enlarged to the point of incoherence, the Russian's sentences sputter out inconclusively: "And he would say yes—and then he would remain—go off on another ivory hunt—disappear for weeks—forget himself amongst these people—forget himself—you know" (56). Still, his almost passionate protest of Marlow's almost articulate interpretation of what he had almost said indicates an awareness that his vague formulations do not exclude the possibility, "amusing" to the worldly seaman Marlow, of a homoerotic referent. Homosexuality, or rather a comprehensive proximity to, even penetration by, the other that might include intercourse—"it appears," Marlow writes about the Russian and Kurtz, "their intercourse had been very much broken by various causes"—represents an inadmissible and yet omnipresent potentiality in identification, the knowledge that is unknown because it is subject to immediate cancellation or repression, the ultimate affirmation of a self-destroying sameness, the purest and most dangerous "adventure" (*HD* 55).

As Judith Butler points out, the presumption that homosociality and homosexuality are mutually exclusive "serves a heterosexual matrix" ("IGI" 26). Conservative readers of Conrad's conservatism, readers who see in the Marlow-Kurtz relation an asexual reciprocity, trust in the brightness and clarity of the line between the two. Marlow, however, does not. Marlow understands how an awakened desire can inhabit even such innocent gestures as "forgetting" oneself or "forgetting" to sleep, how a particular need can insinuate itself into discourse of love "in general." Marlow understands, in short, how the Russian's identification with Kurtz could fail to screen out a homoerotic dimension. He understands the ultimate compatibility between feelings of affinity and active desire, a compatibility that makes identifications, as Butler says, "not simple to describe" ("IGI" 26).

To read *Heart of Darkness* as a narrative of identification rather than of knowledge is to reconfigure, or rather to *un*configure, the story's sex, to liberate potentialities and permit them to mingle with each other so that the Congo River, for example, with its reeking stench of corruption, could include among its symbolic possibilities the rectum as well as the vagina. Identification rectifies the classic narrative paradigm in which a male adventurer or quester pursues a feminized object of knowledge or value not by replacing it with another, but by enlarging it, by permitting it to mingle with its Other. In this uncertain atmosphere, the "mere shadow of love interest just in the last pages" that Conrad mentioned in a letter could fall between Marlow and the Intended, Kurtz and the Intended, or Marlow and Kurtz (*CL*, 2:145–46). As the subject of identification in *Heart of Darkness* as well as *Lord Jim*, Marlow introduces into the narratives he tells a lively if uncrystallized homoerotic attraction, the basis for which is hinted at in *Chance*, where an older and less vigilant Marlow speaks with some feeling of "the woman in my nature" (42). However revealing, this explicitness and self-consciousness contribute to the mediocrity, in all respects but the strictly technical, of that novel. In the Marlow of *Heart of Darkness* and *Lord Jim*, Conrad had inaugurated British literary modernism in part by exploring a masculine way of being that "included" the feminine, a more sophisticated because "unconscious" form of inclusiveness than that of the mannish Mrs. Travers, the Hassim-Immada quadruped of *The Rescue*, or the artificially feminized James Wait. Considered as a novelist of identification,

Conrad qualifies as the greatest explorer of male-male attraction in the English language, far more interesting, subtle, and even candid than the elusive Wilde. If Conrad's position in a homophobic canon, a canon organized around the quest for (conscious) knowledge, the pursuit of the (acceptable) object of desire—organized, in a word, around the "heterosexual matrix"—is not thereby jeopardized, this is because his emphasis on the river's mouth, while it suggests and entails both the open sea and the Inner Station, does not designate or insist on them, making them—for those who wish to avoid them—avoidable.

Sex at the Beginning of Time

Given that water is the site of an aboriginal homosociality, it might appear that Conrad believes that the male comes before the female, with all the privilege and stature that anteriority implies. At the beginning of time, Conrad might seem to be saying, there are men, men afloat. This aspect of Conrad's work perhaps accounts for the eagerness with which psychoanalytically inclined critics have always seized on his narratives. For in Freud, too, the male is treated as the norm and the female as a derivative; and in Lacan, the phallic function is made to account for both sexes, the difference between which is articulated with respect to this term. But, while, for Conrad, forms of homosociality including the homoerotic appear to be primary and primordial, and women are "out of it," living "in a world of their own," this appearance is overshadowed by something—a force, an element, a medium, a structuration—even more archaic, something bodied forth by the sea itself.

In the sea, we witness, Conrad says, a first formation of creation, a darkness so utter that it seems to have been "created before light itself," an original condition that is subsequently confirmed and varied in the psychosocial arrangements of human beings. We can, for example, perceive in the sea's depths the rudiments of sexual difference. "The sea, O Nina, is like a woman's heart," Dain tells Nina in *Almayer's Folly* (174). Sometimes Conrad is more explicit and less poetic. The sea, he says in *The Mirror*, is like a woman in that it is unstable and fickle: "Impenetrable and heartless, the sea has given nothing of itself to the suitors for its precarious favours." Nor can it be "subjugated"; hence, despite the "fascination that has lured so many to a violent death, its immensity has never been loved as the mountains, the plains, the desert itself, have been loved" (*MS* 136). If the sea is unworthy of a man's love, the reason may be that it is not a true woman at all, but merely possesses some traits—infidelity, fickleness, deadliness, remoteness—popularly associated with women. Indeed, the sea may well be more mannish than womanish, a "savage autocrat" who "cannot brook the slightest appearance of defiance" (*MS* 137). But it is just as unsatisfactory a man as it is a woman, for it has, Conrad says directly, "no display of manly qualities" (*MS* 137). This may be why Conrad sometimes reverts to the neutral *it:* the sea gives nothing of *itself* to the suitors for *its* favors; *it* cannot be subjugated, etc.

All the sea's sex markings are on display during that most archaic of events, the storm. And it is during the storm that human beings, too, revert to the original condition under the mighty influence of the sea. This, at least, seems to be the implication of Conrad's one story devoted primarily to the storm at sea, *Typhoon* (1902). This tale has been interestingly described recently by Francis Mulhern, who stresses not the mighty accomplishment of the stolid, literal-minded Captain MacWhirr in bringing the ship through the storm by refusing to alter his set course, but the various unravelings that occur during the storm itself.

> The ship has been transferred from the British to the Siamese flag; and the 'cargo' on this occasion is human—200 Chinese coolies. . . . Sailing under 'queer' colours, its crew outnumbered by their freight of alien bodies, the *Nan-Shan* heads into 'dirty' weather. The storm attacks every established social relationship of the vessel. Masculinity is abandoned for hysteria; linguistic order fails, as speech turns figural or obscene, is blocked by superstition or swept away by the gale. MacWhirr and his first mate, Jukes, reach for each other in encounters that mingle duty and desire, resolution and bewilderment; while in the hold the Chinese have apparently gone berserk. . . . and *Homo Britannicus* is abandoned to a chaos of effeminacy, homoeroticism, and

gibberish—the terrifying counter-order of the Chinese labour-
ers below. The ship survives. But the restoration of order is understood as a furtive improvisation, the hurried winding-up of
an incident better forgotten. (255–56)

The details of *Typhoon* are even more unexpectedly interesting than
this synopsis implies. In the first blast of the typhoon, Jukes dons his
coat, going, as the narrator puts it, "through all the movements of a
woman putting on her bonnet before a glass" (224). Then, battered
by a great volume of water, he finds himself "mixed up with a face,
an oilskin coat, somebody's boots. He clawed ferociously all these
things in turn, lost them, found them again, lost them once more,
and finally was himself caught in the firm clasp of a pair of stout
arms. He returned the embrace closely round a thick solid body. He
had found his captain" (229–30). Later, he catches hold of MacWhirr
by the waist, and the two stand "clasped thus in the blind night, bracing each other against the wind, cheek to cheek and lip to ear, in the
manner of two hulks lashed stem to stern together"—rubbing sides
at last, like Kurtz and the Russian (233). Later still, the boatswain
finds Jukes's legs "with the top of his head. Immediately he crouched
and began to explore Jukes' person upwards with prudent, apologetic
touches, as became an inferior" (236). During the storm, the crew
is hypermasculinized as it performs arduous duties heroically, and
hyperfeminized as it embraces and is embraced; and, as sexuality is
irrelevant and even inconceivable in such circumstances, it is neut-
ered as well.

During the storm, Mulhern implies, the British command structure on the deck is "abandoned to"—by which he apparently means
"is symbolically conflated with"—the "counter-order" represented by
the Chinese tumbling about in the darkness below the deck, scuffling
for loose coins in what Conrad's narrator describes as a "mound of
writhing bodies . . . an inextricable confusion of heads and shoulders,
naked soles kicking upwards, fists raised, tumbling backs, legs, pigtails, faces" (244). In this desperate condition, self-interest rules even
in the absence of identifiable selves. But the confusion of British limbs
and identities on the deck does not merely echo the anarchy down
below. Although a regression from the ordinary circumstances of

navigation, the situation on the deck is still more "advanced," more differentiated, than that below, and both are superior to the wordless violence of the sea itself, which represents an ultimate dedifferentiation, the first confused stirrings of life, an index of the primitive condition Conrad refers to as "creation." "I have come to suspect," he writes in *A Personal Record*, "that the aim of creation cannot be ethical at all. I would fondly believe that its object is purely spectacular. . . . The rest"—which would include Mulhern's "social relationships," "masculinity," and "the linguistic order"—"is our affair" (*PR* 92). Creation begins in the turbulence of the sea with an unsorted and agitated jumble of attributes informed by no purpose other than the "spectacular." The first *human* formation, the first modification of this original condition in human material, comes with the general melee, the roiling heap of human parts below the deck of the *Nan-Shan*. Within this frantic and homogeneous mass arise the rudiments of individual difference, expressed in the primitive form of scuttling after money. Mulhern also discerns here "effeminacy, homoeroticism, and gibberish," but really only the last applies. The other two make their first identifiable appearance above the deck, in the gropings and embraces among the crew. Sexual difference as such "begins" not only in the "white" race, but in hierarchy, in the clutch of superior and inferior males (although it may have been announced in the "pigtails" of the Chinese). Eventually, there are discrete women, such as MacWhirr's complacently obtuse wife, who receives his understated accounts of the storm in her secure inland home, fearful not that he won't return but that he will. In Conrad's fantasia of the origin, then, the male is not original. First comes the sea; then an undifferentiated ("yellow") humanity; then, not men exactly, but ("white") women-men and men-men; *then* men and women.

The storm at sea reminds us that the origin is ever present. In a different way, so does the act of identification, a de-differentiation stimulated by primitive surroundings, whether at sea or upriver. Both recall the nonethical aim of creation, and each fresh act of creation reintroduces this primordial anarchy into the world. "My task," Conrad says in his most famous critical utterance, is purely spectacular; it is, "before all, to make you *see!*" (*NN* 147). He might have said, and indeed almost did say, "to make you sea," for as creations, his texts return their readers to the original position, confronting them with a perpetual challenge to interpretive and ethical mastery.

"Ethical" readings of Conrad underestimate the spectacular force of the sea in his work. When, for example, Albert Guerard, one of Conrad's most canonical critics, argues that James Wait is the object of "irrational identification" by the men, and must be seen as "*something the ship and the men must be rid of before they can complete their voyage*," he reads into the text—that is, he claims that the text reflects—his own need for order and stability (109). Paradoxically, Guerard's reading is actually reflected—that is, repeated in inverted form—by the reading of those such as J. Hillis Miller who, in *Poets of Reality*, depicts Conrad as an unremitting nihilist. Both err by positioning Conrad on one side or the other of the threshold of the invisible. Conrad at his greatest has no determinate position, any more than the earth has hemispheres, the sea has boundary lines, or Marlow has a discrete identity.

Who is Marlow at the end of his travels? Where is the line drawn between him and Jim, him and Kurtz, him and anybody else? We would be thinking along Conradian lines if we conceived of identity on the model of the world's water, which is one, encompassing the earth, but has acquired names as though it were comprised of separate units, distinct "bodies of water." "Beneath" these fantasmatic yet necessary and effective designations, beneath the words and lines on maps, the water, a liquid entity, or rather, the liquidity of all entities, slides indifferently.

THREE
To Write in English

One is sensible of one's native word in a completely different way or, to be more precise, one is ordinarily not sensible of one's native word. . . . Native word is one's "kith and kin"; we feel about it as we feel about our habitual attire, or, even better, about the atmosphere in which we habitually live and breathe. It contains no mysteries; it can become a mystery only in the mouth of others, provided they are hierarchically alien to us—in the mouth of the chief, in the mouth of the priests.

—V. N. Vološinov, *Marxism and the Philosophy of Language*

ENGLISH AS A SEVENTH LANGUAGE

"It was then"—Conrad was to recall nearly thirty-five years after an event that happened in the port of Marseilles in 1875—"that, for the very first time in my life, I heard myself addressed in English—the speech of my secret choice, of my future, of long friendships, of the deepest affections, of hours of toil and hours of ease, and of solitary hours too, of books read, of thoughts pursued, of remembered emotions—of my very dreams!" The address itself was brief: "it consisted precisely of the three words 'Look out there,' growled out huskily above my head" (*PR* 136). The first words spoken to him in English, the first time he was addressed in the English language, coming from the first English ship he ever touched, the very ship soon to throb under his open palm—truly an inaugural moment.

By the time he wrote this passage in May 1909, he was almost finished with his life's work. Within nine months, he would finish "The Secret Sharer" and *Under Western Eyes,* his last significant texts (a class in which the overworked *Chance* and the underdramatized *Victory,* both attempts to recover lost inspiration from former times by returning to Marlow and the South Pacific respectively, do not belong). He was beginning to look at his career retrospectively, and to understand that prior to this greeting, or warning, he had just been waiting. He had spoken, but he had been waiting to speak; he had been at sea, but he had been waiting to become a seaman. He learned both language and seamanship simultaneously on British ships, beginning with the *Mavis* in 1878, and told the old captain who administered his British Master's examination that from the very first stirrings of his wish to go to sea, he had determined ("of course, in the Polish language") that, "if a seaman, then an English seaman" (*PR* 122). "Only an Englishman," he told an interviewer in 1917, "can be a real sailor" (Najder, *CUFE* 198). It was certainly true that more sailors were English than any other nationality, and true, too, that the vast majority of commercial transactions involving the sea were conducted in English (Bailey 109). It was also the case that the immense British merchant fleet, as well as a longstanding British tradition of hospitality towards political exiles (and support for the Polish uprisings), provided Conrad with a professional opportunity he was unlikely to get elsewhere. But what Conrad seems to be pointing to in such comments is some larger and more intimate affinity between the island nation and the sea. The intuition of such an affinity had been implanted in Conrad, it appears, in adolescence. In *A Personal Record,* Conrad recounts how, while traveling in Switzerland with his tutor, he encountered an Englishman notable for his exposed calves, which "dazzled the beholder by the splendour of their marble-like condition and their rich tone of young ivory"; and somehow, "all at once," an ongoing debate about whether the fifteen-year-old orphan should go to sea was resolved in his favor (40, 44). It is, I will begin by contending, this identification of England with the sea, established not just by the sight of ivory English calves, and not just by the merchant marine, but also by the Royal Navy and again by a celebratory literary tradition—it was all this that solicited or, to use the Althusserian terms, "hailed" or "interpellated" Conrad as a writer. In going to sea and learning English, Conrad was doing the same thing twice—being adopted, attempting to master the unmasterable, following (as he told Ford Madox Ford of the profession of writing) a "*métier de chien*" (Ford, *JC* 275). All these energies and factors converge in the utterance issuing, in 1875, from the warm lips of a British sailor speaking the English language directly to him: "Look out there."

At that moment, Conrad was fluent in Polish and in French, which he used in conversation and correspondence all his life. Moreover, he knew some Russian, and had studied Latin, German, and Greek (see Najder, *JC* 38). Some eminent writers (Wilde, Julian Green, Rilke, Beckett, Manuel Puig, Wole Soyinka) have written in two or more languages; a very few (Koestler, Nabokov, Brodsky) have written primarily in a language different from their mother tongue. The cosmopolitan Nabokov produced novels and translations in Russian, German, and French, besides English, moving through languages, as George Steiner has said, "like a traveling potentate" (7). Steiner's term for Nabokov and other writers who found themselves displaced by war and social upheaval is "extraterritorial." Conrad does not fit this description. Having settled in England, he never seriously thought of living anywhere else, or of writing in any other language. Considering himself a "Kentish man," he was more provincially "territorial" in this respect than Wilde, Joyce, Shaw, Yeats, or Ford Madox Ford, and this despite the overwhelming fact that in the history of world literature, Conrad is unique in having written exclusively in his seventh language.

Working as an ordinary seaman, Conrad's speech developed on a different schedule from that of his writing. It was not until 1885 that he began to write letters, very few and very awkward, in English ("old Father Time always diligent in his business has put his eraser over many men" [*CL*, 1:11]). And although he may have written a story, "The Black Mate," for a contest the following year for the best article by a seaman on "My Experiences as a Sailor," he did not begin *Almayer's Folly* until the fall of 1889, by which time he had been speaking English almost exclusively for over eleven years. One of the first peculiarities of Conrad's growing command of English, then, is the discrepancy between his speech, which rapidly became serviceable but remained a lifelong marker of foreignness, and his writing, which he wrenched from himself as an exquisite, self-inflicted torture, but which earned him a reputation as an undisputed master of the English language, someone to be compared, with respect to sheer stylistic command, to Henry James.

His speech was a separate freak. His best friends found him difficult to follow, and he knew it. A reading of the manuscript of *An Outcast of the Islands* to Edward Garnett in 1895 was a failure because his accent was so peculiar Garnett couldn't understand his words, much less appreciate their felicity. After meeting him, one visitor wrote home to her husband that "his voice is very clear and fine in tone, but there is an accent which I have never heard before. It is an accent which affects every word, and gives the most extraordinary rhythm to phrases. And his verbs are never right. If they are in the place they should be—which is seldom—they are without tense; a new facet for the miracle" (qtd. in Najder, *JC* 411–12). A character invariably described as "high-strung," "nervous," and "sensitive"— traits uncommon among the literary class in Britain—made his speech even more discomposing. Less than two years before his death, he hesitated to commit himself to an American tour because he feared displaying his accent before an audience gathered to hear a man by then famed as a great stylist. "I will disclose to you that this really is the sorrow of my life," he wrote to the man who had proposed the tour; "for if it were not for that shrinking I would love nothing better than to give readings from my works" (Karl, *JC* 878). No recording was ever made—a terrible oversight!—but we can imagine what he must have sounded like based on attempts by friends to render his accent, if not what Ford Madox Ford calls his "caressing, rather dragging voice," orthographically (*JC* 33). One of his biographers attempts a partial inventory of his idiosyncrasies:

> He found the English "th" sound troublesome and—like so many foreigners—would say "dis" and "dat." He transposed "v" and "w" so that "vowel" became "wowvel"; said "used a sword" as "úsit a súword." "Iodine" he pronounced "uredyne," which his young son once took to mean "you are dying." Hugh Clifford . . . heard him describe an editor as a "*Horréeble* Personalitee! *Horréeble* Personalitee!" He would also say: "I thought he was afr*aïd* (as in Port Saïd), so I ask*èd* him, but I was *ütt*erly [ooterly] wrong" and "It is uncomfortable. *On komm for tarble for them!*" . . .
>
> Acutely sensitive about his faulty accent, Conrad parodied his own way of speaking English in his fiction. He wrote of the half-caste captain of the ship that takes Lord Jim to Patusan: "His flowing English seemed to be derived from a dictionary compiled by a lunatic." In "Falk," the English pronunciation of the German merchant Mr. Siegers "was so extravagant that I

can't even attempt to reproduce it. For instance, he said 'Fferie strantch.'" (Meyers, *JC* 128–29)

In "The Doldrums" (1897), Conrad's friend John Galsworthy put Conrad's speech into the mouth of the first mate Armand: "'Dosé fallows, you know' (he pronounced it 'gnau'), said the mate in his slightly nasal, foreign accent, evidently resuming, 'it's very curious you know, day [Chinese] rraally haven't any feelings'" (188). Conrad pronounced the silent "w" in "wrong," said "moosic" for "music," Sal-*is*bury for Salisbury, and "desè auks" for "these oaks." Soon after shipping on the *Mavis,* he began to read English literature, including Shakespeare and Trollope, and he evidently formed mistaken sound impressions that were not corrected by exposure to the limited and specialized discourse of seafaring that constituted his daily experience of the language. When he began writing, he had never heard many of the words he was using. Besides, as he acknowledged, he had "unluckily no ear" (Jean-Aubry, 2:125).

He had an eye, however, and could gauge the visible effects produced by the Polish language on English ears. In "Amy Foster" (1901), he depicted the initial fascination and then revulsion felt by local townspeople for the émigré Pole, Yanko Goorall, whose speech seems to them "so disturbing, so passionate, and so bizarre" (187). A strong Polish accent must have seemed to his literary friends like an invasion of the English language by an alien force. In 1910, his agent, friend, and longtime creditor J. B. Pinker wounded Conrad with a comment that Conrad recalled in a letter: "As it can't have escaped your recollection that the last time we met you told me that I 'did not speak English' to you I have asked Robert Garnett to be my mouth-piece— at any rate till my speech improves sufficiently to be acceptable" (*CL*, 4:334).

In the early days, confusion began with his name, Korzeniowski, which baffled the most attentive English listeners. Once over this hurdle, he must have been asked to repeat himself constantly, and must have observed the annoyance or amusement of his listeners as they attempted to adapt what they thought they had heard to the conventions of English pronunciation. There were surely countless gaffes and malapropisms, his meaning changing as he spoke, constantly sliding beyond or beneath his control as it was submitted to the guesswork of his audience. A series of unpredictable lesions in his discourse created by unintended puns and homonyms must have set the received meaning of his utterances constantly at odds with his intentions. Eventually, however, Conrad discovered a way to make this crippling incoherence, this constant exposure and vulnerability, into a condition of creation. The major phase of his career begins, we must note, with a request for repetition following on an unintended pun.

> "Wait!" cried a deep, ringing voice.
>
> All stood still. Mr. Baker, who had turned away yawning, spun round open-mouthed. At last furious, he blurted out:—"What's this? Who said 'Wait'? What . . .".
>
> . . . After a moment he said calmly:—"My name is Wait— James Wait." (*NN* 10)

The most famous bit of dialogue he ever penned is a repetition: "The horror! ["Pardon?"] The horror!"

When he was at his ease, his accent could even be a component of his general fascination. He could be an astonishing verbal presence. Counseled by Henry James in 1913 not to visit Conrad ("But, dear lady . . . but dear lady . . . He has lived his life at sea—dear lady, he has never met 'civilized' women" . . .), Lady Ottoline Morrell risked it, and found herself confronting a man and a manner

> so nervous and sympathetic that every fibre of him seemed electric . . .
>
> He talked English with a strong accent, as if he tasted his words in his mouth before pronouncing them; but he talked extremely well. . . . It seemed difficult to believe that this charming gentleman with . . . the unmistakably foreign look . . . was . . . such a master of English prose. . . . He talked on apparently with great freedom about his life—more ease and freedom indeed than an English would have allowed himself. . . . I was vibrating with intense excitement inside; and even now, as I write this, I feel almost the same excitement, the same thrill of having been in the presence of one of the most remarkable men I have known. (232–34)

In Conrad's speech, language acquired a distinctive carnality by pausing, as it were, in the mouth before issuing forth as signification. Its sensory being was stressed, and this, perhaps, liberated energies that Conrad might have found difficult if not impossible to express in the languages he knew better. As Najder says of Conrad, the very unfamiliarity of English, "resistant like every object that is strange and newly discovered, and at the same time softly pliable because not hardened in schematic patterns of words and ideas inculcated since childhood," enabled him to treat expression almost impersonally, like a game. Communicating in a foreign language, Najder notes, "admits a greater temerity in tackling personally sensitive problems, for it leaves uncommitted the most spontaneous, deeper reaches of the psyche" (*JC* 116).

The "ease and freedom" of Conrad's verbal performance contrasted not only with that of most English citizens, but also with his own practice of writing. A master of the language, he wrote with an agonized slowness made even slower by afflictions of gout in his writing hand. His letters are eloquent if repetitive monuments to writer's block, writer's cramp, writer's exhaustion, writer's panic, writer's masochism. On at least two occasions, however, his complaints become interesting. Having begun *Heart of Darkness,* he writes to William Blackwood, editor of *Blackwood's Magazine,* on 13 December 1898, to apologize for his "inefficiency," saying that "it is such a pleasure for me to appear in the *Maga* that you may well believe it is not laziness that keeps me back. It is, alas, something—I don't know what—not so easy to overcome. With immense effort a thin trickle of MS is produced" (*CL,* 2:129). At just this time, he was working on the beginning of his novella, including the scene with the Accountant, who keeps his books in apple-pie order while "Everything else in the Station was in a muddle—heads, things, buildings. Caravans. Strings of dusty niggers with splay feet arrived and departed; a stream of manufactured goods, rubbishy cottons, beads, and brass-wire set into the depths of darkness and in return came a precious trickle of ivory" (*HD* 21). The connection between the trickles of text and ivory is strengthened in other letters of this period, including one to Edward Garnett written just five days after the one to Blackwood, where he mentions "a short story for B'wood which I must get out for the sake of the shekels" (*CL*, 2:132). Whereas most commentaries on *Heart of Darkness* presume a filiation between Conrad and the garrulous seaman Marlow, these passages hang a wire between Conrad and Kurtz. The incredibly arduous effort required to produce English prose—which would then be sold—enabled Conrad to apprehend a connection between himself and those who plundered the African interior for ivory. Simply writing in English (the language of ivory calves) provided Conrad with a first identification, a sense of affinity that was then reworked in the text in the relationship between Kurtz and Marlow. To the latter, the former's (undoubtedly accented and "foreign") speech could only be described in terms that Conrad's friends may have used to describe Conrad's own speech, as "common everyday words" that nevertheless "had behind them, to my mind, the terrific suggestiveness of words heard in dreams, of phrases spoken in nightmares" (*HD* 65). As a raconteur, Conrad may have been, or wished he could be, a Marlow; but his exotic accent aligned him with Kurtz, a connection confirmed by his writing.

The second image to which I want to draw attention is contained in a 1908 letter to Arthur Symons, where Conrad says, with a touch of self-pity, "I have been quarrying my English out of a black night, working like a coalminer in his pit. For fourteen years now I have been living as if in a cave without echoes" (*CL*, 4:114). This, too, recalls a figure of Marlow's, a commentary on the "sordid buccaneers" of the Eldorado Exploring Expedition: "To tear treasure out of the bowels of the land was their desire, with no more moral purpose at the back of it than there is in burglars breaking into a safe" (*HD* 32, 32–33). Even more directly, this retrieves the central image of *Nostromo* (1904), the San Tomé silver mine, with its own precious trickle, the stream of silver that flows from the gorge of the mountain, "yielded to the hazards of the world by the dark depths of the Gould Concession" (*N* 98). Casting his own writing in this mold, Conrad, the passionate critic of material interests, constructs a kind of triangle, identifying his own labor with that of the degraded Kurtz and the deluded Charles Gould.

The innocent phrase "quarrying my English out of a black night" points to a tacit and perhaps unconscious alignment of the objects of his criticism with the criticism itself. Both are wrenched by force from a cleft, a gorge, an archaic or anarchic interiority radically incompatible with the idea of "culture" no matter how thoroughly "cultural" the finished product will be. His own work can be seen, he suggests, as a concession to "dark depths" that produces a morally neutral entity—a "spungy lump" of silver, say, or a narrative text—that can then be "endowed" by readers with a "justificative conception," as the silver is by Mrs. Gould, "as though it were not a mere fact, but something far-reaching and impalpable, like the true expression of an emotion or the emergence of a principle" (*N* 98). The literal activity of plunderers turns out to be a remarkably apt metaphor for the process of writing in English, one that imposed on him a sense of his own complicity and compelled him to experience in the process of creation itself the sense of inextricability that in one form or another dominates his best work. Moreover, this powerful but unwilled identification with the objects of his moral and political outrage effectively inhibits the kind of complacent or self-applauding moralizing characteristic of criticism of imperial hypocrisy and rapacity. Conrad wrote no tracts, recognizing, perhaps, that the aim of all creation, including his own, was not moral but spectacular.

Conrad's work qualifies as "modernist" partly because of the sheer effort his pages cost him, a labor that indicates a dedication to craft, the exercise of discipline and skill in the construction of aesthetic form. But the pursuit of formal perfection may not have been Conrad's only goal as he put himself through the agonies of authorship. For most writers, language may be deployed in the service of an idiosyncratic, fugitive, or exile sensibility, but as speech, it still guarantees a preliminary personal acceptance by the community of native speakers as "one of us." For most people, speech itself is a gift so commonplace as to be unremarked in any inventory of worldly blessings. For Conrad, however, speech, natural speech, was an impossible object of desire. His writing yearns for it, seeks to be taken for it, fetishizes it. He is, I would argue, laboring to quarry from the obdurate medium of writing an oratorical style, a discourse that could never issue from an "impersonal" or "omniscient" narrative voice. Conrad's "modernist" innovation, the conversational narrator, constitutes a technical breakthrough—and also a poignant confession of a powerful desire to speak easily, naturally, inconspicuously. The modernism of Flaubert, James, and Joyce, superficially like that of Conrad in combining a high aesthetic polish with a powerfully "realistic" attention to literal, concrete detail, is sophisticated in a way that Conrad's is not, and not just because they try, in Ezra Pound's phrase, to "make it new," while Conrad writes about trips to the beginning of time, and seems to regard narrative as "a ceremonial invocation of tribal gods and heroes" (Watt, lxii). Their modernity consists precisely in the triumph of writing, the humbling of the spoken word before the purity of the text, the submission of spontaneous storytelling to narratological mastery or craft. Conrad's modernity is more complex, for his texts, while acknowledged to be miracles of pattern and form, largely present themselves as transcriptions of the spoken word, with both the teller and his audience folded into the narrative.

While modernism celebrated the written word, it did not surrender the massive confidence in language entailed by operating in the mother tongue. Modernism may have invented the "arbitrariness" of the sign, but for the most part it trusted in the capacity of craft to render the world, not to unravel it, and even to erect an edifice of language that could stand not just as a plausible representation but as a freestanding and substantial construction. Conrad's colleagues in verbal experimentation might have comprehended Marlow's outraged incredulity at hearing African natives described and punished as "enemies" and "rebels" by an imperial force with no legitimacy in the land. They would not, however, have shared Conrad's desperate and comprehensive fears about what he called the *unreality* of language. They would not, for example, write, as Conrad does on the first page of *Under Western Eyes*, "Words, as is well known, are the great foes of reality" (55). Nor would they write, in the ambivalent form of a confession and a plea for sympathy, that "My efforts seem unrelated to anything in heaven and everything under heaven is impalpable to the touch like shapes of mist. Do you see? Even writing to a friend . . . does not give me a sense of reality. All is illusion—the words written, the mind at which they are aimed, the truth they are intended to express, the hands that will hold the paper, the eyes that will glance at the lines" (*CL*, 2:198). In such a mood—and this was more a periodically crippling conviction than a mood—Conrad felt language's unreality to be contagious or contaminatory, spreading from the marks on the page out to the hands, the eyes, the mind, the entire physical and metaphysical being, of the reader. "Words," Conrad writes in a marginally more positive tone to Hugh Clifford in 1899, "groups of words, words standing alone, are symbols of life" that possess a disturbing self-sufficiency: "The things 'as they are' exist in words" (*CL*, 1:200).

According to Said, Conrad marks a transition from "storytelling as useful, communal art to novel writing as essentialized, solitary art" (*WTC* 101). He does this, Said says, by emphasizing the medium—a heard or reported speech whose utility is doubtful and in fact actively doubted by listeners who are themselves dramatized as participants in a framing narrative whose subject is the presentation and reception of the primary narrative. By dramatizing this framing narrative, Said says, Conrad seeks "to move toward the visual" and away from writing (106). A textual representation of speech, Conrad's writing thus "negated and reconstituted itself, negated itself again, and so forth indefinitely," all as part of a strategy to achieve the "transcendence of writing" (108, 109). But despite his compulsive representation of the scene of speech, Conrad's doubts about the reality of language do not stop at the margin of writing; they extend to all of language including speech, and from there to language users, and from there to the world referred to by language, including the world of meaning. His doubt achieved this maximal comprehensiveness because it was rooted not in a philosophical skepticism about the mimetic power of language, nor in an awed appreciation of the power of language to construct a rival world, but in a detailed apprehension of the phenomenal proliferation of differences, definitions, distinctions, and structures in human language as such. For Conrad, unreality was entailed by the constant and intimate experience of thinking and expressing himself in a medium that had no claim to being "natural" to him, a language that existed at a great remove from his original language (which was, even in his childhood, the discourse of exiles and was now, when he was an adult living in England, of little use to him), with the patternings, rhythms, and categories of several other languages, both living and dead, intervening. To the extent that such a thing is possible, Conrad was, when he began the study of English, a man without a mother tongue.

As a writer of English, then, Conrad was "taken out of his knowl-edge." This sad and revealing phrase occurs, and recurs, in "Amy Fos-ter," where Conrad attempts to describe the effect on a simple Pole of linguistic deprivation. To be displaced linguistically is to be yanked from certainty itself and repositioned in a milieu where things float, where they are not just differently named but differently conceived, defined, and evaluated. Conrad's own situation was more extreme, for Yanko Goorall had only two languages, one in which he was adept and the other in which he was not. He could function by translating the second into the first, re-experiencing, after an interval of uncer-tainty and confusion, the sense of ease and naturalness of the native speaker. More radically alienated from native tongue and native land—and immensely more gifted, more capable of adaptation—Conrad could not so easily revert to an original, nonforeign language. In his peculiarity, he exemplified, especially at the beginning of his experience with English, the cultural-linguistic condition Homi Bhabha calls "hybridity." In "DissemiNation," Bhabha notes Renan's account of the obligation to forget the inaugural repression of differ-ences that founds the nation, and links this obligation, a "minus in the origin," to a condition of signification that emerges as a problem whenever cultural differences are being negotiated (310). Registered as a loss in meaning, a failure of the function of translation to over-come the opacity of language, this linguistic impediment testifies to a larger cultural condition, a positive inmixing of otherness. Differ-ence can be repressed or oppressed, but cannot, short of genocide or massive communal amnesia, be altogether obliterated. Thus, a culture obliged—as cultures, especially nations, are—to forget its own hy-bridity will, Bhabha argues, be structurally vulnerable to uprushes of uncertainty, "the perplexity of the living as it interrupts the represen-tation of the fullness of life" ("DN" 314).

This conversion of the problems of a few beleaguered Others into an explanatory model of cultural life generally constitutes Bhabha's real point. It is not the fact that a particular immigrant, émigré, or migrant must confront a foreign language that enlists Bhabha's atten-tion, but rather the fact that such people present a mirror to the na-tives, disclosing to them "the foreignness of languages" as "the ines-capable cultural condition for the enunciation of the mother-tongue"

(317). A talismanic figure for Bhabha as for Said, Conrad may have been out of his knowledge, operating in a foreign language with the mother tongue many languages, miles, and years away, but he was perfectly positioned to grasp this concept.

In fact, in his multipositionality, he may have been somewhat better placed than Bhabha himself, whose identifications emerge in occasional moments of moral certainty. The mute Other standing at the margin of the cultural-linguistic community, evokes, Bhabha argues, "an archaic anxiety and aggressivity by impeding the search for narcissistic love-objects in which the subject can rediscover himself, and upon which the group's *amour propre* is based" ("DN" 316). Does not Bhabha's tone here suggest a certain investment in the figure of the dangerous and unsettling outsider, and a certain aggressivity against "the group," driven by its primitive need for reflections of itself? But other names for the dandified and foreign term *amour propre* might be as neutral as "self-awareness," "self-definition," a "way of life," a "discourse," a distinctive psychosocial "cognitive style"—in a word, a "language." To the extent that the group is a group, it must have a language in which it "discovers itself," in which the familiarity of familiar things is established and the strangeness of the strange is marked. The group cannot help itself in this respect, nor can one help forming a group with those with whom one shares a language. The charismatically silent, monolingual Other would surely gabble away happily if any of his countrymen were around to listen. Some form of identification, a kind of narcissism, seems to have warped Bhabha's theoretical discourse. On strictly theoretical grounds, there is no cause, in the circumstance of the stranger in town, for admiration or reprobation, judgments that necessarily reflect the kind of confidence in one's categories and evaluations that, in any event, characterizes not the Other but "the group." One cannot form common cause with the Other without forming a new group, with its own mother tongue.

In one respect, Conrad is a poor candidate for the title of the Other. His social conservatism and pronounced patriotism places him squarely in the center of the polis. When the *Daily Chronicle* wanted a boosterish article on the accomplishments of the Royal Navy at the end of the Great War, they turned to one of the most famous British seamen since Nelson, the laureate of the Merchant

Service—Joseph Conrad, who readily complied with a laudatory piece called "Well Done." On the other hand, however, Conrad is a truly radical or Kurtzian outsider, for there is, in his work and even in his letters, virtually no discernible nostalgia for his own mother tongue, no attempt to reconstitute, on the basis of narcissism or *amour propre,* his own lost group: he has simply left these "love-objects" behind. One is tempted to say that he has "gone to sea," that he has found (or lost) himself in an indescribably ancient place where no language is natural and all are equally foreign, a place, or "cave," from which, nevertheless, all languages have emerged. On this point, Bhabha's description of the "archaic anxiety and aggressivity" provoked by the Other is exact, for what the foreigner, the *pure* foreigner, dimly represents is an aboriginal wordlessness associated not just with another place but with a *time* before language. From this place-less time, as a Polish sailor who never met another with whom he could enjoy the community of the homeland (except for the "slow-witted" compatriot encountered in the Sailor's Home in London—was there a conversation?), Conrad had a privileged access to a hidden metaphor of linguistic life: that the natural language was not a thing of nature at all, but a kind of ship, a product of human craft and dedication precariously afloat on mighty waters, pitching on the heaving surface of a chaos that constantly threatens to overwhelm it.

This chaos must be considered pre- or proto-linguistic rather than antilinguistic. Conrad among the British is bereft not of language but of "content." He is not wordless, but surfeited with words, with a vast proliferation of words all of which seem possessed by the aspiration to grasp something, to stand for something, to *be* something—all of which seem to think of themselves narcissistically as the only such words in the world, and to think of their referents on the model of "solid ground." No language has priority: taken out of his knowledge, Conrad knows this. Henry James, with his exquisite sensitivity to issues of knowledge, knew it too. "No one has *known*—for intellectual use—the things you know," James wrote, "and you have, as the artist of the whole matter, an authority that no one has approached. . . . You knock about in the wide waters of expression like the raciest and boldest of privateers" (James 368). James recognized that what Conrad knew was not best described as "the sea" or "sea life," but "expression"—the sea of language, language as such, a form of language, a form of *form,* which underlies and underwrites the crystallized natural languages that people speak. A natural language, a native language, is not a sea. Human language itself, however, is, or could be. This "itself" is not easy to describe or even to imagine, since language only exists in its various particular forms. But Conrad, with his singular experience and aptitudes, might have been approaching it when he spoke, in the preface to *The Nigger,* of art's attempt to discover "the truth, manifold and one," underlying the various appearances of the visible universe. The artist's rendering of the world is, he says, "an attempt to find in its forms, in its colours . . . what of each is fundamental, what is enduring and essential—their one illuminating and convincing quality—the very truth of their existence" (*NN* 145). Manifold in its instantiations, language is yet "one." Conrad may, in other words, be contemplating an analogy: as appearances are to visuality, so are languages to language.

This analogy, which argues the derivative equivalence of all languages, is available to a native speaker only in theoretical form. Even the person who learns a second language from the assured base of a first is not required to think it; and to think it without compulsion, to think it freely, to *entertain* the thought, is not truly to think it at all. Years before he learned English in his twenties, Conrad had relinquished Polish and was operating almost exclusively in French, which he had learned as a child (over the space of a few months from a governess, not from having been "educated in France," as Said inexplicably claims [*B* 110]). The native language was, in other words, already buried deeply, functioning not as a center of silent ease and *amour propre* but more like a pulse, an involuntary muscle whose sustaining contractions could be detected only with conscious effort. He did not simply transfer his mastery of Polish, after an interval of learning, to English. Nor was a mastery of English simply a way of forgetting the miseries of Poland. Nor, for that matter, does his English ever display the tranquil clarity expressive of a perfect mastery: as Kipling commented, his prose reads like an excellent translation of a foreign writer—of which nationality Kipling did not say (qtd. in Najder, *CUFE* 162). Beneath the trivial syntactical errors that Conrad committed in his first novels, errors involving prepositions, word order, verb tense, articles, etc., one can sense a more radical displacement of another language, another story, that one cannot quite identify but which disturbs everything, just as Conrad's accent affected every word. Jameson notes how, in certain passages of "purer" description, "Conrad's sensorium virtually remakes its objects," fashioning a "new space and a new perspective," and suggesting "forms of libidinal gratification as unimaginable to us as the possession of additional senses, or the presence of nonearthly colors in the spectrum" (230, 231). With its alien combination of curiously weighted terms, ideological slogans, strange adjective-noun combinations ("opaque air" [*HD* 41]), and tangled constructs, Conrad's discourse, he argues, "must be regarded as a foreign language that we have to learn in the absence of any dictionary or grammar, ourselves reconstructing its syntax and assembling hypotheses about the meaning of this or that item of vocabulary for which we ourselves have no contemporary equivalent" (245–46).

For Jameson, all this reflects a "strategy of aestheticization," as though Conrad were plotting his effects, assiduously burying History beneath a mass of Art (231). Jameson's description of the effect of Conrad's language is original and suggestive, but his attribution of the cause ignores the element I am trying to bring out. Conrad's intentions, conscious as well as unconscious, were necessarily and deeply conditioned by his grasp of the language, a grasp that was of a different order than that of a native speaker, or even of a polyglot who has learned a second or third language. Conrad is in fact best considered a master not of English but of what might be called "language itself." At their most distinctively "Conradian," the peculiarities in his English seem to flush out or grope towards not an approximation of an expression proper to Polish or French, but some thought, object, or sensation that lies elsewhere, that is proper to no natural language, that is drawn from the primordial sea of language itself. In the first chapter, I suggested that Conrad occupied Bhabha's "Third Space," which I defined at that time in terms of the binary of colonizer and colonized. It must be noted, however, that the Third Space is, for Bhabha linguistic in a theoretical sense: it is the gap between the subject of a proposition and the subject of enunciation that constitutes, as Bhabha says, "the discursive conditions of enunciation," a general

circumstance of ambivalence that underlies all articulation whatsoever (*LC* 37). Conrad's linguist space is just as general as Bhabha's,
but more mysterious because less theoretical, more historical. When
Marlow speaks, in a single passage, of the "still and earthy atmosphere
as of an overheated catacomb," of the Congo River invading "the con-
torted mangroves that seemed to writhe at us in the extremity of an
impotent despair," of his "weary pilgrimage amongst hints for nightmares," he seems to be trying to give countenance to something that,
like the Third Space, is "unpresentable in itself" (*LC* 37). He does not
hollow out a space in English for the Polish sensibility, but probes
English for effects and possibilities previously unsuspected in either
Polish or English, groping for thoughts and sensations that come
from the beginning of time, as a paleontologist will pore over the
familiar dirt in search of the fossilized bones and teeth of some forgotten antediluvian monster (*HD* 17). Conrad's practice suggests a
retrospective approach to the origins of language itself as revealed by
"paleontological analysis." This term was employed in the 1920s by
the Soviet linguist N. Marr and again by V. N. Vološinov, who argued
that language could be said to begin with the phenomenon of the
"alien world," that is, with intertribal linguistic "crossings" necessi-
tated by historical turbulence and economic needs (76).

The dislocations of history and the contingencies of the merchant
service took Conrad on a voyage at once spectacularly idiosyncratic
and virtually universal, into the unknown future and back, linguistically speaking, to the beginnings of time, landing him finally in England, one of those dark places of the earth where literature was produced. Steeped in the experience of occupying alien lands, of hearing
and speaking alien words, Russians seem to be highly attuned to the
strangeness of literature, which, the Formalist Viktor Shklovski wrote,
should provide a bracing "defamiliarization" of customary modes of
understanding through its "strange, surprising quality." Literature,
Shklovski contended, constitutes a "translation" of ordinary language; indeed, "it is often a foreign language" (qtd. in Ray 85). For
Conrad, these phrases were not metaphorical speculations but literal
facts: translation was for him a condition of being, as well, I would
argue, as a positive spur to creation. Bereft of his native tongue, Conrad found himself face to face with the foreignness of languages, an

unmasterable and barbaric tongue unfit for civilized women, not quite a language but a kind of magma that, under propitious circumstances—breakfast and voyages done, table cleared, writing instruments at hand—erupts, bursting through the crust to the surface, producing—culture, art, literature.

THE LANGUAGE OF MASTERY

> . . . I had elected to be [a British seaman] very deliberately, very completely, without any looking back or looking elsewhere. The circumstances were such as to give me the feeling of complete identification, a very vivid comprehension that if I wasn't one of them I was nothing at all.
>
> —Conrad, "Well Done"

In terms he clearly intended to be definitive, Conrad refuted in the "Author's Note" to *A Personal Record* the notion that he had "exercised a deliberate choice between French and English" (iv). In fact, French was impossible because "so perfectly 'crystallized,'" and English was compulsory.

> The truth of the matter is that my faculty to write in English is as natural as any other aptitude with which I might have been born. I have a strange and overpowering feeling that it had always been an inherent part of myself. English was for me neither a matter of choice nor adoption. The merest idea of choice had never entered my head. And as to adoption—well, yes, there was adoption; but it was I who was adopted by the genius of the language, which directly I came out of the stammering stage made me its own so completely that its very idioms I truly believe had a direct action on my temperament and fashioned my still plastic character. . . . All I can claim after all those years of devoted practice, with the accumulated anguish of its doubts, imperfections and falterings in my heart, is the right to be believed when I say that if I had not written in English I would not have written at all. (v–vi)

In one of a series of such adoptions—the first being by his relatives after the death of his father, and another being by the British seaman who administered his Master's examination—the language claimed him as its own, or rather, forcibly made him its own at a time when he was still "plastic," with no resistance from him or from any of the other languages that had had their chance at him. His first identification was not with Britain or the British, but with the language, on learning which he discovered that his "faculty to write in English"—a charmingly "foreign" way of putting it—was natural to him. He was "adopted" by his own nature.

At the time he learned English, his entire written *oeuvre* consisted of a few letters and notes, some in Polish and some in French. He continued to use French in conversation as an international language of culture and *politesse,* addressing Henry James as "Cher et bon Maître," and even, on one occasion, praising a Polish author to a Polish interviewer who had been conducting the interview in Polish as "l'âme de toute la Pologne, lui" (Najder, *CUFE* 199). In fact, Ford Madox Ford maintained that Conrad's English was never as strong as his French, and that he translated from French into English when writing all but the simplest passages (*JC* 169; see Hervouet). Conrad's English, Ford suggests, was but French in drag, and herein lay an extraordinary artistic advantage. The unfamiliarity of the language compelled Conrad to question the adequacy of every phrase that presented itself, to scour the lexicon in a restless and hyperconscious search for the right word with a keen, one might almost say "artistic," attention to nuance. While Conrad's account stresses nature, Ford's emphasizes learning and conscious effort. Must we conclude that one or the other is simply wrong—or can we reconcile the old friends by saying that it was Conrad's nature to be foreign, that he could only discover and express himself, with much labor and uncertainty, in an alien language?

If so, we must still acknowledge the crucial role of English. A mere attention to detail of the sort that would be required of any non-native speaker is not in itself literary, nor had a knowledge of other languages compelled him to write narrative fictions. It was only with the sustained exposure to English that he became possessed of a specifically literary drive. His books, he nearly suggests, are the products not of his intentions or creative will alone, but messages to the world passed through him from the heart of the English language. If, as I argued in the preceding section, Conrad at his most Conradian evokes a universal "language itself," then the burden of the following will be that Conrad discovered, or was discovered by, the universal in the form of the English.

The idea that language defined a people was almost a commonplace in Conrad's time. In the middle of the nineteenth century, Ernest Renan argued for the idea of a "linguistic race" as a more enlightened conception than that of a physical or anthropological race, a race based on blood, as it had been for Gobineau. The Semitic race, the Aryan race, the "race that speaks Sanskrit," all represent for Renan instances of linguistic races possessed by a definite "spirit." For Renan, language provided the form of a race's thought. French, for example: "[The French language] will say quite diverse things, but always liberal things. . . . It will never be a reactionary language, either. . . . Fanaticism is impossible in French" (*OL*). To the extent that Conrad might have agreed with Renan, this would be one more reason he never wrote in French—the language accorded with Polish liberalism but not with *szlachta* conservatism. (The young Conrad was politically disappointed with the contemporary French nation because of the feebleness of its imperial effort [Najder, *JC* 53].)

The project of describing the characteristics of a language seems quixotic, for all languages must display and be capable of representing an immense range of phenomena, and to isolate some few of these as characteristic of the language as a totality must entail a certain arbitrariness. What, after all, counts as a "feature" of the language? Which features are dominant and truly expressive of the entire language? Nonetheless, the project has a certain appeal. One can, after all, maintain that dogs are essentially masculine and cats essentially feminine despite bitches and toms. In any event, linguistic explanations of the British national spirit have not been wanting. In *Growth and Structure of the English Language* (1905), the great Danish linguist Otto Jespersen contended that English was virtually a *métier de chien*: "There is one expression that continually comes to my mind whenever I think of the English language," Jespersen wrote: "it seems to me positively and expressly *masculine*." By contrast to the "consonant-rich" sound of English, the Hawaiian language, for example, seems "childlike and effeminate . . . adapted only to inhabitants of sunny regions [where life] does not bear the stamp of a hard struggle against nature and against fellow-creatures" (3–4).

English has been accused of many things, but never of being a sissy. "Virility," especially in comparison with the feline French, is perhaps its most commonly attributed characteristic; "greatness" is another; "universality" is a third (see Claiborne). This rather sinister combination informs, in fact, the thinking of one of Conrad's early champions, F. R. Leavis, who enshrined Conrad with George Eliot and Henry James as the three pillars of "the great tradition" of the English novel. Leavis constructs a kind of Book of Manly Virtues— vigor, strength, raciness, concreteness, moral seriousness, "spiritual fineness," "maturity"—that are both claimed as the specialties of English language and culture and also labeled essential "human" values. Conrad, Leavis claimed, belongs to this tradition because his "themes and interests demanded the concreteness and action—the dramatic energy—of English" (17). Indeed, a tradition so constructed would virtually have to include Conrad, whose works express an untroubled confidence in the adequacy of English to the task of representing the most alien peoples, sensations, intuitions, and concepts. Almayer speaks in Dutch and Malay, but his speech is rendered in English, as is the speech of the Malay characters. The very first page of *The Nigger* contrasts "the feverish and shrill babble of Eastern language" as it "struggled against the masterful tones of tipsy [British] seamen" (1). Kurtz speaks French, although as a citizen of the world, he speaks English as well, and it is all rendered in English. The others Marlow meets en route to Kurtz must all speak French; otherwise, Marlow would not be so starved to speak English by the time he reaches him. *Under Western Eyes* speaks of the Russian fascination with language and the Russian language itself—in English. No matter where Conrad's novels are set, English is the lingua franca. In his early adulthood, Conrad felt himself to be adopted by a language that had long specialized in adoption. His works are faithful to the language in this respect, that while they clearly belong to the English tradition, they claim the world as their proper subject. In Conrad's works, we can actually see English in the process of becoming a "world language," a medium as limitless as the sea itself. In fact, Emerson had already made this comparison, likening English to "the sea which receives tributaries from every region under heaven" (qtd. in McCrum, Cran, and MacNeil 11). Deracinated, the youthful Conrad was imprinted with the character of the language and immediately engaged with the vast opportunities it presented; to express himself in English was all at once to become a man, a seaman, a Brit, and a cosmopolitan citizen of the world. If we grant Leavis and Jespersen their points, we might understand Conrad's relation to English in this way: as a conspicuously virile author with a "universal" message, he took the features of the English language as his main themes.

However, other features, or factors, were at work as well. He might "not have written at all" if he had not learned English, but English by itself was not entirely sufficient to compel him to take up his pen. The story of how that happened is the subject of many pages in *A Personal Record,* where he narrates, with a bewildered attention to detail, the events—the clearing of the breakfast dishes, the filling of the pipe, the arrangement of writing materials, the mood of "absolute irresponsibility"—on the morning that he began to write *Almayer's Folly.* What was he thinking of? Not, he assures his reader, of writing a novel, of becoming a novelist, of rendering the vibrations of life, of establishing a link with "that humanity so far away." Rather, "it is possible and even likely that I was thinking of the man Almayer" (74). To be more exact, he was thinking of the name Almayer. For some time, Almayer had been just a name for him.

> I had heard of him at Singapore; I had heard of him on board; I had heard of him early in the morning and late at night; I had heard of him at tiffin and at dinner; I had heard of him in a place called Pulo Laut from a half-caste gentleman there. . . . I had heard of him in a place called Dongola. . . . At least I heard his name distinctly pronounced several times in a lot of talk in Malay language. Oh, yes, I heard it quite distinctly—Almayer, Almayer. . . . Upon my word, I heard the mutter of Almayer's name faintly at midnight. (75)

This was not, in fact, the man's name, but it was close. Conrad had met Charles William Olmeijer, a Eurasian Dutchman, in Borneo two years before, in 1887, had delivered a pony to him, had received a goose from him, had conversed with him about Olmeijer's "very large interests"—all unrealized—"up the river" (*PR* 86). Olmeijer is clearly a proto-Kurtz at this point, but the novel's epigraph, from

Henri Frédéric Amiel, suggests another possibility as well: "Qui de nous n'a eu sa terre promise, son jour d'extase et sa fin en exil" (Who of us has not had his promised land, his day of ecstasy, and his end in exile?). Ian Watt claims that Conrad's use of this sentence signals both a "hidden identification" between Conrad and his first hero, and a "universality of theme".—perhaps even a personal identification enabled by universality ("I" lxi). Watt does not mention language, but Almayer and English are coupled from the start. The book, and the career, begin with the young Almayer leaving home "with a light heart and a lighter pocket, speaking English well, and strong in arithmetic; ready to conquer the world, never doubting that he would" (*AF* 5). (The recent Penguin edition, mindful of sales, quotes this sentence on the back as though it were representative of a book that actually chronicles unrelieved defeat and depression.) A Hollander from Java and Macassar, married to a Malay, Almayer still knew that local connections would take him no further than the locale, and that English was the key to success in "the world."

Even before he learned English, Conrad might well have understood Almayer's sentiments. British missionary and imperial activity had long been responsible for the spread of English, and such activity, having accelerated throughout the nineteenth century, was reaching a peak around the time that Conrad began his career at sea. At this time, too, powerful claims were being made by jingoists and linguists alike for English as a "universal" or "world" language. Often, as in South East Asia or South Africa, the struggle for linguistic dominance paralleled a struggle for material dominance, as Britain sought in both cases to establish a presence in a region previously controlled by the Dutch. Since Britain was generally successful in its commercial ventures, the language usually prevailed, becoming the second language of choice in numerous countries. Even where British interests did not prevail, however, the English language often maintained a powerful presence. In South Africa, for example, English held on even after the retreat of the English, even after 1925, when Afrikaans was established as the official state language. Most blacks used English as a second language in preference to Afrikaans, which they associated with apartheid. If the Afrikaans government saw English as the language of local protest, South African blacks saw English as an "international" language that would enable them to forge links with other black communities as well as appeal to the conscience of the West in their struggles. In the South East Asia Conrad saw, English advanced inexorably, permitting itself to be worked by local interests and variations, assimilating bits of other languages as a glacier picks up trees, houses, villages in its advance. It is in fact possible that the superior adaptability of English contributed to the colonial success of the British, and that the success of the local population in mastering English—not just learning it but appropriating it, adding to it and making it their own even as they became its own—encouraged a readier acquiescence in the process of their own domination. As compensation for material exploitation, English could offer a greatly expanded access to the world.

Linguists are reluctant to explain the global success of English as a function of intrinsic linguistic features, although English does have a number of unusual traits, including its huge vocabulary, its uninflected pronouns, its genderlessness, the flexibility of its word order, the ease with which compound words are formed, and its superabundance of synonyms. However, the history of the language actually provides a surer guide to its dominance. English is distinguished by the complexity of its origins. Conrad's still "plastic" character was formed by a language whose most salient historical characteristic is plasticity. At the base lies a now almost entirely buried Celtic language (or languages) that, like the Celts themselves, was brutally suppressed first by the Romans, in struggles memorably recalled by Marlow at the beginning of *Heart of Darkness*, and then by the Angles, Saxons, Jutes, and perhaps Frisians. For some reason, Latin did not strike deep roots in England as it had elsewhere in Europe, leaving the language to be freely influenced by the invading Germanic tribes who followed the Romans' departure. Thus, both Celtic and Latin had been effectively "forgotten" by the time of the Viking invasions, which produced a new flood of words, especially place-names, chiefly in the north. Most remarkably, English borrowed basic elements of syntax, including pronouns, from the Danes. Even before 1066, when an entirely new linguistic trauma arrived, the language had been conquered and reconquered, adapting itself constantly. For their part, the Normans did not simply import "French." They were Vikings who had lived in France for about two hundred years, forgetting their original language entirely and coming to speak a rural dialect that was so sharply divergent from Parisian French that it is referred to as "Anglo-Norman." Then came the chaos of Middle English dialects that precipitated and yielded to Modern English (see Burgess 231–57; Bryson 46–66). By the beginning of the great English diaspora of the eighteenth century, when it set out from its island home to impose itself as the language of "choice" not only in the American and Canadian colonies, but in Ireland and Wales as well, English could claim a singularly rich history: a child of the "masculine" Germanic and the "feminine" French, English also counted among its ancestors languages long dead and wholly forgotten. All Europe contributed to the making of English.

Long understood to be a "mongrel, independent, idiosyncratic" affair, English has always resisted efforts to preserve and purify it (Bryson 152). French intellectuals might seek to protect the integrity of French through the activities of a French Academy, but, despite the efforts of Jonathan Swift to institute a comparable Academy for English, none has come into being, perhaps for the reason that Defoe adduced in *The True-Born Englishman:*

> Thus from a Mixture of all kinds began,
> That Het'rogeneous Thing, *An Englishman:*
> In eager Rapes, and furious Lust begot,
> Betwixt a Painted *Britton* and a *Scot:*
> Whose gend'ring Offspring quickly learnt to bow,
> And yoke their Heifers to the *Roman* Plough:
> From whence a Mongrel half-bred Race there came,
> With neither Name nor Nation, Speech or Fame.
> In whose hot Veins now Mixtures quickly ran,
> Infus'd betwixt a *Saxon* and a *Dane.*
> While their Rank Daughters, to their Parents just,
> Receiv'd all Nations with Promiscuous Lust.
> This Nauseous Brood directly did contain
> The well-extracted Blood of *Englishmen.* . . .

So sedimented and traditional in some respects, British culture, like its language, is a hardy hybrid accustomed to struggle. A Nietzschean "genealogy of language" would uncover, beneath the surface of the universal language a series of skirmishes won and lost, bloodshed, mastery gained by force and by stealth. English is the mother tongue to which foreignness is most proper, the language most indicative of the foreignness of languages, the photographic negative of a culture that prides itself on its island solidarity.

If English is adaptable to local purposes no matter what the locality, the reason may be that, linguistically speaking, English is already "one of us": it makes its way, recommending itself as a language already mastered, a victim's language and yet a victor's language as well. Above all, it is a survivor's language that makes an immediate appeal to a culture facing defeat. If, "tomorrow the advancing civilization will obliterate the marks of a long struggle in the accomplishment of its inevitable victory," as Conrad says in the first paragraph of *The Rescue,* then one way for the imperiled local culture to preserve itself would be to make English its own (15). And it could do so in part because English is historically more hospitable to such appropriations than, for example, Dutch, French, or Spanish, the self-consistent languages of self-consistent groups. Already a "foreign" language, English might not seem, to an Indian or a black South African or a Filipino, quite so foreign as these others. In fact, English is structurally vulnerable to countercolonial insurrection. In a provocative 1982 article, "The Empire Writes Back with a Vengeance," Salman Rushdie pointed out that English is "no longer an English language," that it "now grows from many roots; and those whom it once colonized are carving out large territories within the language for themselves." While others, especially African writers such as Ngugi wa Thiong'o and Conrad's enemy Chinua Achebe have felt uncomfortable with the "territories" available to postcolonial writers in English, the sheer size of the audience that can be reached in English generally proves irresistible, in part because an "international" language is the appropriate medium for making "universal," that is, ethical claims. As Achebe himself wrote in 1975, the African writer should seek to transform English, not to reject it, to fashion "an English which is at once universal and able to carry his peculiar experience" (*MYCD* 62; see Bailey 151–77).

The extraordinary transformability of English is allegorized in *The Secret Agent,* where Conrad explores the phenomenon of England's traditional hospitality to anarchists from other lands. For Conrad himself, English must have seemed an incomparable opportunity, a language that really understood the partitioned sensibility, a language finally adequate to the scale of the sea, a language that mastered all others precisely because it has been mastered and remastered countless times, a language in which he could find a home. The idiosyncrasy of his English, so different from that of native speakers, mines, in a way they could not, the historical heterogeneity of the language. This is why it is often impossible to tell whether some especially "incomprehensible" phrasing represents an utter mastery in the form of a sublime transcendence of the literal, or a simple foreigner's inability to achieve plain English. The most unmistakably Conradian passages in Conrad's work are those in which the function of reference is disturbed, in which language seems to point towards some supercharged dimension of being where vulgar discord (possibly) becomes sublime concord. The conceptual-stylistic feature I have called, generically, oxymoron, in which unlikenesses are stapled together, often suggests both a fantastic linguistic mastery *and* a failure to achieve even mere reference or coherence.

*

In the ideology of empire, the British, like the Belgians, had traditionally aligned colonial power with superior virtue, mastery with self-mastery. The imperial mission was justified by the self-evident truth that the British deserved to rule: they ruled the seas because they ruled themselves. However, as Conrad was winding down his maritime career, this equation was beginning to become destabilized. Although British imperial might was at its apex in the last half of the nineteenth century, it was not unchallenged. The founding of the nationalist Indian National Congress in 1885, the Boer War, and the ongoing crisis of the Irish Home Rule movement threatened British rule overseas. At home, the aesthetic movement in the arts, and the widespread concern at the fin de siècle with cultural "degeneration," suggested that British self-mastery was in doubt as well (see Greenslade 106–19; Hynes 15–53; Showalter, 169–87). On the one hand, then, Britain was experiencing the shock of seeing the empire writing back, asserting its own claims in a robustly "British" discourse of rights and entitlements; on the other, Britain was seeing its own culture, especially its artistic culture, ripening into a hypersophisticated and foreign-influenced decadence.

Immensely impressed by British imperial successes and its stable culture, Conrad was also keenly sensitive to signs of softening. His formative experiences of British authority were at sea, and, to appropriate the name of one of his short stories, in "outposts of progress," in places where Britain was establishing its interests against other would-be imperial powers and an often resistant native population. What he witnessed as a British seaman was shipboard discipline, with the ever-present threat of mutiny against a power that was, by enlightened standards, excessive; and the subtle, complex, often indirect and only partially effective, dominance entailed by the gradual imposition of a mercantile apparatus whose claims to moral warrant were not altogether persuasive to the disinterested observer. In both instances, the issue was emphatically not decided in advance, and it is this circumstance of uncertainty that he reproduced in his writing. Take for example, the combination of *The Nigger* and its famous preface. With its emphasis on the sensuousness of art, the "blending of form and substance," the "shape and ring of sentences," the "magic light of suggestiveness," the fleeting moment, the preface has been described as "impressionist," "aestheticist," even "Paterian"—and this despite the fact that the book itself is a militantly masculine celebration of the stiff-upper-lip ethos.

Nowhere is this highly stimulating combination of mastery and its Other more apparent than in the paean to Lord Nelson in the last section of *The Mirror of the Sea*. The embodiment of "the heroic age," Nelson brought a very particular quality to the national spirit: exaltation. Conrad dwells on this term, reserving it exclusively for Nelson. "Other men there were ready and able to add to the treasure of victories the British navy has given to the nation," he writes. But "it was the lot of Lord Nelson to exalt all this glory. Exalt! the word seems to be created for the man" (185). The mere thought of Nelson seems to push Conrad over the edge; his rhetoric becomes slightly excessive, irrational, even hysterical. The glory of Nelson, his "nobleness of mind," his "splendid and matchless achievements"—all this is "too great for mere pride" (184, 184, 185). Rather, the appropriate feeling, the one evidenced by Nelson himself, is love, specifically love of Fame. "He loved her jealously, with an inextinguishable ardour and an insatiable desire—he loved her with a masterful devotion and an infinite trustfulness. In the plenitude of his passion he was an exacting lover. . . . Thus he would hug to his breast the last gift of Fame" (186). He also enlisted the love of his men, who, one contemporary reported, invariably confessed the "heartiest expressions of attachment to his person and admiration of his frank and conciliatory manner to his subordinates." "They loved him," Conrad continues, "not only as victorious armies have loved great commanders; they loved him with a more intimate feeling as one of themselves" (187). They loved him because he "knew how to lead lovingly to the work of courage" through his uniquely "uplifting touch" (188). "Verily," Conrad concludes, "he is a terrible ancestor" (187).

Verily, Conrad has become a bit carried away here. Identifying with a master, he has compromised his own self-mastery. The cause, however, is not Conrad's failure, but Nelson's particular kind of greatness. What made Nelson so extraordinary, such a pure instance of the national spirit, so quintessentially one of us was not his surpassing daring, his tactical brilliance, or even the fact that some of his most famous victories came when he acted either without or against orders. The secret of his greatness, according to Conrad, lay in this: that Nelson *trusted to chance.* If, at Trafalgar, the wind had failed, "nothing, it seems, could have saved the headmost ships from capture or destruction. No skill of a great sea officer would have availed in such a contingency"; indeed, Nelson lost his arm at Santa Cruz de Teneriffe because of "a quite unusual failure of the wind" (189, 190). Nelson's greatness, his *British* greatness—which Conrad claims as his own when he remarks on "the fleets opposed to us," or "our daring and our faithfulness"—lay in his abandonment of his fate to the weather (193). Nelson's self-mastery, and thus the basis of the British claim to mastery over others that he asserted, consisted of his ecstatic surrender to the caprices of the wind. Herein lies the essence of the superior virtue of sail as opposed to steam: steam is mastery plain and simple, mastery in which nothing is risked, mastery without reserve or fissures.

Sail, by contrast, is mastery submitted to a puff of wind; and the greatness of the victory at Trafalgar continues to amaze Conrad because, as he says, "I cannot free myself from the impression that, for some forty minutes, the fate of the great battle hung upon a breath of wind such as I have felt stealing from behind, as it were, upon my cheek while engaged in looking to the westward for the signs of the true weather" (192). In such unguarded phrases, occurring as they do just after an extended rhapsody on Nelson as a much-loved lover, Conrad clearly discloses more than he intends. He has, we might say, been overtaken by an affect stealing up on him from behind while he was earnestly "looking west," trying to get to the bottom of Nelson's greatness as a commander. And yet, this slip of the tongue notwithstanding, the prose in this section is—heroic. Conrad might almost be quoting, or adopting, Nelson's formula for success when he writes that "I feel how mysteriously independent of myself is my power of expression. . . . I am, so to speak, only the agent of an unreliable master" (qtd. in *LJ* 293). For Conrad as well as for Nelson, self-surrender, self-forgetfulness, a certain relinquishing of mastery, are the conditions of greatness.

Indeed, for Conrad, they may have been the conditions of creation in the first instance. To see why, we need to return to Almayer's name. In *A Personal Record,* Conrad imagines himself speaking posthumously with the shade of Almayer: "It is true, Almayer," Conrad would say, "that in the world below I have converted your name to my own uses. But that is a very small larceny" (87). Indeed, it is not quite a theft at all, for Olmeijer's name remains his own. Conrad has converted the Dutch name into an English one, putting into "the hollow sound," as he calls it, "the very anguish of paternity" (88). But who is the father, who the son? In the depths of this uncertainty, we arrive at the navel of Conrad's creation. In one sense, Conrad, the younger man, is the father, whose creative agency has produced "Almayer." In another, however, the agency is centered in Almayer, who is addressed as a "Shade"—"What's in a name, O Shade?"—the very term Conrad uses for his own father in the "Author's Note" to *A Personal Record* (87, x). It is Almayer, Conrad insists, who is the true father of his work, "responsible for the existence of some fourteen volumes, so far." "If I had not got to know Almayer pretty well," he asserts, "it is almost certain there would never have been a line of mine in print" (87). The hollowness of "Almayer" accommodates both configurations. But the English version of the name, in which the mystery of paternity is centered, is not merely empty. In English, the name suggests an infinite permissiveness, a nonrestrictive openness to appropriation that is still the law of the father. Within the closed field of compulsion and necessity represented by paternity, Conrad has created, through a pun operative in English, a pocket of freedom, even license.

Thus, neither the English language nor "the man Almayer" by itself provided the necessary energy to clear the table, arrange the writing materials, and begin to write a fictional narrative. Together, however, these two factors provide a bifocal perspective on the inaugural act. Conrad began writing when he discerned, in the English approximation of the name of Olmeijer—an exile in whom he could recognize both himself and his father—a general permission, lawlessness, anarchy. Since this otherness in the "name of the father" was more visible than audible (Almayer sounding too much like Olmeijer to make a difference to the ear) the permission obtained was, specifically, to write, to make you see.

This otherness takes, in Conrad's own account, the most transgressive form possible, a weird *mélange* of homosexuality, incest, and prostitution. Having begged Almayer's forgiveness for pinching his name, Conrad imagines himself urging Almayer to consult with the shade of Shakespeare about such appropriations. "You came to me," he portrays himself saying, "stripped of all prestige by men's queer smiles and the disrespectful chatter of every vagrant trader in the Islands. Your name was the common property of the winds: it, as it were, floated naked over the waters about the Equator" (*PR* 88). The undoubted inaccuracy of Conrad's account of a man Ian Watt calls a "fairly successful and respected" trader foregrounds the unusual energy expended to label him, or at least his unresisting name, a whore (Watt, "I" xxii). "Almayer" seems to represent a secret side of the man Olmeijer, a dimension imperceptible in Dutch, as in the actual man, but available to one who can translate it and reconfigure it to fit, or almost fit, the canonical accents of the national bard. Shakespeare's "disgrace with fortune and men's eyes" becomes "stripped of all prestige by men's queer smiles," a modest adjustment that nevertheless strips Olmeijer not just of his name but of his *name*, his respectability, and permits a certain sort of unarticulated and even unrecognized identification.

Could a "crystallized" language such as French provide the same opportunity for the covert and uncensored act of recognition out of which Conrad's career began? Could any other language have disclosed a radical plasticity so efficiently as did English, in the very first sentence Conrad heard addressed to him? "Look out there": a peremptory command warning of danger—or is it? Maybe the British sailor was trying not to make Conrad take aversive action but simply to look *out there;* maybe he was trying to make Conrad see. Maybe he was simply trying to tell Conrad that a "look-out" was posted in a particular place—"there." The grammatical status of each of the three words is determined by the interpretation of the sentence, which of course cannot be settled without knowing what part of speech each word is.

As Ford tells it, Conrad had numerous complaints about the "inexact, half-baked language that English was" (*JC* 101). "Conrad's dislike for the English language," Ford recalls, was "extreme, his contempt for his medium unrivalled" (226). Why? Because "he was convinced that he would never master English. He used to declare that English was a language in which it was impossible to write a direct statement" (228). All English words, Conrad told Ford, "are instruments for exciting blurred emotions." In French, for example, "oaken" means made of oak; in the heart of English oak, however, lurk "innumerable moral attributes . . . stolidity, resolution, honesty" (229). These sentences register the unmasterability of English, not just from the point of view of a man learning the language as an adult, but from any point of view. For Conrad, however, English was appealing, even imperative, precisely because he had not fully mastered himself, and the language seemed responsive to that fact. A "blurred" personality, Conrad could express himself best, he intuited, in a medium that was itself blurred. Conrad's understanding of the English language is fundamentally different from that of Leavis, but then Leavis remained in his outpost—Cambridge—for nearly his entire life and never had to grapple with English as a foreign or "world" language. Conrad himself gradually grew out of his hostility, Ford reports, and came to wield the language with greater confidence and "fluency," but when his hatred died out, his love did too, and "he then regretted that for him all the romance of writing was gone" (230).

The most interesting comment Ford reports is Conrad's analysis of the consequence of the blurring of the edges of English words, that "a reader is always, for a fraction of a second, uncertain as to which meaning of the word the writer intends" (*JC* 229). Some of Conrad's most disconcerting moments involve just such uncertainty. The phrase "men's queer smiles" is one example. Already, as Elaine Showalter argues (but the *Oxford English Dictionary* does not), a code word for "homosexual" before the 1890s, "queer" is one of those words to which Conrad turns and returns (112). Heyst is introduced as both a gentleman and a "queer chap" (*V* 4); and Jim recalls to Marlow the experience of falling into the boatful of men when he jumped from the *Patna* "with a queer contraction of his lips, like a man trying to master his sensibilities" (*LJ* 70). "It's queer how out of touch with truth women are," Marlow reflects in *Heart of Darkness*, immediately before revealing his own "queer feeling" of being an impostor (*HD* 16). Before the typhoon strikes, and Homo Britannicus tangles its limbs in ecstatic confusion, MacWhirr runs up the Siamese flag, a "queer flag for a man to sail under," according to Jukes (199). Leaving his cabin for the first time since Leggatt, the "secret sharer," entered it, the young captain suspects that the steward has told other crew members that he is "queer" (670). The closest Conrad comes to giving an unequivocal meaning to the term is in *Chance*, where Marlow, just two pages after confessing to the vigor of "the woman in my nature," speculates, vis-à-vis the Fynes, "'Queer enough they were. Is there a human being that isn't that—more or less secretly?'" (45). Even this is still equivocal; the dominant meaning *might* dominate. But the very fact of a secondary meaning, coupled with a certain consistency in the contexts in which the word crops up, must give the reader pause.

In a word, the reader of English must wait. Waiting becomes a constant and characteristic activity, and "Wait," the essential message from the language to the reader. James Wait becomes, by this logic, a token of the English language, and his arrival on board the *Narcissus* inaugurates Conrad's career as a major British author. But Conrad also freighted other names and other words in order to exploit the deferral implicit in the language itself. The name of the crewman who had seen the pants of gentlemen, for example—"dirty Knowles"—suggests, after a moment's reflection, dirty knowledge, dirty holes, and a knowledge of dirty holes. In "Youth," Marlow finds himself on his first voyage to the East, serving as second mate (on the *Judea*—"Queer name, isn't it?") under the elderly Captain Mahon ("his name was Mahon," Marlow comments, "but he insisted that it should be pronounced Mann"), and extraordinarily excited by his destination: "I . . . wanted awfully to get to Bangkok. To Bangkok! Magic name, blessed name" (117, 127). What's in a name? Is it the city itself that enthralls him, or does the name—especially when linked with that of his captain, as in the phrase "Mahon's mate to Bangkok"—contain its own appeal, when uttered by an English speaker? As the narrator begins the story by saying, "This"—the telling of the story by Marlow—"could have occurred nowhere but in England" (115). The real import of the name "Jim," the man with whom one cannot help but identify in *The Nigger* and in *Lord Jim*, was almost surely hidden from Conrad himself, for it was disclosed only in 1905, when he wrote in "Autocracy and War" of Russia as a "dreaded and strange apparition . . . something not of this world, partaking of a ravenous ghoul, of a blind Djinn grown up from a cloud" (*NLL* 89). But the most extended deferral of the meaning of a name occurs in *Heart of Darkness*, where Conrad converted the name of the agent at the Inner Station, Klein, to a German near synonym, Kurtz. The conversion was made not because Conrad hesitated to use the name of a real person—he showed no such delicacy in Olmeijer's case, or in Lingard's—but because "Kurtz," while retaining the sense of Klein, and thus the anchor in reality, also enabled a pun or near rhyme *in English*, a mediation of "Christ" and "cursed" that reinforced the troubling combination of moral splendor and moral squalor that constitutes Kurtz's distinction as a character. Ford reports that, in their conversations about *Heart of Darkness*, he and Conrad always assumed that Kurtz spoke French, and that his last words would be "*L'horreur! l'horreur!*" (*JC* 169). The accentuation of "the horror" seemed, Ford reports, wrong in the terminal position. But there may be a deeper reason for not ending the story with Kurtz's last words, a reason unrecognized by either man. When translated into English, these words throw a line to "whore," to the Whore of Babylon, for example, who may have been an unacknowledged archetype for the Intended—who, Conrad may have recalled, lived in the city Marlow described at the beginning as "the sepulchral city" (full of all uncleanness and dead men's bones). "The horror" thus virtually entailed a final apocalyptic episode following Kurtz's death, an episode that would realize the meaning of Brussels, of the Belgian empire, and of the Intended herself, a whore for whom Kurtz had gone to Africa with the project of enriching himself so he could afford to marry her.

With divergent meanings squirting out on all sides, puns and homonyms represent oxymorons in a state of maximum condensation, a force of anarchy operating within the law of the signifier, a mutiny of sense against the rule of sound. As Jonathan Culler points out, puns "present the disquieting spectacle of a functioning of language where boundaries—between sounds, between sound and letter, between meanings—count for less than one might imagine and where supposedly discrete meanings threaten to sink into fluid subterranean signifieds too undefinable to call concepts" (3). However, as Culler continues, puns are also recognized as a fundamental feature of language, the very "foundation of letters." As a consequence of their primordiality, they can be enlisted in the service of various projects that seek to undo the rule of "phallic" mastery in the name of some force more authentic, original, or profound. If Julia Kristeva were, for example, to go looking in language for the "semiotic," the modality of the signifying process beneath and anterior to the "symbolic," and therefore roiled up by "poetic" language, she might find it in puns, whose indeterminate, polyvocal (and rhyming) signification is a rudimentary form of the poetic. If Luce Irigaray were asked how, precisely, one might follow her prescription for the "feminist" disruption of language, she might reply: make puns, for puns employ a "double syntax," they are "neither one nor two," "other in themselves," subversive of "the seriousness of meaning," they "make it impossible for a while to predict whence, whither, when, how, why" (see *TSNO* and *SOW* passim). Derrida might cite the pun as an exemplary form of *différance,* through which meaning is deferred by differing from itself. The pun, Freud might agree, is a branch of the family of "primal words" whose "ambivalence" led him to suspect that, in the beginning, meanings that are contradictory today were conflated, as in the case of *heimlich,* which once meant both "canny" and "uncanny."

It is difficult to quantify such things, but English is, by common consent, extraordinarily rich in homophones. Even Samuel Johnson, who castigated Shakespeare for his addiction to "quibbles," included puns in his dictionary, a practice inconceivable in a French dictionary. Conrad despised Freud and had a decidedly limited appreciation of humor. They write in different genres, of course, but their writing practice is not *altogether* different: Freud insistently masters an anarchic referent, the unconscious, while Conrad's work is itself visibly, or rather audibly, worked by the unconscious, largely through "unconscious" puns made available to him in English.

Could Conrad possibly have been aware, fully aware, of the range of possible meanings when he wrote that Captain Allistoun "all day long pervaded the poop," and "seldom descended from the Olympian heights of his poop" (*NN* 18, 19)? Was he aware that "poop" meant not only that part of the ship—the stern—where the master and officers are quartered, but also, as the *OED* was shortly to affirm, "the hinder part of a man or animal, the posteriors, rump"? Did he know, as part of his professional vocabulary, another meaning, the verb form "*Naut*.": "Of a ship: to receive (a wave) over the stern; to ship (a sea) on the poop" (*OED*). Could he *not* have known? Doesn't the homosocial/homoerotic streak running through this opening section of *The Nigger*—this section, which moves directly from Allistoun as the autocrat of the poop to impossible stories about admirals, and the seats of gentlemen's pants—proclaim, in fact, a clear and certain knowledge? Doesn't Allistoun himself confirm this when he murmurs to his mate that the crew are a "queer lot"? (84). But such knowledge, if admitted into the field of Conrad's intention, would convulse the entire tale: every particular of the story would change meaning, countless details would take on the status of the *coy* or the *sly;* and, it need hardly be added, the entirety would drop out of the canon like a stone. Inasmuch as the text remains in the canon, the knowledge in question is consigned to the shadows, like a secondary and possibly, probably, unintended meaning—the kind in which English specializes.

Many of the locutions that fall into this category seem so artless that one hesitates to attribute their appearance to an unconscious energy that, we suppose, would surely, in a great artist, find a more circumspect means of expression. It is simply too obvious, isn't it, that the steamer whose owner takes that queer chap Heyst off his island is called the *Sissie?* (The *New English Dictionary* Supplement lists among the very first uses of this term to mean "an effeminate man or boy" an 1893 quotation: "Ware! Sissy men in Society.—Powdered, painted and laced. They swarm at afternoon teas.") And too obvious, too, when Conrad informs his publisher that he is trying to depict the "action of human beings that will bleed to a prick" (*CL,* 2:418). The Golfo Placido in *Nostromo* itself seems, to the sensitized or hypersensitized eye, to have bled to a prick the morning after Nostromo, after spending the night on a lighter with Decoud, has landed the silver on the island: "The great mass of cloud filling the head of the gulf had long red smears amongst its convoluted folds of grey and black, as of a floating mantle stained with blood. . . . The glassy bands of water along the horizon gave out a fiery red glow, as if fire and water had been mingled together," he adds gratuitously, "in the vast bed of the ocean" (*N* 339). Nostromo is then shown awakening as if from bed, after "a fourteen hours' sleep . . . Handsome, robust, and supple" (340). Other instances seem only marginally subtler. In *Lord Jim,* Marlow compares Gentleman Brown—the man who insinuates, in his conversation with Jim, "an assumption of common experience; a sickening suggestion of common guilt, of secret knowledge"— to "his contemporary brother ruffians, like Bully Hayes or the mellifluous Pease, or that perfumed, Dun-dreary-whiskered scoundrel known as Dirty Dick" (235, 214). Strictly contingent in one sense, the roll call of bounders takes its place in a text that seems, from another point of view, largely written in code. "'It was as if I had jumped into . . . an everlasting deep hole,'" Jim tells Marlow, foretelling the terms of Brown's appeal for help on the grounds that they are both on "the dirty earth" in an "infernal hole"; a fellow gentleman, Brown urges, ought to help "a man trying to get out of a deadly hole" (68, 233, 233,

235). The controversial division of the text—the leap, the inquiry, the relation with Marlow in one part, and Jim's travels, ending in his death in Patusan in a second part—may have been structured not as a story in which a man commits a cowardly act and then bravely atones for it, but rather as a tale in which a gentleman jumps into a hole—a difficult position, but also "a secret room in which an unlawful occupation is pursued," as well as "the orifice of any organ or part of the body"—and then tries unsuccessfully to get out (*OED*).

Telling Marlow about his leap only gets Jim deeper in the hole, especially as Marlow tells it. Almost violently susceptible to flutterings "of light . . . of heat!" in the presence of "a youngster of the sort you like to see about you," Marlow reserves a special warmth for the "magnificent vagueness," the "glorious indefiniteness" of the impulse that leads men, including Jim, to the sea (*LJ* 78). This positive taste for blurred emotions is confirmed and realized in his discourse, which is consistently equivocal and seeks out the equivocal in every situation. Marlow is particularly attentive to Jim's recognition that "there was not the thickness of a sheet of paper between the right and wrong of this affair," a formulation that associates the moral equivocality of Jim's leap with the sheets on which he is writing, and, perhaps, with the sheets of the nearby bed. Ostensibly, the initial bond between the two men is a shared commitment to the sea, but the very phrases in which this commitment is articulated are saturated with an ambivalence that is at odds with the simplicities of the maritime life. "In no other kind of life is the illusion more wide of reality," Marlow comments, "[and] the subjugation more complete. Hadn't we all commenced with the same desire, ended with the same knowledge, carried the memory of the same cherished glamour through the sordid days of imprecation?" Hadn't we? And so, "what wonder that when some heavy prod gets home the bond is found to be close; that besides the fellowship of the craft there is felt the strength of a wider feeling" (79). The passage is not only grouped around the ambivalent concept of "wideness," but is full of words that seem inexact or "translated," such as "subjugated" and "sordid," and concludes with the positively strange "heavy prod." However, these terms are strange, as it were, in the same way, so that the whole is precise enough, especially when placed in the context of "a wider feeling," the man-child bond that transcends a mere occupational kinship. Marlow even elicits a certain affection from Conrad himself, as the 1921 "Author's Note" to *Youth: A Narrative, and Two Other Stories* (*Heart of Darkness* and *The End of the Tether*) suggests. Here, Conrad recalls "the first appearance in the world of the man Marlow, with whom my relations have grown very intimate in the course of years." "That gentleman," as he calls Marlow, was one of those "health-resort acquaintances which sometimes ripen into friendships"; and now, years later, "he haunts my hours of solitude, when, in silence, we lay our heads together in great comfort and harmony" ("AN" 71, 72, 72). So often taken as a distinctively "modernist" narrative innovation or "device" by critics such as Watt who are eager to see in Conrad evidence of a highly developed interest in technique, Marlow serves more immediately as a target or bearer of the "heavy prod" of solidarity between men whose desires remain furtive and figural.

So wide is the feeling summoned up by Jim's hole—his predicament, his situation—that "if two men who, unknown to each other, knew of this affair met accidentally on any spot of this earth, the thing would pop up between them as sure as fate" (*LJ* 84). They would be virtually certain to ask each other, as a French officer asks Marlow, what there was "at the bottom of this affair" (88). Jim himself recognizes Marlow as a fellow bottom-dweller, stammering to Marlow, "at bottom . . . you, yourself" (109). Just at this moment, Marlow suffers an anxiety attack as he senses that Jim is about to leave him; or, as he puts it, "I, too, who a moment ago had been so sure of the power of words, [was now] afraid to speak, in the same way one dares not move for fear of losing a slippery hold. It is when we try to grapple with another man's intimate need that we perceive how incomprehensible, wavering, and misty are the beings that share with us the sight of the stars and the warmth of the sun" (109). He persuades Jim to dine with him one last time, and then offers to provide a letter of introduction to a friend, a letter written, he assures Jim, "in terms that one only ventures to use when speaking of an intimate friend" (111). Impressed, Jim bites his lip and frowns: "'What a bally ass I've been,' he said very slow in an awed tone. . . . 'You are a brick!'" (112).

The blooded bed, the heavy prod, the bottom of the affair, getting a slippery hold on another man's intimate need, being a bally ass to a man who is a brick—impressive testimony to the "power of words" to express meanings as definite and systematic as they are "incomprehensible, wavering, and misty." But are words the agent here, or the instrument of a man seeking an expressive outlet by probing fissures in the language, exploiting secondary meanings that tell a wholly different story from the primary or literal meaning? Isn't Conrad himself responsible? Perhaps; but the phrase "Conrad himself" is inexact, for Conrad himself, speaking as himself and for himself, would strenuously disavow any intention to represent, in however covert a manner, a libidinal subplot so utterly at variance with the manifest sense of his works. As Thomas Moser says, "love" of any kind is an "uncongenial subject" for Conrad. But as Marlow says in *Chance,* the refusal of "the embrace" invites "an invasion of complexity, a tormenting, forcibly tortuous involution of feelings." Banished as uncongenial, sexuality remains as a foreign element in Conrad, one that never really finds a home in his work and yet, in involuted forms, is never truly out of it either, as currents of an indeterminate desire flash intermittently along wires designed primarily to carry other messages. The unmentioned subject, sexual desire, and especially homosexual desire, escapes the vigilance of the artist searching after the elusive *mot juste,* concentrating on one kind of exactitude while leaving the chaotic domain of secondary meanings to itself.

What seems to be happening is that—especially in the period of his concentrated greatness, 1897–1900, from *The Nigger* to *Lord Jim*—Conrad makes "mistakes" by failing to perform the kind of "screening" that is performed more or less effortlessly by native speakers. He fails to censor inappropriate or excessively revealing connotations, with the result that his language purchases its extraordinary indeterminacy, resonance, and evocativeness at the cost of a certain bluntness that blooms in the secondary or tertiary levels. Not only a confession of desire, this candor also signals a certain instability of gender identity. Most heterosexual adult native speakers manage their utterances to accord with their established genders; keenly sensitive to unruly nuance, they repress heavy prods and dirty dicks with the same unconscious efficiency with which they repress the homosexual affect itself. People inhabit their gender identities in the same way that they inhabit their linguistic identities: fissures in the linguistic crust can permit an uprush of affective lava, and suppressed gender identifications will seek out such fissures, including not only puns and homonyms, but cognate forms, connotations, oxymorons, associations of all kinds. Conrad's writing demonstrates this in countless richly varied ways, and leads to the general conclusion that the more linguistic resources one has at one's disposal, the more meanings are *not* "at one's disposal." The more masterful one's command of language and languages, the more one's meaning becomes unmasterable, subject to mistakes and subversive implications that escape the psycholinguistic vigilance that accompanies and enforces a normative heterosexual identity. (By the same logic, Kurtz is both "above" the Africans who worship him and "below" them, degraded in a way they are not.) This universal truth has recently been rediscovered by another Eastern émigré living in the West, Kristeva, who argues that the most highly evolved use of language, poetry or literature in general, is also the most primitive, the most intimate with the rhythms and musicality of the semiotic, the most closely associated with "drives." Literature advances, or undergoes a "revolution," not through the discovery of some new principle, but through "an irruption of the drives" that returns language to a "natural" state. "What remodels the symbolic order," she writes, "is always the influx of the semiotic" (113). English (she does not add) is, because of its mixed genealogy, its inexplicable toleration of foreign anarchists in its midst, predisposed to such a transgression of the "phallic" order of the signifier, predisposed to revolution. This is what Conrad—who was both "English" and a "foreign anarchist"—makes us see.

Not that all who see know what, or even that, they see. One of the most intriguing features of Conrad criticism is the recurrence of the invisible homoerotic trope. Albert Guerard, for example, describes—in the course of a general defense of Conrad's way of leaving Kurtz's unspeakable secrets unspoken—the movement of *Heart of Darkness* as a "groping, fumbling" process of "penetration and withdrawal"—and then again as "the tracing of a large grand circle of awareness" that includes Marlow and his mates, as well as the Romans, all "men enough to face this darkness" (42, 44, 44, 45). When Guerard says that Marlow meets Kurtz "in the flesh, and wrestles with his reluctance to leave," one can glimpse a deeper and unspoken affinity between author and critic on the altogether tacit ground of a fascination with the abomination, with "unspeakable lusts" and "the dark places of the earth." To take a more recent and complex instance, consider Terry Eagleton's account of literary value in *Marxism and Literary Criticism*. Seeking to place value on a more secure conceptual footing than a traditional critical impressionism had been able to provide, Eagleton points to the famous, extended scene in *Nostromo* where Nostromo and Decoud find themselves together at night on a lighter in the Golfo Placido. The scene is "artistically fine," Eagleton argues, because Conrad's "ideological perspective" and his sense of individuals as "impenetrable and solitary," gave him unique access to the "crisis in the ideology of the Western bourgeois class" and in the "history of imperialist capitalism" (8, 8, 7, 7, 8). Conrad may have felt this way about capitalism, but to focus on the political and economic skirts a more immediately pertinent source of pessimism in the buried awareness that men, especially when alone together in the dark, were indeed "penetrable," if it were not for social and ethical strictures, the organization of society, the necessity of the species to reproduce itself—and, perhaps, at a stretch, imperialist capitalism. What Eagleton registers as "artistic" quality is not Conrad's deep macroeconomic insight, but rather the effective sublimation of the impulse to penetrate, the finessing of the question of "the embrace."

Conrad does not qualify as an early "modern" investigator of the underside of the psyche merely because his work explores obscure motivations or guilt feelings. His real contribution in this arena comes from the way in which his texts display slippages and irruptions of meaning that plainly elude his conscious control and thus demonstrate the imperfectly effective operations of "repression." I would insist on this elementary point in response to those who would see a pattern of double entendres as a triumphantly evasive declaration of sexual, especially homosexual, energy in the face of some external censoring agency, the construction of an "open secret," as D. A. Miller puts it. As Miller and Eve Kosofsky Sedgwick use the concept of the secret, the emphasis falls on the discrepancy between the all but universally acknowledged truth of desire and the still-necessary prohibition against disclosure. The stress falls, in other words, on a truth known but denied, and the political or polemical thrust of their (very different) arguments derives from the injustice and incoherence attendant upon this denial. By contrast, nothing good can come of the example of Conrad, who was surely oblivious to the systematic intimations of the homosexual embrace legible in his work. Conrad speaks not as the victim of hypocrisy and prejudice but as a man who feels himself to be free, albeit a man whose only access to his desire is linguistic and figural. His case, in other words, is more pathetic than progressive.

I would urge this argument as a kind of appendix to the argument of Wayne Koestenbaum, who claims, with respect to male-male collaborations in the early modern era, that "double writing" represents a "metaphorical sexual intercourse" (3). In his brief discussion of *Romance,* one of Conrad and Ford's joint ventures, Koestenbaum tracks a number of instances of such words as "queer," "gay," and "fagot," in order to argue that the collaboration itself invested simple words with multiple meanings whose erotic import "can never be justified and that sustain a dreamy half-life, impossible to dismiss and impossible to prove" (173). Koestenbaum's argument seems to me indisputable as far as it goes, but for the true lineaments of the Conradian phenomenon to be apprehended, it must be widened. Conrad did not need Ford to experience the erotic possibilities of polysemy. In fact, his collaborative efforts are duller, smaller, more conventional works than his greatest individual efforts because, one might infer, collaboration untangled the involutions of his language and enabled a somewhat more straightforward or frontal approach to desire. Donkin does not whisper, "I like you, James Wait"; nor does Leggatt, as he prepares to scramble over the railing, kiss the young captain "lightly on the cheek"; nor does Nostromo report that Decoud's handshake "thrilled me like a woman's." The occurrence of all these things in *Romance* is just one index of that work's mediocrity, and their absence in those other, far greater and more interesting works is one key to their resonant capaciousness, their "universality." In Conrad's greatest works, sexuality is expressed on the condition that it is not expressed, not expressed *as such.*

It is essential to the interior structure of the homoerotic in Conrad that the author does not fully realize what kind of identifications he is representing, much less experiencing himself. Within Conrad's work, sexuality is "chastened" by being sublated—canceled, preserved, and transcended—and rerouted both into stylistic deformations and into the thematics of solidarity, tests of fortitude, law and anarchy, colonial activity, explorations of dark places, the encounter with a "double," and unspeakable mysteries shared among men who are functionally asexual. The apparent issue in many of Conrad's works is indicated by Singleton's challenge to the crew: "What do you know?" What one knows, what one believes, what one learns—these are, in many texts and in a great deal of the criticism of those texts, the key questions. But the question of knowledge is just the beginning. Especially in the very greatest works—*The Nigger, Heart of Darkness, Lord Jim,* and *The Secret Agent*—the pivot of the plot is a moment when, as the narrator of *The Nigger* says, "all our certitudes were going" (26). The agent of the dissolution of knowledge, I am arguing, is unconscious sexual desire—What do you want?—with its cognate question of gender identity—Who are you? With respect to sex and gender in Conrad, the status of "knowledge" is far from simple, for what is "known" is, for the most part, presumptively heterosexual male self-sufficiency, but what is "done" by both author and characters is unacknowledged homoerotic male desire. Homosexuality is done but not known, while heterosexuality is known but not done.

In a "Conradian" account, desire and gender identity are always at odds with knowledge. Such an account is itself at odds with the understandings prevalent among gender theoreticians today, who often approach a Conradian position only to veer away from it in the end, perhaps because it is too dark altogether. In *Gender Trouble: Feminism and the Subversion of Identity,* Judith Butler notes that, within the discourse of that combination of misogyny and homophobia she calls "compulsory heterosexuality," a need for coherent and discrete gender identities dictates the steady repression of a primary libidinal disposition, an original bisexuality/homosexuality, which it renders not just unacceptable but incoherent. As Butler puts it in virtually Conradian terms, homosexuality is made "unthinkable" and "unsayable," a concrete cultural possibility that is refused and redescribed as impossible. Bisexuality/homosexuality is, then, both produced and negated, defended and defended against; and any possible "subversion of identity" coming from that quarter is foreclosed, becoming no more than a "futile gesture, entertained only in a derealized aesthetic mode which can never be translated into other cultural practices" (78).

From this influential account, which is still basically consistent with the "unthinkability" of homosexuality represented in Conrad, two possibilities emerge. In the first, "indirect" or "negative" alternative, homosexuality is victimized by paranoid misprision, but because the dominant view of homosexuality is so manifestly wrong, it is left essentially unaffected, untouched, untroubled. Diana Fuss, quoting Butler for support, takes this position: "heterosexuality secures its identity by at once disavowing and perpetually calling attention to its abject, interiorized, and ghostly other, homosexuality"; and "heterosexuality is profoundly unstable, tenuous, and precarious, and must therefore be continually reinforced and resecured" by marking its own contrasts to homosexuality (732, 734). To describe the heterosexist view of homosexuality as defensive propaganda is implicitly to secure a negative but defiantly stable and "normal" homosexual identity as that which is *not* the weird hetero phantasm. The homosexual knows oneself without reference to any particular acts one may have performed. Butler herself, however, takes her story to a different denouement by moving, in her concluding chapter, "From Parody to Politics." If gender identity consists of a pattern of imitations, selections from an inventory of culturally coded gestures, then gender is structurally vulnerable to parody. Indeed, it is nothing other than parody, a function of gesture, imitation, and performance, a "*stylized repetition of acts*"; and parodic gestures, meeting no resistance from a biologically determined identity, can be proliferated to the point where new configurations of political agency will emerge to displace the very norms that make gender so oppressively intelligible in the first place (140). These new configurations will renounce any claim to determining a truth of homosexuality, devoting itself instead to outlining a performative carnivalization in which the problem of knowing who one is will be resolved by action—in which, that is, knowing is determined by doing. Homosexual identity will be secured by positive opportunities for agency and self-determination, and "knowing" as such will simply disappear as a problem.

Both Butler and Fuss have, to be sure, a certain power to illuminate Conrad's fictive productions, which, with their "ghostly, abject,

interiorized" Others, their imponderable mysteries, sordid transgressions, and unspeakable lusts, seem devoted to representing "the unsayable" in general, reinscribing in ever more luridly alienated forms
what Butler might call the unthinkability of gender that lies darkly at
the heart of identity itself. All the blurs, mists, smudges, fogs, or
storms in Conrad could be explained as symptoms of a disturbance
Conrad was unwilling or unable to confront directly. But Conrad's
fictions reciprocally illuminate, or perhaps darken, contemporary
gender theory as well, for the emphasis in both Fuss and Butler falls
ultimately on a utopian overcoming of the split between knowledge
and action. Either one knows who one is (Fuss), or one does who one
is (Butler). In both cases, the problem vanishes. In Conrad, however,
knowing and doing are never coincident, and desire and gender identity, the primordial forms of this noncoincidence, are always trouble.

The terms with which I have been wrestling, "doing" and "knowing," are taken from a sentence in Marx's *Capital*: "they do not know
it, but they are doing it." Appropriated by Žižek, this sentence has
been given a second life in contemporary theory as a definition of
ideology, or what he calls the "social symptom": "*a social reality whose
very existence implies the non-knowledge of its participants as to its essence*" (*SOI* 21). Against those who claim that we now inhabit a "post-
ideological" world of unified surfaces, Žižek insists on the Lacanian
account of the subject as essentially divided or fissured, constituted
by an unconscious that, when transposed into social terms, becomes
ideological. Especially as represented in Conrad, the sex-gender complex might be considered a "psychosocial symptom" in these terms,
disturbing the surface of "knowledge." The further point, however, is
that the energies that cannot be reduced to knowledge, that trouble
knowledge, that lie outside of knowledge also function as exemplary
objects of knowledge; they are what knowledge is ostensibly about,
what knowing wants to know. Only when knowledge is about something other than its own operations is it persuaded of its objectivity,
its grip on the "external" world. The same is true of gender "performance." The term "performance" suggests a certain emptiness, an
absence of deep determination, in the act, and also a perfect concen-
tration in the moment, an eager desire "to make you see," and
an indifference to what cannot be seen. Both suggestions presume the

character of freedom. But nobody performs a gender identity "freely." If a gender performance is not felt to represent a libidinal predisposition, it is not performed at all, or at least the performance has a decidedly limited run. To stress, as Butler does, the decision to perform, the selection of certain gestures, the plotting of strategy, constitutes a repression of dispositional necessity that flattens out and simplifies identity by eliminating the factor of the unconscious, the factor of the fissure. To see gender as cognate with ideology, as something that people do without knowing, is, on the other hand, to posit a structure of "Conradian" complexity, in which a force of repression intervenes between knowing and doing.

It is, I hope, apparent that I am not suggesting that Conrad's various thematic concerns can all be reduced to the status of mere covers for sexual drive. Rather, I claim that a fugitive sexual energy, clustering in the fissures between primary and secondary meanings, provides Conrad's work with a personal urgency that it would not otherwise have, and gains, itself, in gravitas by being confused with public and political themes that seem remote from it. It is not the flickering and uncertain presence of sexuality as such that marks Conrad's work, but the partial exposure of a larger field of the repressed or transgressive in general that gives his work at its best its distinctive quality. Sexuality, homosexuality in particular—the uncongenial form of the uncongenial subject—stands as a fair representative of this larger field. The force of sexuality and sexual identity not only disturbs the surface of Conrad's work, giving it a hallucinatory intensity, but also widens its significance and appeal. Neither meditations on "Man," nor the use of the "quest motif," nor themes of heroism, self-knowledge, or a descent to the underworld, nor settings in distant lands fully account for the "universality" of Conrad's work. It is rather the undefined and therefore unrestricted desire that underwrites, even as it undermines, these public and sanctioned themes that accounts for the sense of magnitude, of expansiveness, of general human significance that readers continue to discover. It is the unacknowledged, unthematized, and almost invisible combination of desire and fidelity, sex and solidarity, that has earned for Conrad's work an honored place in the canon not just of British but of world literature.

ON GREATNESS

> For an intellectual product of any value to exert an immediate in-
> fluence which shall also be deep and lasting, it must rest on an inner
> harmony, yes, an affinity, between the personal destiny of its author
> and that of his contemporaries in general. Men do not know why
> they award fame to one work of art rather than another.... the real
> ground of their applause is inexplicable—it is sympathy.
>
> —Thomas Mann, *Death in Venice*

Conrad is a writer about whom it is remarkably easy to be pious
or reverential. His accomplishments have an impressive weight and
magnitude. He virtually invented, for example, the idea of a placeless
"universality" as an aim of literary representation. His heroes explore
not drawing-rooms, salons, villages, cities, palaces, even nations, but
a "deeper region of the mind." They embark, as his critics say, on "a
spiritual voyage of self-discovery," a heroic "quest," a "night journey
into the unconscious," an "initiation into the primitive sources of
being." Conrad liberated literature from naturalism and realism,
and wrote, with an ambition unmatched by his contemporaries, of
"Man." After Conrad, Western literature begins to think of itself as
deracinated, as properly belonging not to a national tradition but to
a more comprehensively conceived human community that can best
be represented by the exile or émigré. While James introduced into
the novel the "international theme," he never imagined a non-
national or acultural kind of human being. Conrad did. When Stephen Daedalus went forth to forge the uncreated conscience of his
race, he was thinking of Ireland as an instance, not as the race itself,
and was following in Conrad's footsteps. When another large-minded
émigré, T. S. Eliot, wanted to announce his ambition to represent a
general crisis of Western culture in *The Waste Land,* he thought of
using a Conradian epigraph: "The horror! the horror!" (Pound rejected it, arguing that Conrad wasn't "weighty" enough.) Conrad enlarged the scene of Western literature immensely, first through his
Malay novels, but more tellingly through his "discovery" of Africa,
which predated by several years the fateful and decisive encounter
with African masks by Vlaminck, Derain, Picasso, and Matisse. He
enlarged that scene almost infinitely through his imagination of the
sea, which made it, for the first time really, big—not just a big stage

for an ego or a voyage, but big in itself. The esteem in which his work is held reflects, then, the expansiveness of his imagination, his willingness to think as a human being rather than as a citizen of some nation, a resident of some place. Even his technical innovations testify to an extraordinary spaciousness of conception. Unconstrained by parochial traditions, habits, or values, Conrad, it has been argued, was free to explore the technical resources of fiction, and succeeded in pushing back the frontiers of literature itself by developing the broken time line, the use of multiple narrators and points of view, the nesting of narration within narration, the use of irony.

So capacious is his craft that there is a Conrad for all seasons—an earnest moralist, a stylist, a critic of the West, a representative of the West, an explorer of the dark side, a modernist, a postmodernist, a structuralist, a poststructuralist, a deconstructionist, a psychoanalyst, an anarchist, a popular entertainer, a Tory, an antifeminist, an existentialist. There is a Conrad of the nineteenth century, the twentieth, and, if the present work has any influence, the twenty-first. One might think, then, that his stature in the canon would be guaranteed, because he would always have defenders no matter what the prevailing critical fashion. That is probably true, but the curious thing about Conrad's reputation is that, while his importance, his greatness, is invariably conceded, it is just as invariably contested. "His place," Jameson writes, "is still unstable, undecidable, and his work unclassifiable, spilling out of high literature into light reading and romance, reclaiming great areas of diversion and distraction by the most demanding practice of style and *écriture* alike, floating uncertainly somewhere in between Proust and Robert Louis Stevenson" (206). To an extraordinary degree, Conrad criticism has been obsessed with the issue of evaluation; also to an extraordinary degree, the question of quality remains unsettled. No other author of comparable stature is the subject of such a compulsive evaluating energy, or of such wildly divergent evaluations.

Of no other author whose position is comparably secure can it be said that so much of his or her work is considered unworthy. Even Conrad's most zealous proponents, those convinced that he belongs with the immortals, are persuaded that, at some point, Conrad lapses into the tasteless, the slack, the disheveled, the inept, the frankly execrable. Leavis begins his pathbreaking discussion of Conrad in *The Great Tradition* by conceding that the proposition "that Conrad has done classical work is as certain as that his classical status will not rest evenly upon his whole *oeuvre*. . . . He has, of course, long been generally held to be among the English masters," but "the greatness attributed to him tended to be identified with an imputed profundity, and . . . this 'profundity' was not what it was taken to be, but quite other, and the reverse of a strength" (173). Leavis regards Conrad as one of cornerstones of the English novel, but thinks highly only of *Nostromo* and *The Secret Agent*. Much of his discussion is concerned to debunk such supposed masterworks such as *Heart of Darkness*, which offends for its "adjectival and worse than supererogatory insistence," for the "cheap insistence" on "glamour," for "a certain simplicity of outlook and attitude," and for the way in which unfortunate mannerisms tend to "cheapen the tone" (179, 189, 183, 179). Said, too, rejects the doxa of the syllabus, preferring *Nostromo* to *Heart of Darkness*, and complaining about the distractions presented by Marlow's narration in the latter, its "breathless insistence, its ill-timed jocularity" (128).

Between the Conrad that everybody should be required to read and the Conrad that nobody should be required to read there is, by consensus, a vast gulf, but where, exactly, is this gulf? Does it lie between phases of his career (a period of apprenticeship followed by one of achievement, and then by "decline"), between individual books, or within texts themselves? Nothing, it seems, is above suspicion, not even *Heart of Darkness*. There does seem to be a consensus that *The Nigger of the "Narcissus," "The Secret Sharer," Heart of Darkness, Nostromo,* and *Lord Jim* stand on one side of the great divide, and *An Arrow of Gold, The Rover,* and *An Outcast of the Islands,* on the other. But this leaves such works as *The Secret Agent, Typhoon,* "Youth," *Under Western Eyes,* and *Victory* in limbo. Debates often consist of competing declamations, of a passionate exchange of terms of praise and condemnation, as when Frederick Karl asserts that *Victory* is "one of Conrad's greatest achievements ("V" 23)," and Cedric Watts responds that the book is, on the contrary, "cumbrously heavy-handedly, and at times ludicrously allegoric . . . [containing] appallingly bad passages of dialogue" (76, 78).

Most typically, such debates occur intracritically, within a single text. One of Conrad's first American champions, Guerard found in the last novels "a sad, tired resignation," "an indifference bred of fatigue," "failing syntax and diction" (293). He thought *Nostromo* "without question Conrad's greatest creative achievement," "the central novel of Conrad's career," one of the finest novels in the language—but found the last half, some three hundred pages, much inferior to the first, and had serious objections even to that (176, 210). In this undoubted masterpiece, Guerard discovered "an indifference to technique," a "refusal to commit himself," evidence of blundering, awkwardness, evasiveness (207, 208). "From beginning to end," he concluded, *Nostromo* "exposes more clearly (or fails to conceal through rhetoric and narrative device) what Conrad could not yet do well: above all, the handling of dramatic action and the rendering of intense emotion" (216). These are large qualifications, and gross deficiencies to discover in one of the greatest novels in the language. And yet, in the context of Conrad criticism, they are more representative than one might think possible. No critic, it seems, can rest with an unqualified judgment: to praise Conrad is to commit oneself to criticizing him, as if Conrad attracted to himself both poles of judgment, as if only he could provide the comparison by which he could be either praised or condemned. The result has been a certain quivering or trembling quality in Conrad's reputation that reflects an unease about the placement and integrity of the boundary that separates greatness from mediocrity. But a century after Conrad began to write, we might now consider a fresh possibility, that Conrad's singular stature, unlike that of most writers, is based not on a careful discrimination between the pure and the corrupt, the sublime and the vulgar, the achievement of a remarkable goal and the failure to achieve a routine one—but on the strict impossibility of such a discrimination.

The dedicated reader of Conrad criticism must be struck from time to time by the manifest unsuitability of Conrad for the versions of the canon in which he is positioned. Leavis enlists him—ahead of Dickens, Hardy, and Lawrence—in a nativist tradition predicated on concreteness of presentation and moral certainty, a tradition which, according to one school of thought, Conrad not merely opposed but destroyed. Ian Watt discusses Conrad as a participant in a cosmopolitan climate of cultural and philosophical thought, a technical wizard, and a proponent of a traditional and largely unproblematic morality. For Marlow, Watt says, "the issue is clear. Marlow must determine whether wilderness and darkness have an invincible power over man's moral being" (*CNC* 232). Indeed, everywhere Watt looks in Conrad, the issue is clear. The "total disconnection in Kurtz between words and reality reflects a general tendency in Western culture"; the "lie" Marlow tells the Intended is to be placed in the context of a nineteenth-century philosophical meditation on lying; Kurtz is "a symbol for the faithless and inner emptiness of the modern world in general"; *Lord Jim* is directly comparable to the epic of Gilgamesh; and Conrad's work generally can be thoroughly explained by reference to its "universal themes," and emphatically without recourse to the unconscious (*CNC* 235, 234). But if all this is so, then much of Conrad becomes simply a perverse distraction from the main point. Correlatively, we could say that Watt's dedication to what he calls "the literal imagination" in the case of a writer whose characteristic effects so extravagantly exceed the literal seems almost perverse of Watt himself (*CNC* x). In a larger sense, it is at least curious that Watt should argue so strongly for the canonical stature of a writer with whom he seems to be radically out of synch. But it is precisely at this point that Watt is most exemplary, serving as a kind of spokesman for those critics who cherish commitments and interests Conrad did not, but who seem nevertheless compelled to regard him as one of the greatest of authors.

Even more interesting than the compulsive disrespect shown to Conrad by his most ardent advocates is the equally compulsive admiration begrudged him by his detractors. Jameson's interest has a distinctively Marlovian cast, a fascination with the abomination. Rescuing from *Lord Jim* and *Nostromo* the shadow-image of larger political and historical processes, Jameson recognizes that Conrad's tastes, values, convictions, and apparent intentions run in precisely the opposite direction from his own, tending to celebratory tales of heroic individuals confronting tests of character. Jameson understands, that is, that the discrepancy between his own methodology and Conrad's texts risks a double shattering in which the texts are destroyed and criticism is rendered useless by its refusal to take the novels on their own organizational terms (243). And yet, Jameson finds much to respect in Conrad, according him more attention than any other writer, and honoring him as the one crucial literary figure in the mighty world process by which "the political" finally becomes "unconscious." Even Pound, whose political orientation was rather different from Jameson's, gave ground when Eliot protested that "The horror! the horror!" was the best thing he could find: "Do as you like about Conrad," Pound said; "who am I to grudge him his laurel crown?" (qtd. in Eliot 125).

The fiercest attacks, and most grudging concessions, have come from those offended by racism and misogyny. I have already referred to Chinua Achebe's 1975 assault on Conrad as a "bloody racist," a brief essay that has enjoyed a great prominence, largely because it is a rare instance of the empire writing back, refusing the names and attributes stapled to it by a colonizing West. Achebe accuses Conrad of bad faith, vulgar prejudice, xenophobia, complicity in a massive system of cruelty, "preposterous and perverse arrogance," and even liberalism ("IOA" 257). Achebe sidesteps the questions of what Conrad *ought* to have said, of what impressions the Congo *must* have made on the mind of anyone of Conrad's background, or of whether *any* person can encounter people so utterly unlike oneself and consider them—as Achebe suggests—as "quite simply . . . a continent of people—not angels, but not rudimentary souls either—just people" (261). Achebe implies that Conrad should have embraced Africans as brothers, that Marlow should have described his cannibal helmsman as one of us, that the differences between Europe and Africa should have been registered as differences without distinctions, that a better book would have been titled *Heart of Grayness.*

But would a novel composed on such principles, a novel about "just people," have the resonance, the energy, or the stature of the book Conrad actually wrote? Does Achebe really believe that that stature can be called into question on the grounds that the book proves its author to be a racist? He certainly seems to, raising the issue of "whether a novel which celebrates this dehumanization, which depersonalizes a portion of the human race, can be called a great work of art." His answer: "No, it cannot." In the first publication of this lecture, Achebe followed this judgment with a personal denunciation of Conrad (see Hamner 125). I have already, in the first chapter, indicated my own dissent from this account. But my dissent interests me less and is less significant than Achebe's own reservations, which became manifest when he edited his essay for a 1988 critical edition of *Heart of Darkness*. In the old version, he compared Conrad to a slave trader, a doctor who poisons his patients, and Nazis; in the new version, Achebe took a different approach: "I do not doubt Conrad's great talents," he wrote; "Even *Heart of Darkness* has its memorably good passages and moments. . . . Its exploration of the minds of the European characters is often penetrating and full of insight. But all that has been more than fully discussed in the last fifty years" ("IOA" 257–58). Intended as empty compliments, these words are both revealing and provocative. What, we might ask, does Achebe mean by "good," "penetrating," "full of insight"? Are these "aesthetic" virtues only, which leave the ethical and human questions he has raised untouched? Or has Achebe stumbled on an uncomfortable—or as Conrad would say, "on komm for tarble"—truth in the intervening eighteen years between the first and final versions of his essay, years in which "difference" has become the most prominent term in the critical discourse of postcolonial literature? Has he tacitly renounced his original belief in "just people" as an illusion of the bourgeois West; does he now hold that differences intervene, and structure all apprehension of the Other? Has he learned to appreciate Conrad's intense registration of this fact as a function of "penetrating insight" rather than of perversity and racist arrogance? Has he, in short, come at last to agree wholeheartedly with his own assessment, included even in the earliest version of his essay, that Conrad is "undoubtedly one of the great stylists of modern fiction and a good storyteller into the bargain," and that "his contribution therefore falls automatically into [the class of] permanent literature" ("IOA" 252)?

The fact that Achebe begins his essay with this judgment indicates not just an unresolved conflict between ethics and aesthetics, but something much more profound, a glimmering intuition that what he admires in Conrad might finally be indistinguishable from what he condemns, that the very presentation that strikes him as preposterous and racist at one moment impresses him as "penetrating" and "insightful" at another. The greatness of a work—Achebe all but understands—is largely a function of its ability to solicit such divergent responses or readings, and still to appear to possess "unity" or "wholeness." One of the mysteries of art is how a mass of conflicting textual energies and readerly responses can acquire an aesthetic unity by huddling together under the cover of such terms as "style" and "storytelling." "Permanence" in literature may well be a function first of the strength and interest of a work's ideological, ethical, or political contradictions, and second of how well those contradictions reconcile themselves, in the eyes of beholders, to coexistence under the formal rule of "style." The practice of condemning an artist as a human being but reserving admiration and respect for his art suggests that there is a partial disconnect between aesthetic and nonaesthetic dimensions of a work, a difference that sometimes registers as a distinction and sometimes doesn't. In one mood, Achebe can condemn the man and the work in a single gesture, but in another, he cannot; the art stands on its own. Neither mood dominates: Achebe's original recognition of Conrad's artistic greatness returns to trouble his conviction of Conrad's moral unworthiness, which itself returns to disturb his recognition of Conrad's artistic greatness.

Nowhere is this dilemma experienced more sharply than in the case of feminist criticism, which generally approaches Conrad as a monolith of the patriarchy and its associated institutions of dominance. In a provocative article, Nina Pelikan Straus charges Conrad with "complicity in the racist, sexist, imperialist . . . world he has inhabited with Kurtz" (135). Treating *Heart of Darkness* as "a kind of mainstream male experience associated with traditional Western high art"—the "penetration into a female wilderness, confrontation with monstrosity, male rites of passage"—Straus suggests that the stature accorded the novel reflects a "narcissistic identification" that is portrayed in the text between Marlow and Kurtz, and repeated in the (presumptively male) critic's appreciation of Conrad's accomplishment (123). *Heart of Darkness*, she contends, is structured to confirm, in a specifically male setting, a kind of critical heroism marked by affirmations of identity and solidarity between critic and Marlow or Conrad, affirmations modeled on the Marlow-Kurtz coupling. The necessary response to the masculine domination of the fictive and critical scenes is, Straus says, for women "to recognize that in *Heart of Darkness* women are used to deny, distort, and censor men's passionate love for one another." And not only this text: "high art" in

general must be seen as "in some way a confirmation of the one gender's access to certain secrets (in this case the secret conjunction of art
and horror)" (134). What must above all be resisted, she concludes, is
"the ongoing critical insistence that this work is in some way moral.
Art is not moral. High art may be especially immoral. Its province is
pleasure," especially the pleasure of the self-mystifying, gynophobic
male, against whom feminist criticism can only seek to generate "new
artistic conventions which are able to serve both art *and* truth" (135).

Straus is silent on the configuration of these new conventions, but
the limits of optimism have been set very low in her severe character-
ization of "art" as being opposed to "truth" and "justice." Unresolved
is the question of how, given the status of "art" as immoral and untrue, the new, progressive conventions will still be "artistic," or, for
that matter, how they will become "conventions" at all. Mercilessly
particular in her analysis of Conrad and his readers, Straus seems at
the end powerless to imagine a way to overcome a certain obduracy,
a sullen resistance to reformation or enlightenment in "art" itself, an
entrenched affinity between the aesthetic and the ethical-ideological
dark places of the earth. Allied, for Straus, to injustice and misrepre-
sentation, high art, and Conrad's in particular, yet provides a critical
purchase on the self-mystifying and self-amplifying machinations of
patriarchal culture by the way in which it compulsively represents an
"other," unmastered set of forces, which it is powerless either to eliminate or accommodate. Having reached this conclusion, however, she
encounters Achebe's question: what is the stature of Conrad's art?

"Does *Heart of Darkness* become less authentic," she asks at the
very end, "when it is recognized that it is less the comprehensive human Id that is disclosed than a certain kind of male self-mystification
. . . ?" It is a bold question, but one she cannot bring herself to answer,
even though her entire argument seems to be designed as evidence
for a resounding and unequivocal "Yes." (Or is it? Is she suggesting
that it is possible to disclose a "comprehensive human Id," something
analogous to Achebe's universal "people"? Given patriarchy, wouldn't
an "authentic" masterwork have to represent male self-mystification?
Would a female self-mystification be preferable?) What is impressive
and troubling about Straus's inability to answer her own question is

that she, like Achebe, rejects certain traditional grounds for Conrad's stature but cannot bring herself to reject the stature itself.

Why not? Why does Conrad seem to be the Man of the Canon, when his work seems to attract every kind of criticism? Is it possible that the vulnerability of his work—its all too obvious flaws, its manifest unevenness, the dubiousness of its "views"—actually contributes to his reputation as a master of the language, a master storyteller? Is it possible that the very act of according a work high praise entails, as a dialectical counterbalance, a certain revulsion? Is it possible that what is perceived as greatness, the quality Eagleton calls "artistic fineness," consists in part of a recognition of precisely those values or attitudes that the culture defines itself by repudiating? Is it possible—to put the question more sharply—that one can only accord one's highest praise to an author whom one finds in some ways repellent, unworthy, incompetent, defective?

It is often suggested that a writer's greatness is independent of his or her unworthy prejudices or deplorable opinions, that literary achievement is a different kind of thing from personal virtue. Jameson rejects such a notion as a mark of a naïve liberalism that distinguishes between the primary or authentic artistic work and the contingent details of one's political convictions. A decidedly nonliberal response to the problem represented by the scoundrel genius would affirm that greatness is *in*separable from certain kinds of reprehensibility. A glance at the canon does not disconfirm this hypothesis. Dickens is (found by many to be) sentimental and cheap, George Eliot depressingly high-minded, Hardy clumsy and provincial, Wilde indifferent to suffering other than his own, Joyce inhuman and elitist, Woolf snobbish, D. H. Lawrence obsessed with the phallus, T. S. Eliot cold and academic, Pound bigoted—to name a few. But couldn't one name them all? Can one imagine a figure of canonical stature—other than, perhaps, Jane Austen and the immensely tantalizing figure of Shakespeare—whose work does not suggest to some the mind of a bounder, a boor, an egocentric, a domestic bully, an ingrate, a sexist, a hectoring puritan, a shrew, a fraud? Isn't this element of reprehensibility what E. M. Forster, for example, is missing, and why his reputation never breaks the surface of true greatness? Isn't the problem that, with his sympathetic attention to women, to the socially and economically stressed, and to India, Forster is simply *too enlightened* to engage the darker regions of the cultural psyche, and his appeal suffers as a consequence from a certain shallowness? Isn't—to take the case of Shakespeare—the picturesque image of the immensely prolific playwright-actor living and working among gifted and well-compensated people so unsuited to the company of the canon that many believe the man from Stratford could not have written those plays? Isn't this image also responsible, for those who believe in his authorship, for the singular position he holds not exactly *in* but *atop* the canon? As a man, Shakespeare may be surcanonical, but his work is canonical because, in addition to such happy writerly virtues as intellectual acuity, verbal accomplishment, and fertility of invention, it displays an immense range of imaginative sympathy that extends from the virtuous and heroic all the way down to evil, despair, perversion, impotence, waste, cowardice, misogyny, and anti-Semitism.

As a canonical figure—*the* canonical figure—Conrad exemplifies the unsorted mix of attributes, the ambivalence proper to our notion of eminence. Modern, western culture does not revere those who write solely from within the culture, reproducing only narcissistic images of its best moments or most admirable traits. In *Exiles and Emigrés*, Eagleton points out that, at least in terms of the English canon, the weightiest writers are socially marginal people when they are not actually foreigners like Conrad. In British literary modernity, those who, like Bennett, Galsworthy, or Wells, take an identifiably English point of view on life in England follow the very recipe for minor literature. The perspective provided by the outsider has this advantage, that it not only confirms the centrality of one's own culture as an object worthy of attention, but also gratifies a distinctively modern appetite for self-criticism by calling the legitimacy or normativity of the culture's prevailing customs and attitudes into question. This fairly obvious and conventional point actually entails another, far more problematic one—that the dominant culture of modernity is eagerly receptive to representations of the transgressive or disavowed impulses it has supposedly overcome. Literature is the site of this return of modernity's repressed, and one of the common threads running through canonical literature is an invitation to identify with that which has been stigmatized as morally or socially unacceptable. Jameson takes this point to an extreme, declaring that "all the works of class history . . . have all had a vested interest in and a functional relationship to social formations based on violence and exploitation; and that . . . the restoration of the meaning of the greatest cultural monuments cannot be separated from a passionate and partisan assessment of everything that is oppressive in them and knows complicity with privilege and class domination, stained with the guilt not merely of culture in particular but of History itself as one long nightmare" (299). I would argue instead that "the greatest" monuments of modern culture expand, enlarge, or (better yet) widen the mind by soliciting a full and uncensored act of identification with both the forces of enlightenment and with those extremities of thought, feeling, and action that have been sacrificed to enlightenment. A strong equivocality in the image, one that permits a narcissistic identification and a mirroring inversion of narcissism, is a crucial component of "greatness" conceived in these terms.

*

There are two classic accounts of literature's essential function. In the first, literature disturbs or troubles us, awakening us from our customary slumbers, our moral complacency, our inertial and routinized habits of feeling and reflection. In the second, literature introduces us to new friends, extends our horizons, enriches our sensibility, and enables us to explore other worlds, other ways of life, other minds. How does literature, especially "great" literature, do both? How does it destabilize and enrich, disturb and consolidate; how can a single work seem subversive and classic? Conrad's work, I have argued, negotiates this problem in three ways: (1) by invoking the image of the nation, the political community, but doing so in a way that germinates an intuition of the arbitrariness of the national idea, the permeability of the bounded society; (2) by summoning up what might be a reassuring or "grounding" spectacle of nature, the precivil or prepolitical sea, but doing so in a way that discloses both nature's politicality and its destructiveness; and (3) by deploying language in a way that inspires pride and awe in the British reader at the resources of the English language and Conrad's mastery of it, but doing so in a way that also inspires doubt about Conrad's control of a host of unintended and manifestly unwanted meanings that the language itself seems to impose on him. In other respects, too, Conrad stands in the theoretically inconceivable position of occupying both sides of a contradiction, as between heterosexual and homosexual, realist and symbolist, popular adventure writer and master of modernist *écriture,* defender of authority and anarchist, a man whose imagination was crowded with images of impersonal centrality (the Mint, the Observatory, the mine, the metropolis) and of people being blown to bits. In the disorderly spectacle of Conrad, we can see the conditions and contradictions of literary greatness writ small.

It is ultimately the public apprehension of an otherness that is both *internal* and *common* that generates the "sympathy" that Thomas Mann (in an account of the career of the great artist and homosexual pedophile Gustave von Aschenbach) describes as the "real ground" of fame. Neither Conrad nor the idea of greatness is degraded by this truth. Instead, Conrad is rendered at once a more poignant, impressive, and even more representative figure. The canon he graces is altered, too, seen no longer as either transcendental or narrowly political, but rather as a massively collective production that yet reflects the deepest urgencies and anxieties of individual identity and desire.

WORKS CITED

Note: Abbreviations used in the text appear here in brackets following the author's name.

Achebe, Chinua. ["IA"] "An Image of Africa." Hamner 39–58. (Originally published, 1977.)

———. ["IOA"] "An Image of Africa: Racism in Conrad's *Heart of Darkness*." Conrad, *Heart of Darkness* 251–62.

———. [*MYCD*] *Morning Yet on Creation Day.* London: Heinemann, 1975.

Acton, John Emerich Edward Dalberg, Baron. *Selected Writings of Lord Acton.* Vol. 1 of *Essays in the History of Liberty.* Indianapolis: Liberty Classics, 1985.

Anderson, Benedict. [*IC*] *Imagined Communities: Reflections on the Origin and Spread of Nationalism.* London and New York: Verso, 1991. (Originally published, 1983.)

———. ["NN"] "Narrating the Nation." *Times Literary Supplement* 13 June 1986: 659.

Bailey, Richard W. *Images of English: A Cultural History of the Language.* Ann Arbor: University of Michigan Press, 1993.

Baines, Jocelyn. *Joseph Conrad: A Critical Biography.* London: Weidenfeld and Nicolson, 1960.

Bakunin, Mikhail. *Statism and Anarchy.* Trans. and ed. Marshall S. Shatz. Cambridge, UK: Cambridge University Press, 1990.

Berthoud, Jacques. Introduction. Conrad, *Almayer's Folly* xi–xxxix.

Bhabha, Homi K. ["DN"] "DissemiNation: Time, Narrative, and the Margins of the Modern Nation." Bhabha, *Nation and Narration* 291–322.

———. [*LC*] *The Location of Culture.* London and New York: Routledge, 1994.

———, ed. [*NN*] *Nation and Narration.* London and New York: Routledge, 1990.

Bradbury, Malcolm. *The Modern World: Ten Great Writers.* London: Secker & Warburg, 1988.

Brennan, Timothy. "The National Longing for Form." Bhabha, *Nation and Narration* 44–70.

Breuilly, John. *Nationalism and the State.* Manchester, UK: Manchester University Press, 1993.

Bryson, Bill. *Mother Tongue: English & How It Got That Way.* New York: William Morrow and Company, 1990.

Burgess, Anthony. *A Mouthful of Air: Language, Languages . . . Especially English.* New York: William Morrow and Company, 1992.

Butler, Judith. [*GT*] *Gender Trouble: Feminism and the Subversion of Identity.* New York and London: Routledge, 1990.

———. ["IGI"] "Imitation and Gender Insubordination." *Inside/Out: Lesbian Theories, Gay Theories.* Ed. Diana Fuss. New York and London: Routledge, 1991. 13–31.

Cave, Terence. *Recognitions: A Study in Poetics.* Oxford: Clarendon Press, 1988.

Cixous, Hélène. *Three Steps on the Ladder of Writing.* Trans. Sarah Cornell and Susan Sellers. New York: Columbia University Press, 1993.

Claiborne, Robert. *Our Marvelous Native Tongue: The Life and Times of the English Language.* New York: Times Books, 1983.

Connor, Walker. *Ethnonationalism: The Quest for Understanding.* Princeton: Princeton University Press, 1994.

Conrad, Joseph. [*AF*] *Almayer's Folly.* Ed. Jacques Berthoud. Oxford and New York: Oxford University Press, 1992.

———. "Amy Foster." Zabel 155–91.

———. ["AN"] "Author's Note to *Youth: A Narrative, and Two Other Stories.*" *Conrad's Prefaces to His Works.* New York: Haskell House Publishers, 1971. 71–74.

———. *Chance.* New York: Signet, 1992.

———. [*CL*] *Collected Letters* (see under Karl, Frederick R., ed.).

———. *Congo Diary and Other Uncollected Pieces.* Ed. Zdzisław Najder. Garden City, NY: Doubleday & Co., 1978.

———. ["GR"] "Gaspar Ruiz." Conrad, *A Set of Six* 3–72.

———. [*HD*] *Heart of Darkness.* 3d ed. Ed. Robert Kimbrough. New York and London: W. W. Norton and Company, 1988.

———. [*LJ*] *Lord Jim.* Ed. Thomas Moser. New York and London: W. W. Norton and Company, 1968.

———. [*MS*] *The Mirror of the Sea. The Mirror of the Sea and A Personal Record.* Ed. Zdzisław Najder. Oxford and New York: Oxford University Press, 1988.

———. [*NN*] *The Nigger of the "Narcissus."* Ed. Robert Kimbrough. New York: Norton, 1979.

———. [*N*] *Nostromo: A Tale of the Seaboard.* New York, Chicago, San Francisco: Holt, Rinehart and Winston, 1964.

———. [*NLL*] *Notes on Life and Letters.* Garden City, NY: Doubleday, Page & Co., 1926.

———. "An Outpost of Progress." *Tales of Unrest.* Harmondsworth: Penguin, 1987. 83–110.

———. *An Outcast of the Islands.* Ed. J. H. Stape and Hans Van Marle. Oxford and New York: Oxford University Press, 1992.

———. [*PR*] *A Personal Record. The Mirror of the Sea and A Personal Record.* Ed. Zdzisław Najder. Oxford and New York: Oxford University Press, 1988.

———. "Poland Revisited." Conrad, *Notes on Life and Letters* 141–73.

———. *The Portable Conrad.* Ed. Morton Dauwen Zabel. New York: Penguin, 1976.

———. ["*P*"] "Prince Roman." Conrad, *The Portable Conrad* 58–84.

———. ["*PC*"] "Proust as Creator." Conrad, *Congo Diary* 105–06.

———. [*R*] *The Rescue: A Romance of the Shallows.* Harmondsworth, UK: Penguin, n.d.

———. ["*SS*"] "The Secret Sharer." Conrad, *The Portable Conrad* 648–99.

———. [*SA*] *The Secret Agent: A Simple Tale.* Ed. Martin Seymour-Smith. London: Penguin, 1990.

———. [SS] *A Set of Six.* Garden City, NY: Doubleday, Page & Company, 1926.

———. *The Shadow-Line. A Confession.* Ed. Jeremy Hawthorn. Oxford and New York. Oxford University Press, 1992.

———. "To My Readers in America." Conrad, *The Nigger of the "Narcissus"* 167–68.

———. [*T*] *Typhoon.* Zabel 192–289.

———. [UWE] *Under Western Eyes.* London: Penguin, 1985.

———. [*V*] *Victory.* New York and London: Anchor Books, 1957.

———. "Well Done." Conrad, *Notes on Life and Letters* 179–93.

———. ["*Y*"] "Youth." Conrad, *The Portable Conrad* 115–54.

Coolidge, Olivia. *The Three Lives of Joseph Conrad.* Boston: Houghton Mifflin, 1972.

Culler, Jonathan, ed. *On Puns: The Foundation of Letters.* Oxford: Basil Blackwell, 1988.

Curle, Richard. *Conrad to a Friend.* Garden City, NY: Doubleday and Company, 1928.

Dabrowski, Marian. "An Interview with J. Conrad." Najder, *Conrad under Familial Eyes* 196–201.

Davies, Norman. *Heart of Europe: A Short History of Poland.* Oxford: Clarendon Press, 1984.

Debray, Regis. "Marxism and the National Question." *New Left Review* 105 (Sept.-Oct. 1977): 24–41.

DeKoven, Marianne. *Rich and Strange: Gender, History, Modernism.* Princeton: Princeton University Press, 1991.

Diamond, Larry, and Marc F. Plattner, eds. *Nationalism, Ethnic Conflict, and Democracy.* Baltimore, MD and London: The Johns Hopkins University Press, 1994.

Dvornik, Francis. *The Slavs in European History and Civilization.* New Brunswick, NJ: Rutgers University Press, 1962.

Eagleton, Terry. [*EE*] *Exiles and Emigrés: Studies in Modern Literature.* New York: Shocken Books, 1970.

———. [*MLC*] *Marxism and Literary Criticism.* Berkeley and Los Angeles: University of California Press, 1976.

Eliot, T. S. *The Waste Land: A Facsimile and Transcript of the Original Drafts Including the Annotations of Ezra Pound.* Ed. Valerie Eliot. New York: Harcourt Brace Jovanovich, Inc., 1971.

Fleishman, Avrom. *Conrad's Politics: Community and Anarchy in the Fiction of Joseph Conrad.* Baltimore, MD: The Johns Hopkins University Press, 1967.

Ford, Ford Madox. [*JC*] *Joseph Conrad: A Personal Remembrance.* New York: The Ecco Press, 1989.

———. [*PL*] *Portraits from Life.* Boston: Houghton Mifflin, 1937.

Forster, E. M. *Abinger Harvest.* New York: Harcourt Brace, 1964.

Freud, Sigmund. "Mourning and Melancholia." *General Psychological Theory: Papers on Metapsychology.* Ed. Philip Rieff. New York: Collier Books, 1963. 164–79.

Fried, Michael. "Almayer's Face: On 'Impressionism' in Conrad, Crane, and Norris." *Critical Inquiry* 17.1 (Autumn 1990): 193–236.

Fuss, Diana. "Fashion and the Homospectatorial Look." *Critical Inquiry* 18.4 (Summer 1992): 713–37.

Galef, David. "The Heart at the Edge of Darkness." *Journal of Modern Literature* 17.1 (Summer 1990): 117–38.

Galsworthy, John. "The Doldrums." *From the Four Winds.* Rpt. in *Forsytes, Pendyces and Others.* London: W. Heinemann, 1935.

Gellner, Ernest. *Nations and Nationalism.* Oxford: Oxford University Press, 1983.

Gombrowicz, Witold. "The Statue of Man upon the Statue of the World." Najder, *Conrad under Familial Eyes* 273–76.

Gomulicki, Wicktor. "A Pole or an Englishman?" Najder, *Conrad under Familial Eyes* 193–96.

Goonetilleke, D. C. R. A. "Conrad's Malayan Novels: Problems of Authenticity." Hamner 39–58.

Greenfield, Liah. *Nationalism: Five Roads to Modernity.* Cambridge, MA: Harvard University Press, 1992.

Greenblatt, Stephen. *Shakespearean Negotiations.* Berkeley and Los Angeles: University of California Press, 1988.

Greenslade, William. *Degeneration, Culture and the Novel.* Cambridge, UK: Cambridge University Press, 1994.

Greenwood, Dr. "Poetry and Mystery of the Sea." Quoted in Frank Goodrich. *The History of the Sea.* Philadelphia: Hubbard Bros., n.d. 27.

Guerard, Albert. *Conrad the Novelist.* Cambridge, Ma: Harvard University Press, 1958.

Hamner, Robert D., ed. *Joseph Conrad: Third World Perspectives.* Washington, DC: Three Continents Press, 1990.

Haugh, Robert F. "*Heart of Darkness:* Problem for Critics." Conrad, *Heart of Darkness* 239–42.

Hervouet, Jules. "Conrad and the French Language, Part One." *Conradiana* 11.3 (1979): 229–52.

———. "Conrad and the French Language, Part Two." *Conradiana* 14.1 (1982): 23–50.

Hobsbawm, E. J. *Nations and Nationalism since 1780: Programme, Myth, Reality.* 2nd ed. Cambridge, UK: Cambridge University Press, 1994.

Hroch, Miroslav. *Social Preconditions of National Revival in Europe: A Comparative Analysis of the Social Composition of Patriotic Groups among the Smaller European Nations.* Trans. Ben Fowkes. Cambridge, London, New York: Cambridge University Press, 1985.

Hynes, Samuel. *The Edwardian Turn of Mind.* Princeton: Princeton University Press, 1968.

Ignatieff, Michael. *Blood and Belonging: Journeys into the New Nationalism.* New York: Farrar, Straus and Giroux, 1994.

Irigaray, Luce. [*SOW*] *Speculum of the Other Woman.* Trans. Gillian C. Gill. Ithaca, NY: Cornell University Press, 1985.

———. [*TSNO*] *This Sex Which Is Not One.* Trans. Catherine Porter with Carolyn Burke. Ithaca, NY: Cornell University Press, 1985.

Irving, Washington. "The Voyage." Tanner, *The Oxford Book of Sea Stories* 15–20.

James, Henry. *Selected Letters.* Ed. Leon Edel. Cambridge, MA and London: Belknap Press of Harvard University Press, 1987.

Jameson, Fredric. *The Political Unconscious: Narrative as a Socially Symbolic Act.* Ithaca, NY: Cornell University Press, 1981.

Jean-Aubry, G. *Joseph Conrad: Life and Letters.* 2 vols. Garden City, NY: Doubleday, 1927.

Jespersen, Otto. *Growth and Structure of the English Language.* New York: D. Appleton and Company, 1931.

Karl, Frederick R., ed. [*CL*] *The Collected Letters of Joseph Conrad.* 4 vols. New York: Cambridge University Press, 1983–.

———. [*JC*] *Joseph Conrad: The Three Lives. A Biography.* New York: Farrar, Straus and Giroux, 1979.

———. ["V"] "Victory: Its Origin and Development." *Conradiana* 15.1 (1983): 23–52.

Kedourie, Elie. *Nationalism.* 4th exp. ed. Oxford, UK and Cambridge, MA: Blackwell, 1993.

Koestenbaum, Wayne. *Double Talk: The Erotics of Male Literary Collaboration.* New York and London: Routledge, 1989.

Komornicka, Maria. "*Lord Jim.*" Najder, *Conrad under Familial Eyes* 192–93.

Kristeva, Julia. "Revolution in Poetic Language." *The Kristeva Reader.* Ed. Toril Moi. New York: Columbia University Press, 1986. 89–136.

Lacan, Jacques. "Kant avec Sade." *October* 51 (Winter 1989): 55–104.

Leavis, F. R. *The Great Tradition.* New York: New York University Press, 1963.

Lednicki, Waclaw. *Life and Culture of Poland.* New York: Roy Publishers, 1944.

Levinas, Emmanuel. *The Levinas Reader.* Ed. Seán Hand. Oxford: Basil Blackwell, 1989.

Mann, Thomas. *Death in Venice and Seven other Stories.* New York: Vintage Books, 1989.

Marryat, Captain. *Mr. Midshipman Easy.* New York and London: G. B. Putnam's Sons, 1895.

Marx, Karl. *The First International and After.* Ed. David Fernbach. Harmondsworth, UK: Penguin, 1974.

———, and Friedrich Engels. ["DP"] "Democratic Panslavism." Marx and Engels, *The Russian Menace to Europe* 67–84.

———. *The Russian Menace to Europe.* Ed. Paul W. Blackstock and Bert F. Hoselitz. Glencoe, IL: The Free Press, 1952.

———. ["WC"] "What Have the Working Classes to Do with Poland?" Marx and Engels, *The Russian Menace to Europe* 95–104.

McCrum, Robert, William Cran, and Robert MacNeil. *The Story of English.* London and Boston: Faber and Faber, 1986.

Mencken, H. L. "Joseph Conrad." *A Book of Prefaces.* Garden City, NY: Garden City Publishing Company, 1927. 11–64.

Meyers, Jeffrey. [*FCE*] *Fiction and the Colonial Experience.* Ipswich, UK: Boydell Press, 1974.

———. [*JC*] *Joseph Conrad: A Biography.* London: John Murray, 1991.

Michnik, Adam, and Jürgen Habermas. "'More Humility, Fewer Illusions'—A Talk between Adam Michnik and Jürgen Habermas." *The New York Review of Books* 24 March 1994: 24–29.

Miller, D. A. *The Novel and the Police.* Berkeley, Los Angeles, London: University of California Press, 1988.

Milosz, Czeslaw. "On Nationalism." *Partisan Review* 59.1 (1992): 14–20.

Morf, Gustav. *The Polish Heritage of Joseph Conrad.* London: Sampson, Low, Masston, [1930].

Morrell, Lady Ottoline. *Memoirs: A Study in Friendship, 1873-1915.* Ed. R. Gathorne-Hardy. New York: Alfred A. Knopf, 1964.

Moser, Thomas. *Joseph Conrad: Achievement and Decline.* Hamden, CT: Archon Books, 1966.

Mulhern, Francis. "English Reading." Bhabha, *Nation and Narration* 250–64.

Nairn, Tom. *The Break-up of Britain.* London: New Left Books, 1977.

Najder, Zdzisław, ed. [*CPB*] *Conrad's Polish Background: Letters to and from Pol-*

ish Friends. Trans. Halina Carroll. London, New York, and Toronto: Oxford University Press, 1964.

———, ed. [*CUFE*] *Conrad under Familial Eyes.* Trans. Halina Carroll-Najder. Cambridge, UK: Cambridge University Press, 1983.

———, ed. [*JC*] *Joseph Conrad: A Chronicle.* Trans. Halina Carroll-Najder. New Brunswick, NJ: Rutgers University Press, 1984.

Nietzsche, Friedrich. *Ecce Homo. "On the Genealogy of Morals" and "Ecce Homo."* Trans. Walter Kaufmann and R. J. Hollingdale: Ed. Walter Kaufmann. New York: Vintage Books, 1969.

Perłowski, Jan. "On Conrad and Kipling." Najder, *Conrad under Familial Eyes* 150–70.

Pfaff, William. *The Wrath of Nations: Civilization and the Furies of Nationalism.* New York, London, Toronto: Simon and Schuster, 1993.

Ray, M. S. "The Gift of Tongues: The Languages of Joseph Conrad." *Conradiana* 15.2 (1983): 83–109.

Reddaway, W. F. J., H. Penson, O. Halecki, and R. Dybeski, eds. *The Cambridge History of Poland from Augustus II to Pilsudski (1697–1935).* Vol. 2. Cambridge, UK: Cambridge University Press, 1951. 2 vols.

Renan, Ernest. [*OL*] *De l'Origine du langage.* Quoted in Tzvetan Todorov. *On Human Diversity: Nationalism, Racism, and Exoticism in French Thought.* Trans. Catherine Porter. Cambridge, MA and London: Harvard University Press, 1993. 145–46.

———. ["*WN*"] "What is a Nation?" Trans. Martin Thom. Bhabha, *Nation and Narration* 8–22.

Reynolds, J. N. "Mocha Dick Or The White Whale of the Pacific: A Leaf from a Manuscript Journal." Tanner, *The Oxford Book of Sea Stories* 47–67.

Ricoeur, Paul. *Oneself as Another.* Trans. Kathleen Blamey. Chicago and London: University of Chicago Press, 1992.

Rousseau, Jean-Jacques. *The Government of Poland.* Trans. Willmoore Kendall. Indianapolis, IN and New York: Bobbs-Merrill Co., 1972.

Rushdie, Salman. "The Empire Writes Back with a Vengeance." *Times* [London] 3 July 1982: 8.

Said, Edward W. [*B*] *Beginnings: Intention and Method.* Baltimore and London: The Johns Hopkins University Press, 1978.

———. [*CI*] *Culture and Imperialism.* New York: Alfred A. Knopf, 1993.

———. [*WTC*] *The World, the Text, and the Critic.* Cambridge, MA: Harvard University Press, 1983.

Schama, Simon. *Landscape and Memory.* New York: A. A. Knopf, 1995.

Sedgwick, Eve Kosofsky. [*BM*] *Between Men: English Literature and Male Homosocial Desire.* New York: Columbia University Press, 1985.

———. [*EC*] *Epistemology of the Closet.* Berkeley and Los Angeles: University of California Press, 1990.

Serres, Michel. "The Natural Contract." Trans. Felicia McCarren. *Critical Inquiry* 19.1 (Autumn 1992): 1–21. From Michel Serres. *Le Contrat naturel*. 1990.

Showalter, Elaine. *Sexual Anarchy: Gender and Culture at the Fin de Siècle*. New York: Viking, 1990.

Stalin, Joseph. "Marxism and the National Question." *Marxism and the National and Colonial Question*. New York: International Publishers, 1942.

Steiner, George. *Extraterritorial: Papers on Literature and the Language Revolution*. New York: Athaneum, 1971.

Straus, Nina Pelikan. "The Exclusion of the Intended from Secret Sharing in Conrad's *Heart of Darkness*." *Novel* 20.2 (Winter 1987): 123–37.

Szporluk, Roman. *Communism and Nationalism: Karl Marx versus Friedrich List*. New York: Oxford University Press, 1988.

Tamir, Yael. *Liberal Nationalism*. Princeton: Princeton University Press, 1993.

Tanner, Tony. ["I"] "Introduction." Tanner, *The Oxford Book of Sea Stories* xi–xviii.

———, ed. [*OBS*] *The Oxford Book of Sea Stories*. Oxford and New York: Oxford University Press, 1995.

Vološinov, V. N. *Marxism and the Philosophy of Language*. Trans. Ladislav Matejka and I. R. Titunik. New York and London: Seminar Press, 1973.

Walicki, Andrzej. [*BMN*] *The Enlightenment and the Birth of Modern Nationhood: Polish Political Thought from Noble Republicanism to Tadeusz Kosciuszko*. Trans. Emma Harris. Notre Dame, IN: University of Notre Dame Press, 1989.

———. ["PN"] "Polish Nationalism in Comparative Perspective." Ms. read at Tulane University, April 1994.

Watt, Ian. [*CNC*] *Conrad in the Nineteenth Century*. Berkeley and Los Angeles: University of California Press, 1979.

———. ["I"] "Introduction." *Almayer's Folly*. By Joseph Conrad. Ed. Floyd Eugene Eddleman and David Leon Higdon. Cambridge, UK: Cambridge University Press, 1994.

Watts, Cedric. "Reflections on *Victory*." *Conradiana* 15.1 (1983): 73–79.

Zagorska, Aniela. "A Few Reminiscences of Conrad." Najder, *Conrad under Familial Eyes* 210–23.

Žižek, Slavoj. [*EYS*] *Enjoy Your Symptom! Jacques Lacan in Hollywood and out*. New York and London: Routledge, 1992.

———. [*TKN*] For they know not what they do: Enjoyment as a Political Factor. London and New York: Verso, 1991.

———. [*SOI*] *The Sublime Object of Ideology*. London and New York: Verso, 1989.

———. [*TWN*] *Tarrying with the Negative: Kant, Hegel, and the Critique of Ideology*. Durham: Duke University Press, 1993.

INDEX